I0822024

REPERTORIUM COLUMBIANUM

Volume IX

OVIEDO ON COLUMBUS

REPERTORIUM COLUMBIANUM

Publication of this volume was made possible by the generous support of the

THE AHMANSON FOUNDATION
Los Angeles

COMITATO NAZIONALE PER LE CELEBRAZIONI DEL V CENTENARIO DELLA SCOPERTA DELL'AMERICA
Rome

SOCIEDAD ESTATAL QUINTO CENTENARIO
Madrid

Published under the auspices of the
UCLA CENTER FOR MEDIEVAL AND RENAISSANCE STUDIES

SERIES PREFACE

The Repertorium Columbianum is a collection of contemporary sources relating to Columbus's four voyages, and the interpenetration of the hitherto separate worlds that resulted from them. This multivolume series will provide in readily accessible form the basic documents that are the starting point for research into this pivotal moment in world history; they form the indispensable tools for all scholarly inquiry into the encounter. The series provides accurate editions of the essential texts in their original languages, for the use of specialists, while at the same time making them available to students and scholars in related fields through parallel translations into modern English.

The Repertorium Columbianum was originally conceived by the late Professor Fredi Chiappelli, former director of the Center for Medieval and Renaissance Studies at the University of California, Los Angeles. The series is respectfully dedicated to his memory. He intended it to be an up-to-date, greatly expanded version of the Raccolta Colombiana, published on the occasion of the Columbian quatercentenary in 1892. He laid down the basic lines of editorial policy that are being followed in these volumes in an approach that blends philological and historical methodologies. Because of the dual approach, the editing of most volumes is an interdisciplinary undertaking among specialists in the field represented by the source materials in that volume. The Repertorium's scope is generally limited to sources from the period between Columbus's first voyage and the Spanish conquest of Mexico in 1519–1521, although certain volumes, by their nature, may extend the chronological range of the series beyond these dates.

Since 1892 historical perspectives on the Columbian encounter have shifted, and the techniques of philological analysis have made enormous strides. The Repertorium's presentation of the sources reflects these changes. Centennial commemorations such as the Columbian quincentenary serve to remind us of the way in which scholarly methods and concerns have altered over the intervening years; they are occasions for taking stock of the past century's achievements, for seeing how interpretations have changed, for scrutinizing new material that has come to light, and for charting the course for future research. These are the purposes that inform the editorial policy of the Repertorium Columbianum. It seeks to sum up what has been achieved in the field of Columbian studies over the past century, to throw new light on the encounter and its immediate aftermath, to collect in a standardized format the essential materials for research, and to suggest lines of inquiry for the years ahead.

The original Columbian ventures were international in conception and execution, and in this same spirit the Repertorium Columbianum is an international undertaking. The contributing scholars and the members of the editorial board are drawn from both sides of the Atlantic, and the costs are being borne with the help of generous funding from the United States National Endowment for the Humanities, the Italian Comitato Nazionale per le Celebrazioni del V Centenario della Scoperta dell'America, and the Spanish Sociedad Estatal para la Ejecución de Programas de Quinto Centenario. The administrative and editorial work for the series is being performed by the UCLA Center for Medieval and Renaissance Studies, under whose auspices these volumes will appear. As general editor it is my pleasant duty to acknowledge a profound debt of gratitude to the three government sponsors, without whose generous and enlightened support this project would have been impossible.

Geoffrey Symcox
General Editor

THE REPERTORIUM COLUMBIANUM

VOLUME I.
We People Here: Nahuatl Accounts of the Conquest of Mexico
James Lockhart, Editor and Translator

VOLUME II.
The Book of Privileges Issued to Christopher Columbus by King Fernando and Queen Isabel, 1492–1502
Helen Nader, Editor and Translator
Luciano Formisano, Philological Editor

VOLUME III.
The Book of Prophecies *Edited by Christopher Columbus*
Roberto Rusconi, Editor
Blair Sullivan, Translator

VOLUME IV.
Christopher Columbus and His Family: The Genoese and Ligurian Documents
John Dotson, Editor and Translator
Aldo Agosto, Textual Editor

VOLUME V.
Selections from Peter Martyr on Columbus
Geoffrey Eatough, Editor and Translator

VOLUME VI.
A Synoptic Edition of the Log of Columbus's First Voyage
Francesca Lardicci, Editor
Valeria Bertolucci Pizzorusso, Textual Editor, *Historie*
Cynthia L. Chamberlin, Translator
Blair Sullivan, Translator

VOLUME VII.
Las Casas on Columbus: Background and the Second and Fourth Voyages
Nigel Griffin, Editor and Translator
Introduction by Anthony Pagden

VOLUME VIII.
Testimonies from the Columbian Lawsuits
William D. Phillips, Jr., Editor and Translator
Mark D. Johnston, Philologist
Anne-Marie Wolf, Translator

VOLUME IX. *Oviedo on Columbus*
Jesús Carrillo, Editor
Diane Avalle-Arce, Translator
Preface by Anthony Pagden

IN PREPARATION:

VOLUME X. *Italian Diplomatic Documents*
Geoffrey Symcox, Editor
Peter Diehl, Translator
Giovanna Rabitti, Philologist

VOLUME XI. *Las Casas on Columbus: The Third Voyage*
Jesús Carrillo, Editor
Michael Hammer, Translator

VOLUME XII. *Contemporary Italian Accounts*
Luciano Formisano and Gabriella Airaldi, Editors
Ted Cachey, Translator

REPERTORIUM COLUMBIANUM

Volume IX

OVIEDO ON COLUMBUS

Jesús Carrillo
Editor

Diane Avalle-Arce
Translator

Preface by
Anthony Pagden

BREPOLS

D/2000/0095/39
ISBN 2 - 503 - 51030 - 2

Printed in the E.U. on acid-free paper

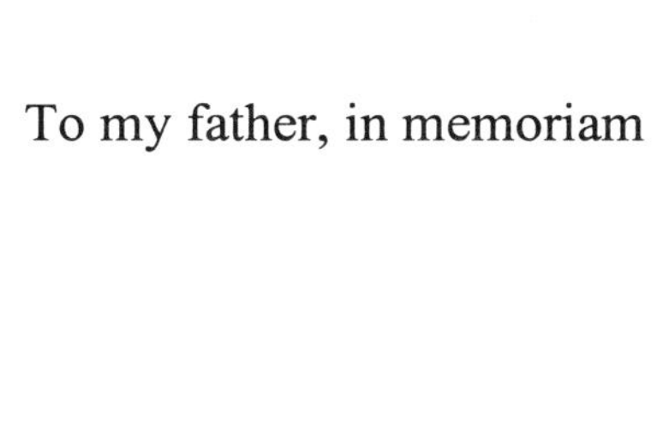

To my father, in memoriam

CONTENTS

ACKNOWLEDGMENTS

I would like to thank Dr. Blair Sullivan for all her patience and encouragement and Dr. Anthony Pagden for giving me the chance to discover a whole new world.

Jesús Carrillo
September 2000

PREFACE

Anthony Pagden

PREFACE

As eighteenth-century historians were fond of saying, Columbus's discovery of America in 1492, and Vasco da Gama's circumnavigation of the globe in 1498, changed the entire world. They ushered in the modern age, the age of navigation, transoceanic trade, of the great European empires, and, ultimately, of the world economy and mass communications, with which we are still living. Columbus has been a hero to many generations, often accredited with scientific understanding he could never have possessed and a vision of the future which would have been meaningless to him. He has also been as consistently vilified as the man who set in motion a historical process which would end in the widespread destruction of tribal peoples across the globe and the unrestrained exploitation of the natural resources of the planet.

These two antithetical images of the significance of the Columbine voyages both date from the years immediately following Columbus's death. The latter, the source of what came to be know as the "Black Legend," owed much of its inspiration to the work of the Dominican Bartolomé de las Casas, "Defender and Apostle to the Indians" and the most controversial figure in the long and troubled history of Spain's American empire. For Las Casas, Columbus had begun his career as the agent of God, a latter-day Saint Christopher, the *Christum ferens*, the "Christ carrier" who would make possible the conversion of countless peoples who, until the coming of the Europeans, had lived outside history, outside time, and had been condemned, through no fault of their own, to everlasting damnation. But he had ended his career as the perpetrator of the first great act of injustice (and many subsequent ones) against the indigenous peoples of the Antilles which, as Las Casas phrased it, "marked the beginning of the spilling of blood, later to become a river of blood, first on this island and then in every corner of these Indies." This had been the great betrayal which had transformed what had been intended—at least in Las Casas's interpretation of the motives behind the initial voyages—as a benign mission of evangelization into a ceaseless and sanguineous act of exploitation, against which he was to struggle for all his very long life.

Ever since the late eighteenth century, when Europeans first began to reassess the legacy of their colonial past, Las Casas has been, and for many still remains, a hero, the one benevolent man, as Denis Diderot put it, in "a century of ferocity." But during much of his own lifetime, and for long after, he was more loathed than loved, more ridiculed than admired. When the French, the Dutch, and the English followed the Spanish, first into the Americas, then into Asia, Africa, and the Pacific, Las Casas's image of Columbus was all but effaced in favor of the figure of the navigator hero, the man who had expanded our knowledge of the terrestrial globe—in the same way as Galileo had expanded our knowledge of the heavens—and who had opened the way for the European conquest of the planet. This image of Columbus as both the initiator of a new scientific era and the agent of imperial expansion survived until well into the last century. It was first suggested, however, by the author of the writings collected in this volume, Gonzalo Fernández de Oviedo. Oviedo was a natural historian who in the opinion of the great nineteenth-century natural historian, explorer, and geographer Alexander von Humboldt, was the first to have attempted a truly systematic descriptive account of the flora and fauna of the Americas. And it is largely for his collection, description, and depiction (many of his works were heavily illustrated) of the plants, animals, and peoples with which he came in contact during the many years which he spent in the Indies that he is best remembered to day. But he was also, as Jesús Carrillo explains in the Introduction to this volume, the tireless champion of the Spanish conquest and occupation of the Americas, what came in subsequent years to be called "the enterprise of the Indies." Oviedo's work is certainly, as Jesús Carrillo points out, one of the earliest in which the objectives of science and empire are yoked together in ways which, in the eighteenth and nineteenth centuries, would become a distinctive feature of much botanical, zoological, and, of course, anthropological writing.

It is, therefore, no coincidence that it was against the works of Oviedo, whom he called that "utterly vain trifler" (*vanissimus hic nugator*), that unashamed fabricator of "monstrous lies . . . from which he stupidly promises himself immortality" that Las Casas had had to struggle to persuade the world of the enormities of what Spain had done in America. Both men had clear and pronounced political objectives behind what were in both cases offered as the immediate and direct fruits of personal experience. Yet both also, in their own ways, contributed massively to the formation of what were later to become the central descriptive branches—natural history and ethnology—of the modern human sciences. The two great sixteenth-century histories of America, neither published in their entirety until the nineteenth century, Las Casas's *Historia de las Indias* and Oviedo's *Historia General y Natural de las Indias* owed more to one another than the similarity in their titles. They were, in a sense, the two voices in a dialogue, a dialogue which, particularly in those sections which deal with the figure of Columbus, is one that is still being conducted to this day.

The editor of this volume, Jesús Carrillo, is one of a number of young Spanish historians who have done so much to revitalize the history of the Spanish conquest and occupation of America, which for had so long lain moribund in the hands of the apologists for General Franco and their pupils. His work on Oviedo, which is now beginning to appear in articles, and the massive study, *The Representation of the Natural World in the Early Chronicles of America: the 'Historia General y Natural de las Indias'* which will soon, I hope, be published in English, draws, as no previous studies of Oviedo have, on unpublished, and some hitherto unknown, material and on the whole range of Oviedo's encyclopedic writings. (In addition to the *Historia General y Natural de las Indias* he wrote genealogical studies, works of aesthetics and art-criticism, a romance of chivalry, and numerous short biographies.) Carrillo also deals with the entire scope of Oviedo's own ambitions, from his use of Renaissance rhetorical techniques and his reflections on the role of representation in modern and ancient painting to his attempt to capture, both figuratively and politically, what he called this new half of the world.

Oviedo, as Humboldt recognized but many subsequent historians seemed to have forgotten, is a major figure in the history not only of the European overseas expansion, but also in the history of science. As Carrillo says, despite "his central place in the processes of discovery, conquest, and early colonization of America, Oviedo and his immense work have so far escaped the attention of international scholarship." With Carrillo's own work, of which this edition constitutes an important part, this sad state of affairs is destined soon to change.

INTRODUCTION

Jesús Carrillo

INTRODUCTION

1. Gonzalo Fernández de Oviedo between Two Worlds

The life and writings of Gonzalo Fernández de Oviedo (Madrid 1478–Santo Domingo 1557) are paradigmatic of the complex ways in which the "New World" entered the cultural universe of sixteenth-century Europeans.[1] Royal chronicler of the Indies since 1532, Oviedo embraced the ambitious task of incorporating the new territories of the Spanish crown into the written records of the European tradition.

The fifty books of his *Historia General y Natural de las Indias* (1535–ca. 1549) were intended to contain any relevant information concerning the West Indies: geography, natural phenomena, and the customs of its inhabitants, as well as to provide a detailed historical account of the submission of those lands to the authority of the Spanish monarchy. Oviedo's work provides, in this regard, an early instance of the western tendency to accompany military and political expansion with an equally expansive corpus of knowledge.

The systematic description of American nature for which the *Historia General y Natural* is best remembered prefigures in many respects the methods of empirical observation which define modern science. The relationship between Oviedo's work as a naturalist and his duties in both the imperial bureaucracy and the official propaganda of Spanish territorial expansion makes his work a good case in which to study the parallel formation of the respective discourses of science, state, and empire in the early modern period.

Oviedo's career reflects the troubled genealogy of both the Spanish imperial expansion and its historical representation. In less than forty years—from 1513, when he left for America the first time, to his final trip to Santo Domingo in 1549—Oviedo crossed the Atlantic nine times and traveled through all of Central America and the Caribbean Islands. Having an itinerant life was a requirement of the imperial overseas office which Oviedo held, but it also was consistent with the desires of an individual who, like many of his compatriots, saw in the receding western horizon an opportunity to expand the scope of his own interests. In the same way, his writings, as any other aspect of his manifold

[1]Some of the points developed in this study have been taken from the Ph.D. dissertation which I submitted to the History Faculty of Cambridge University in April 1997, "The Representation of the Natural World in the Early Chronicles of America: the 'Historia General y Natural de las Indias' by Gonzalo Fernández de Oviedo." Fernández de Oviedo's life has been the object of numerous studies, the first of which was Amador de los Ríos 1851–1855: vol. 1. Pérez de Tudela corrected and complemented Amador's view in the introduction of his reedition of the *Historia*, Pérez de Tudela 1959. In 1957–1958 *Revista de Indias* dedicated two complete issues to commemorate the fourth centenary of Oviedo's death. Most of the articles deal with different aspects of Oviedo's biography: Pérez de Tudela 1957; Peña y Cámara 1957. Manuel Ballesteros Gaibrois reelaborated this material in a biography of Oviedo (1981). In 1988 Fermín del Pino coordinated a more contextualizing view of Oviedo's personality in the two volumes edited to commemorate the fifth centenary of Oviedo's birth: *América y la España del Siglo XVI*. For a complete account of the Oviedo bibliography, see Turner 1966.

activity, have to be regarded equally as the fulfillment of his official duties as official chronicler of the empire and the result of his own personal ambitions as an author.

Oviedo's New World adventure was the continuation of an intense career during which he was able to both witness and participate in some of the crucial events which occurred in Europe at the beginning of the sixteenth century. A member of the Spanish royal household since his childhood, Oviedo was present in 1492 at both the Christian conquest of Granada and the Capitulations of Santa Fe held between Columbus and Queen Isabel.[2] A few years later—from 1499 to 1502—he was involved in the complex affairs which generated a new way of conceiving politics and inspired Machiavelli's *The Prince*: the conflict in Italy among the Spanish, the French, and the Borgias for both international prestige and political supremacy.[3] Back in the Spanish royal court since 1503, Oviedo participated in the gradual replacement of the political and ideological program designed by the Trastámara dynasty with the centralizing and imperialist system newly imported by the Habsburg emperor Charles V.

Oviedo followed all these events from the perspective of a member of an influential lobby of Castilian bureaucrats—secretaries, notaries, and accountants—who had worked in the administration of the royal household of the Trastámara dynasty for several generations. His enduring aspiration to occupy the post of royal chronicler may well have been inspired by his connection with the social and professional circle of notaries and royal secretaries in which he was brought up,[4] but it also reflects the demands of the Spanish monarchy at that particular time. Indeed, the writing of history obtained a special relevance in the transitional years which go from the death of Queen Isabel in 1504 to the definitive installation of the Habsburg dynasty after the revolt of the *comuneros* in 1522. In this context, history was given the important function of supporting and propagating the aspirations of an institution—the monarchy—which had to redefine its role both within and beyond its traditional borders.[5] The intensity and celerity of the changes which occurred during the years in which Oviedo developed his career as a royal historian—the regency of King Fernando, the *comunero* revolt, the transition to the new Habsburg dynasty, and the hazardous construction of the Spanish overseas empire—unsettled in

[2]An event that, in the official historiography, consolidated a new era for the recently united kingdoms of Castile and Aragon.

[3]Sometime after the death of his former patron Prince Juan, Oviedo left for Genoa where he stayed a few months until the Ligurians signed an alliance with the French monarchy. Probably because of his relationship with Messer Giovanni Adorno, Oviedo moved to the court of Lodovico Sforza in Milan until the duke was defeated by the French troops, assisted by Cesare Borgia. After a short period at the court of Isabella d'Este in Mantua, Oviedo followed both Cesare and his cousin the cardinal Giovanni Borgia in their military campaigns in central Italy. In 1500 he arrived in Rome and decided to go on to the south to join the court of Frederick, king of Naples and relative of King Fernando. In 1501, the French-Spanish accord to dethrone Frederick and divide Naples brought Oviedo's Italian career to an end. Oviedo spent one more year with the exiled Neapolitan court in Sicily and finally went back to Spain. See, in this regard, Gerbi 1978: 161–163 and 170ff. An updated view of Oviedo's Italian tour is given in my Ph.D. dissertation (n. 1 above).

[4]The connection between the royal bureaucracy and the writing of history was not as clear in the case of the Castilian monarchy as it was at the neighboring court of the Avis dynasty in Portugal. However, since the reign of John II the post of royal chronicler had been attached to the chancellery, as it was the case of Juan de Mena and Alonso de Palencia. See Bermejo 1980.

[5]See Tate, "La Historiografía de los Reyes Católicos" in Tate 1970: 280–296. See also Tate 1994 and Tate 1996.

dramatic ways both power structures and ideological assumptions.[6] The pessimistic picture of contemporary historiography which Oviedo provided in his writings and his own troubled career as royal chronicler bear witness to the obstacles which the monarchy found in the process of building a unified historical discourse.[7]

Oviedo's activities in America and the opinions which he developed during his long career in the new territories were in many respects a prolongation of the attitudes and loyalties which he had acquired while still in Spain. He joined the first large-scale Spanish expedition to the American mainland in 1513 as the bureaucrat—supervisor of mining and judicial notary[8]—that he was by birth, and he wrote the *Historia General y Natural de las Indias* as part of his duties as a royal historian, the post which he had pursued in Spain for so many years.[9] Notwithstanding the basic continuity of Oviedo's ideology before and after his departure from Spain, some elements in his American writings seem to diverge, however, from the usual conventions of contemporary Spanish historiography. The most remarkable peculiarities in this regard are his exceptionally early view of geopolitics as developed in the *Historia General y Natural*, and the distinct sense of local difference which his vivid descriptions of American nature communicate. The newly revealed region of the world appears on the one hand as a continuum ready to be mapped and described according to the terms of the Spanish imperial expansion. But, on the other hand, this globalizing view is built upon a clear awareness that he was living and writing in a new and, in many respects, different world.

This emphasis on "local" experience is by no means incompatible with the Hispanic imperial sentiment which permeates all his American writings. To an extent, both are the expression of Oviedo's need to strengthen his identity both as an individual and as an author in the unstable context of the early colonial period. The singularity of Oviedo's perspective resulted from a combination of imperial ideas, patriotic sentiments, and a primitive version of Creole zeal, all three basic ingredients of what is usually identified as "colonial."

In spite of his central place in the processes of discovery, conquest, and early colonization of America, Oviedo and his immense work have so far escaped the attention of international scholarship. As Antonello Gerbi quite rightly noted, there have been important historical reasons for this neglect. Oviedo's lifelong confrontation with his more famous adversary Fra Bartolomé de Las Casas (1474–1566) and the shift gradually taken by the official Spanish discourse on the legitimacy of the conquest during the sixteenth century not only resulted in the boycott of the publication of the complete

[6]The rise and fall of the royal chronicler Gonzalo de Ayora (1500–1507), which Oviedo describes as a direct witness, shows clearly the traumatic effects of this instability in the formation of a new historiographic discourse. The story of Gonzalo de Ayora, whom Oviedo met for the first time in Milan in 1499, is recorded on several occasions in the *Batallas y Quinquágenas* (Salamanca MS 359: fol.142) and *El libro de la Cámara del Príncipe don Juan* (1870: 171).

[7]Especially in the *Batallas y Quinquágenas* and the *Quinquágenas*.

[8]See Otte: 11–13.

[9]Fernández de Oviedo was appointed royal chronicler of the Indies in 1532, a job which had been previously performed by Peter Martyr of Anghiera, who never traveled to America. Despite this precedent and the general directives of his appointment, Fernández de Oviedo's specific duties were to a great extent of his own design. The post was vacant until the appointment of Juan López de Velasco by the new president of the Council, Ovando, in 1571.

Historia General y Natural de las Indias during Oviedo's life, but it also caused the subsequent oblivion of his text.[10] For centuries to come, Oviedo was to embody the darker side of the Spanish enterprise in contrast to the figure of Las Casas, the defender of the Indians.

2. Oviedo's Columbus: A Contested Hero

From the opening pages of the *Historia General y Natural de las Indias* Oviedo adopted a double guise to introduce his material to readers. On the one hand, it appeared as a body of data which he claimed to derive directly and exclusively from within the process of discovery and conquest being carried out by the Spaniards. Indeed, the way the information is displayed in the *Historia General y Natural* recalls the official procedure by which reports of conquest and discovery were received and processed by Oviedo himself as official chronicler of the emperor. On the other hand, Oviedo presented the corpus of fragmentary news that he was compiling as pertaining to a single and different entity—a "new world"—comparable in all respects to the three parts of the older and known oikoumené. This new "half of the world," as he calls it, had to be considered by readers as a separate realm which comprised—no less than Europe, Asia, or Africa—a discrete number of peoples, kingdoms, empires, animals, plants, and marvels.[11] The model of Pliny's *Historia Naturalis* followed by Oviedo provided both the authority and the open structure required for such an endeavor.

This initial characterization of the New World as historically dependent upon the intervention of the Spaniards but, at the same time, "naturally" autonomous from any external agency is immediately followed in book 2 by the earliest systematic vindication to appear in print of the central role of Christopher Columbus as "first discoverer." This sequence is by no means coincidental. Oviedo found in the clear and historically probable exposition of Columbus's discovery the most suitable way to unfold the dual picture announced in book 1. Columbus's encounter with the New World was at once a historical fact of incontrovertible significance for the political claims of Spain and the first empirical realization of the natural singularity of the new territories.

Columbus's achievements were strategically placed at the starting point of the process of imperial expansion whose description was the central object of the *Historia General y Natural*. But Oviedo's emphasis on the biographical aspects of the discovery—replacing the general narrative of book 2 with a historical portrait of Columbus—also served his intention to link the discourse on the New World to the testimony of those who, after Columbus, had personally experienced the difference of living in America. For Oviedo, Columbus not only revealed an immense new space which urgently needed to be inscribed in the imperial records; the testimony of Columbus's personal experience inaugurated both a new voice and a new site of utterance which should be distinguished from the many distorted echoes reproduced from Spain.

Bartolomé de Las Casas's *Historia de las Indias* (1527–),[12] together with Oviedo's

[10]Gerbi 1978: 180.

[11]Oviedo 1959, bk. 16, proemio: vol. 2.86.

[12]Las Casas 1992. The *Historia de las Indias* was started in 1527, according Las Casas, and probably finished much later. It remained unpublished until the late eighteenth century.

Historia General y Natural de las Indias, is the earliest attempt to provide a complete historical interpretation of the Spanish enterprise in the New World. It is by no means coincidental that the defense of the role played by Christopher Columbus in the discovery of America was central to their respective projects. Their paths crossed repeatedly from 1519, when they both competed in Barcelona for the government of the region of Santa Marta, until 1548, when Las Casas intervened to prevent the publication of the complete version of Oviedo's *Historia General y Natural*.[13] Each author was highly conscious of the progress of the writings of the other—this is particularly evident in the case of Las Casas—and this reciprocal awareness probably influenced the final form of their respective projects.[14] Despite the long shadow which the legacy of Las Casas has cast over Oviedo's text, his work and personality still provide the best means of approaching Oviedo's account of Columbus and the way he faced the historical questions raised by the discovery.

Bartolomé de Las Casas arrived on the island of Hispaniola in 1502 in one of the earliest expeditions to the Caribbean. Twelve years later, Fernández de Oviedo reached the coast of Panama under the orders of Governor Pedrarias Dávila. Both men spent an important part of their lives in America, but whereas Las Casas finally decided to go back to Spain to continue his crusade against the Spanish exploitation of the Indians, Oviedo remained in America until he died at the age of seventy-nine, having settled his family household in Santo Domingo on Hispaniola. Like Oviedo, Las Casas defended the distinctive value of his writings with the claim that their authority derived from his direct participation in the events he was describing.[15] However, the two historians disagreed quite radically about the ideological foundations of that authority. According to Las Casas, historical truth required complete freedom with regard to any temporal power. For him, God was the only judge and measure of the words of the historian, who thus assumed the role of moral conscience of those having the power.[16] Oviedo, by contrast, considered loyalty to the monarchy to be the main source and guarantee of the truthfulness of his words. He had actually begun writing history for King Fernando long before he left for America, and for many years he strove to obtain the post of royal chronicler at the Spanish court. As it is particularly evident in Oviedo's dedication to the emperor in *De la Natural Historia de las Indias* of 1526, Oviedo liked to present himself as the official spokesman of the empire on any matter concerning the Indies, even before his formal appointment in 1532.

For both Las Casas and Oviedo, writing the history of America was an activity that began late in life. Las Casas had spent some twenty years in the New World before

[13]López de Gómara 1912: 139–140.

[14]Las Casas displayed his negative opinion of Oviedo and his historical work on several occasions, for instance, in the *Historia de las Indias*, bk. 2, chap. 9 and in the eighth reply to Sepúlveda's *Apologia: Estas son las réplicas que el obispo de Chiapas hace contra las soluciones de las doce objeciones que el doctor Sepúlveda hizo contra el Sumario de la su dicha Apología* (Las Casas 1958: 329).

[15]Pagden: 51–89.

[16]On several occasions, Las Casas defended the independence of the historian from any secular power (although he explicitly recognized the right of the authorities either to ban or censure the historical works which contravened against "truth"), and very explicitly in the introduction or *prólogo* to the *Historia de las Indias*: "Diversos motivos y fines que los que historias escriben suelen tener" (Las Casas 1992: vol. 3. 327–338). On Las Casas's view of history, see Anthony Pagden's introduction to N. Griffin 1999.

beginning his *Historia de las Indias*, and Oviedo was already in his late forties when his first book with an American subject matter, *De la Natural Historia de las Indias*—the so-called *Sumario*—appeared in 1526. Neither of them saw their main works printed during their own lifetime. In the case of Las Casas this was because of his decision to bequeath to future generations—like Thucydides—an uncompromising account of contemporary events. Like Herodotus, Oviedo's ambition was, by contrast, to reach the widest possible audience and to obtain the largest possible editorial success. If an important part of Oviedo's historical work remained unpublished, it was only because of his repeated failure to find financial and political support for his publishing projects.[17] Whereas for Las Casas writing had a clear ideological scope, literary activity had for Oviedo very different implications. Indeed, more than half of the books which Oviedo wrote during his long stay in America were on entirely non-American subjects. By the time that his first work on America appeared in 1526 Oviedo had already written a gallery of portraits of illustrious men and a genealogy of the Castilian monarchy—which were never printed in their original form—and had published a chivalric romance, the *Claribalte*.[18]

Despite the radically different objectives and ambitions of the two historians, they both saw Christopher Columbus as central to any interpretation of the Spanish mission in America. Las Casas dedicated the first chapters of book 1 of his *Historia de las Indias* to discovering in Columbus's biography evidence of his destiny as an instrument of God's will. The providential personality of Christopher Columbus—the *Christum ferens* described by Las Casas—was the incarnation of the final cause which should have guided the actions of the Spaniards in America: the conversion of the Indians.[19]

Oviedo's portrait of Columbus was of a rather different nature. In the introduction to the *Sumario* of 1526 he announced that his forthcoming general history of the Indies would start with a detailed account of Columbus's voyages of discovery. As promised, the description of the Columbian enterprise occupies book 2 and part of book 3 of the first part of the *Historia General y Natural de las Indias*, which appeared in Seville in 1535. It was the longest and most exhaustive account so far published on Columbus and his travels. As Oviedo constantly reminded his readers, Columbus's act of discovery was the incontestable point of departure for the long series of episodes of conquest and territorial expansion which he intended to describe in the three parts of the *Historia General y Natural* which were to follow. According to Oviedo, Columbus was the only person who could be truly called "the discoverer." All the successive sightings of new lands made by pilots and captains were, in his view, merely adjuncts to Columbus's foundational act. For Oviedo, the unambiguous characterization of this unique historical achievement was crucial for the Spanish claims of possession, whose defense was the

[17]Oviedo only published the first part of the *Historia General y Natural de las Indias* (Seville 1535). Despite his repeated attempts, the second and third parts, plus a revised version of the first, remained unpublished until the nineteenth century.

[18]On Oviedo's plans to publish a collection of portraits of illustrious men, see the document recorded by Vicente Beltrán de Heredia (vol. 2, no. 394, 399). On his genealogy of the Spanish monarchy, see the letter that his mentor Lope Conchillos sent to Oviedo in March 1518 (Otte: 24). The *Libro del muy esforzado cavallero de la Fortuna propiamente llamado Claribalte* was published in Valencia in 1519. On the *Claribalte*, see Avalle-Arce 1974, Gerbi 1959, and Merrim 1982.

[19]Las Casas 1992: vol. 3, bk. 1, chap. 2.357–359.

main object of his writings.

Oviedo stressed the importance of two events to which, as he informs his readers in book 2, he was a privileged witness when he was a young servant at the court of the Catholic kings. The first was the drawing up of the 1492 Capitulations of Santa Fe by which Columbus was granted both his official appointment and the material means to organize his expedition. The second was the triumphal reception which Columbus was given by King Fernando and Queen Isabel in Barcelona after the discovery one year later.[20] In Oviedo's account of these two occasions there is no sign of the personal saintliness of Columbus or of the divine intervention which pervades Las Casas's narrative. Instead there is a clear reference to the role played by the crown as both promoter and recipient of Columbus's actions. Oviedo's long description of Columbus's life and travels in book 2 was not, as was Las Casas's, a hagiography. It was an encomiastic portrait in the classical style restored in patristic writings and in Il Panormita (Antonio Beccadelli, 1394–1471)in their respective collections of lives of illustrious men. In terms of this particular genre, heroes should be praised and be immortalized by history because of their high services to the commonwealth, which in Columbus's case was the Spanish nation. Oviedo insisted in both the *Sumario* and the *Historia General y Natural* that Columbus's achievements deserved to be celebrated by the Spaniards with a gold statue like those made by the Greeks for Olympic heroes in the Temple of Delphi:

> By the way, Christopher Columbus deserves a much better statue than the one called Holosphiraton and the one by Leoninus, who was the first man to place a gold statue at the Temple of Delphi (in the seventieth Olympic Games), because Columbus was the first discoverer and inventor of these Indies and the first admiral of the Indies in our times.[21]

According to this, Oviedo's historical account of Columbus's achievements served as a monument: an homage paid to the hero for his service and the patent sign of its assimilation within the collective memory of the Spanish nation.

In what Edmundo O'Gorman has called "Oviedo's imperialist thesis,"[22] Oviedo endowed Columbus's achievements with a historical and political relevance equivalent to Las Casas's eschatological characterization of the discovery. One of the most effective means employed by Oviedo to provide his discourse with suitable ideological force was the *imitatio* of Pliny's *Historia Naturalis*, a device which had the effect of presenting Oviedo to his readers as the Pliny of the new Spanish empire. Conscious of the political significance of the Roman model, Oviedo explicitly replaced the cosmological explanation which introduced the *Historia Naturalis* with the detailed account of Columbus's voyage of discovery, the achievement which had made obsolete the narrow limits of the Latin *civitas*.[23] In Oviedo's account, Columbus's discovery both closed a

[20]Oviedo 1959: bk. 1, chap. 7, vol. 1.30.

[21]Oviedo 1959: bk. 6, chap. 8, vol. 1.167. Similar praise can be found in the *Sumario* of 1526: chap. 11, fols. 19 verso–20 recto. The expression "in our times" was added by Oviedo in the manuscripts sometime after the 1535 edition, and it may be related to his theory about a pre-Columbian possession of America by the Spanish monarchy.

[22]O'Gorman: 71–89.

[23]Oviedo 1959: bk. 2, chap. 1, vol. 1.14–15.

chapter in imperial discourse and opened a new one which was no longer identified either with Rome or the past.

Although Oviedo's description of Columbus contains many of the features of the hero as announced by Seneca in the prophetic chorus of Medea—the Promethean master of navigation who showed a new world to humankind[24]—it does not fit completely with the ideal portrait of the hero. On many occasions Oviedo used the conventions of the classical historical genre as found in Cicero, Livy, and Xenophon to introduce judgments on Columbus's behavior. These, disguised as general comments on the difficult role of the ruler, allowed the historian to describe the mistakes and faults made by the admiral as well as praise his virtues. There are secondary characters, such as the Pinzón brothers or Fray Buyl, who are given autonomous voices but are never allowed to contradict Columbus on certain matters. These elements are especially noticeable in the description of the troubled years of Columbus's government in Hispaniola in the last chapters of book 2 and in book 3. Here he is no longer being judged for his discovery, but for his activities as an official of the crown, subject, like any other, to the hierarchy of the royal administration.[25]

This relativistic view of Columbus allowed Oviedo to highlight the part played by the Spanish monarchy in the discovery, a historical device which he had probably learned during his training as chronicler for King Fernando in the years prior to his first trip to America. According to Oviedo, Columbus had given back to the Spanish monarchs a territory which either had already belonged to them by legitimate dynastic rights—in the case of the Caribbean Islands—or which they deserved by the preeminence of the Spanish nation—in the case of the American mainland.[26] In Oviedo's text historical events in this way legitimized both a priori and a posteriori the Spanish domination of the New World. In this respect, Columbus had been the agent of a historical process—the construction of the Spanish overseas empire—which had ultimately escaped from his control and surpassed his understanding. It was a matter of indifference, for the same reason, whether Columbus knew that he was arriving at a new continent. For Oviedo, Columbus could be as wrong about the identity of the Indies as he was about the existence of a navigable passage through the Isthmus of Panama, since the historical value of his actions derived wholly from the political consequences which they had brought about. As Pérez de Tudela once noted, in Oviedo's opinion the importance of Columbus's actions lay in the transcendence they had for the imperial destiny of the Spanish nation, which Oviedo celebrated in his *Historia General y Natural*.[27] It is for this reason that, in chapter 7 of book 2, Oviedo associated Columbus's discovery with the other events took place in 1492—the expulsion of the Jews and the conquest of Granada—which in his view raised the glory of Spain above that of the other Christian

[24]Although he does not refer explicitly to the Medea theme already used by Peter Martyr in his *Decades*, Oviedo develops some of its specific implications, as it is the idea that Columbus was the first to teach the Spanish navigators how to use the astrolabe and the other instruments necessary for transoceanic navigation (Oviedo 1959: bk. 2 chap. 4, vol. 1.20–21).

[25]Oviedo 1959: bk. 2, chap. 13, vol. 1.51 and bk. 3, chap. 4, vol. 1.61.

[26]The thesis of both Iberian and Gothic superiority was developed in the introduction to the second part of the *Historia General y Natural*, which was finished in 1547.

[27]Pérez de Tudela 1952: 148.

nations.

It is not surprising, therefore, that both Las Casas and Columbus's heirs reacted so angrily to some of Oviedo's claims. In chapter 2 of book 2 of the 1535 edition of the *Historia General y Natural* Oviedo recorded the apocryphal story of an anonymous Portuguese pilot who, shortly before dying, told Columbus about the existence of a hitherto unknown western land which he had found by accident.[28] Oviedo did not give much credit to the story—far less than López de Gómara would do two decades later—and it seems to play a peripheral role in Oviedo's whole account of the discovery. The strong criticism, however, which he received for merely propagating the rumor demonstrates how much the priority of Columbus's discovery had become an issue by the first half of the sixteenth century.

Even more contentious was Oviedo's argument that the Spanish monarchy had pre-Columbian claims to the Antilles. Following a loose etymological argument, Oviedo identified the Caribbean islands with the mythical Hesperides, an integral part of a no less mythical ancient Spanish monarchy ruled by King Hespero. Oviedo had based his hypothesis on Berosus's *De primis temporibus et quatuor ac viginti regibus hispaniae et eius antiquitate*. The obscure ancient historian Berosus was actually an invention of Annius of Viterbo, who had created him in order to support his own political claims on behalf of Fernando and Isabel, to whom the work was dedicated. The Hesperides argument appeared for the first time in the *Cathálogo Real*, a manuscript volume that Oviedo offered to Empress Isabel in 1532, three years before the publication of the *Historia General y Natural*.[29] It seems to have immediately attracted the interest of imperial circles since, in a letter signed by Charles V shortly after the reception of the manuscript, Oviedo is required to provide more solid information about it:

> I saw myself as well what you say you have written and that you say you intend to send me with the testimony of five authors that these Indies were ruled by the twelfth king of Spain after Túbal. He conquered these kingdoms after Hercules in the year 1558 before the incarnation of our Redemptor, so that the present year makes 3091 years that these territories have been under the royal scepter of Spain. After so many years, God has returned them miraculously to whom they belong. I shall be very pleased to see the other things that you say about this and the foundations upon which you base your arguments. Thus I order you to send what you have written to me in the first ship departing for these kingdoms, if you have not already done so when you receive this letter; in the case that you have, send a duplicate.[30]

[28]Oviedo 1959: bk. 2, chap. 2, vol. 1.15–16. See the analysis of Oviedo's use of this story in O'Gorman 1976: 75–78.

[29]Library of the Royal Monastery of El Escorial MS h-j-7, fol. 18.

[30]"También yo vi lo que dezis que teneis escrito y entendeis de embiar probado con cinco Autores, que estas Indias fueron del rey de España Duodézimo, contando desde el Rey Túbal, que tomó ciertos reinos después de Hércules, año de 1558 antes que nuestro Redemptor encarnase, de manera que este presente año se cumplen 3091 años que estas tierras eran del Ceptro Real de España; y que no sin gran misterio, a cabo de tantos años, las bolvió Dios a cuyas eran: y todo lo demás que cerca desto dezís: y holgaré de ver el fundamento que para ello teneis: y así os mando si quando esto recibais, no lo huvierades embiado, lo embieis en el primer Navío que para estos Reynos partiere, y duplicado en caso que lo huviéredes embiado." 25 October 1533 (cited in Jos 1940: 18–19).

Probably encouraged by the interest shown by the emperor, Oviedo decided to include a more detailed version of the Hesperides theory along with his description of Columbus's travels in the first part of the *Historia General y Natural* published in Seville in 1535. In spite of the apparently favorable circumstances in which the Hesperides theory appeared, there was actually an influential sector led by Las Casas and Columbus's heirs which contested Oviedo's ideas quite sharply.[31] Las Casas complained that they had earned Oviedo the title of *nocivo lisonjero*—harmful flatterer, the worst attribute for a historian. Las Casas was probably alarmed about the disturbing implications which the hypothetical pre-Columbian sovereignty of America might have for his providential interpretation of Columbus's discovery. The triumph of Oviedo's thesis would imply the priority of the political over the evangelical in the ideological formulation of the Spanish enterprise in America.[32]

Columbus's heirs also had important reasons for rejecting Oviedo's Hesperides theory since it provided arguments that the crown could use in the lawsuit regarding the privileges granted to Columbus since the 1492 Capitulations of Santa Fe.[33] It was shortly after the publication of Oviedo's thesis in 1535—which coincided with the peak of the litigation—when Fernando Colón, or an anonymous biographer according to Antonio Rumeu de Armas, decided to write a biography of Columbus in order to defend the intentional nature of his expedition and his full responsibility for both the discovery and its consequences.[34]

Oviedo had met the two sons of Columbus, Diego and Fernando, when they had been taken under the patronage of Prince Juan—the heir of Fernando and Isabel—for whom the young Oviedo had been *mozo de cámara*—manservant—since 1493.[35] Their relationship continued after the death of the prince on both sides of the ocean and Fernando and Diego are frequently mentioned in the *Historia General y Natural* as firsthand informants on different matters concerning both their father's voyages and their own personal experience in America. Oviedo never explicitly questioned the legitimate rights of Columbus's heirs. In the introduction to part 2 of the *Historia General y Natural* he even expressed his belief in the eternal gratitude owed to Columbus's lineage by both the crown and the Spanish nation. In book 3, Oviedo describes Fernando in the most positive terms: "he is a virtuous gentleman, and besides his great nobility, gentleness and good conversation; he is learned in various sciences, especially in cosmography, and his Catholic majesty relies on him."[36]

The Hesperides hypothesis provided the Spanish monarchy with dynastic rights over

[31]It is impossible to say whether Oviedo modified his theory in the final version of the text of 1549, since the manuscripts containing this passage are lost.

[32]Las Casas 1992: vol. 3.410.

[33]The litigation lasted from 1511 to 1538. On the Columbian lawsuits, see primarily Phillips. See also Jos: 19–22; and Schoenrich 1949–1950. Concerning the documents relating to the privileges granted to Columbus by the crown, see Nader and Formisano.

[34]See Jos, and the chapter dedicated to Fernando Colón in O'Gorman: 91–127.

[35]On Oviedo's friendship with the two sons of Columbus, see Jos: 14; Gerbi 1978: 160; and Fernández Armesto: 57.

[36]"Virtuoso caballero, y demás de ser de mucha nobleza y afabilidad y dulce conversación, es docto en diversas ciencias, y en especial en cosmografía, y de quien la Católica Majestad hace cuenta." Oviedo 1959: bk. 3, chap. 6, vol. 1.67.

the Antilles prior to the 1492 Capitulations of Santa Fe, which were the legal basis of the claims of Columbus's heirs. As a passage added to book 18 around 1540 demonstrates, Oviedo had followed with interest the development of the lawsuit between the crown and Columbus's family and could not thus be unaware of the negative consequences which the publication of his theory might have for the latter's interests.[37] Nevertheless, his will to propagate his original contribution to the general debate on the Indies and the clearly pro-monarchic tone given to the *Historia General y Natural* seem to have prevailed in his decision. Oviedo's main concern in the initial books of the work was to set up a solid historical scaffolding to support the legitimacy of the Spanish domination of America. When Oviedo included his story about the Hesperides alongside the detailed description of Columbus's achievements, he was just adding a further element to his general defense of the political interests of the monarchy. Oviedo could not see any possible contradiction in his account, because the vindication of the historical significance of Columbus and the Hesperides theory were part of the same global strategy. Fernando never forgave Oviedo and devoted an entire chapter of the biography of his father to criticizing Oviedo's claims about the Hesperides; Fernando added to Las Casas's accusation of flattery those of ignorance and naiveté: "We could say as a conclusion that Oviedo is not only forging a new authority in his writings, but that either due to his ignorance or due to his will to please the person who told him those things (which he certainly did not understand), he is conflating two different arguments the manifest incompatibility of which should be enough to demonstrate their mistaken nature."[38]

Despite Oviedo's efforts to please the council and the initial interest of the emperor, his political interpretation of the discovery did not have much success. His attempt to find a compromise between the myth of Columbus and the political interests of Spain was overshadowed by the more eloquent solution given twenty years later by Francisco López de Gómara, chaplain of the emperor, in the *Historia General de las Indias y Nuevo Mundo*. In Gómara's account, Columbus had not been moved by God, by the reading of ancient sources, or by his knowledge of astronomy. He was not even the agent of the *descubrimiento primero*, the first discovery; he had instead been following the indications given to him by the anonymous sailor in whose existence Oviedo had never entirely believed. In this way, Gómara deprived Columbus of the heroic halo which we find in Oviedo's text, as though the myth of the discoverer were no longer necessary for the defense of the legitimate rights of the Spanish monarchy in America. These were sanctioned instead by the papal bull which Gómara transcribed alongside his account of the discovery.[39] However, it was Fernando Colón's more positive view of his father which would prevail from the end of the sixteenth century on, as it follows from the first decade of the *Historia General de los Hechos de los Castellanos en las Islas y Tierra*

[37]Oviedo 1959: bk. 18, chap.20, vol. 2.152.

[38]"(. . .) cosi possiamo conchiudere, che l' Oviedo non solo volle fingere nuove auttorità ne suoi scritti; ma che per inavvertenza, o per voler compiacere a colui, che queste cose gli disse (poi che certa cosa è, lui non le havere intese) si accostò a due contrarii, la sola repugnantia de' quali era sufficiente à manifestare il suo errore." *Historie de S.D.Fernando Colombo; nele quali s' ha particolare e vera relatione della vita e de' fati dell' Ammiraglio D. Cristophoro Colombo suo padre*, trans. Alonso de Ulloa. On Fernando's attack on Oviedo's thesis, see O'Gorman 1976: 96 and 116–117; and Jos 1940: 17ff.

[39]López de Gómara 1555: chaps. 13–15, fols. 6 recto–7 recto.

firme del mar Océano (1601), written by Oviedo's successor as royal chronicler, Antonio de Herrera. Herrera follows his predecessor—and Las Casas—in identifying Columbus and his voyage of discovery as the clear point of departure for his general account of the "deeds of Castilians in the Islands and the mainland of the Ocean sea."[40] It is, however, Fernando Colón's (or the anonymous biographer's) version and not Oviedo's, which should have been the logical referent for the new chronicler. The campaign against Oviedo which both Las Casas and Columbus's heirs promoted immediately after the publication of the *Historia General y Natural* in 1535 was very effective, and not only among their contemporaries. Three hundred years later, when Alexander von Humboldt—who was otherwise very fond of Oviedo's approach to American nature—recorded some of Oviedo's points on Columbus, he described them as mere tales not worthy of further commentary.[41]

The construction of Columbus's historical persona in the first decades of the sixteenth century was not the result of the coordinated efforts of official historiography. As we have seen, Oviedo, Las Casas, and Columbus's family formulated their claims from positions which were not necessarily compatible with each other. The ultimate success of one of the parties and the establishment of Columbus's heroic myth as part of Spanish historiography had more to do with the ability of Las Casas to defend his views than, as López de Gómara's case proves, with the interests of the Spanish monarchy. Oviedo's very failure in defending his view makes patent, on the other hand, the biased ideological position from which he argued. Oviedo's Columbus was the first of the Spaniards living in America—the first "colonist"—a new population which Oviedo was part of and whose distinct voice he wished to be heard and recognized from Spain. As such, Oviedo's Columbus was the first to face the need to give up previous assumptions and to use his personal experience as the main guide in an alien land. At the same time Oviedo's Columbus was also a representative of the crown—like Oviedo himself—whose actions should be judged according to his obedience to the hierarchy and the observance of his official duties. Columbus's every failure or success in either of these two domains—the understanding of the new or the accomplishment of the royal office—was an example for future colonists and officers, who were, in many respects, the ideal audience for the *Historia General y Natural*. Oviedo's Columbus thus appears as a perfect embodiment of the American experience as seen through the eyes of a Spaniard personally living that experience. The glorification of Columbus by Oviedo meant as well the glorification of the Spanish soldier and the Spanish colonist in the New World. Obviously, this purpose was totally absent from both Las Casas's and Fernando Colón's characterization of Columbus.

In spite of Oviedo's efforts to endorse the central imperial discourse, he was writing from the edge of the empire. The longer he stayed away from Spain the more difficult it was for him to defend his views on any subject. This is substantiated by the many unanswered demands which Oviedo addressed to the king and the council in his final years and by the fact that he never saw the publication of the complete version of his

[40]Herrera y Tordesillas: *Década* 1, bk. 1, chaps. 1–3, 1–7.
[41]Humboldt:1.125–126.

Historia General y Natural.

3. De la Natural Historia de las Indias

In 1526 Oviedo dedicated to the emperor Charles V a résumé of what he announced would be a complete natural history of the newly discovered western Indies. This was *De la Natural Historia de las Indias*, the most widely known of Oviedo's works, which he usually referred to as the *Sumario*.[42] The Sumario appeared during the period of political euphoria which followed the victories of Charles V's troops over both the *comunero* rebels in Spain and the French in Italy. The writing of the book coincided with the captivity of Francis I of France in Madrid, the general meeting of the Castilian Cortes in Toledo, and the celebration of the wedding of Charles to Isabel of Portugal in Seville, events which Oviedo was able to attend because of his position as a member of the court of Charles V's cousin, the duke of Calabria. Oviedo left a vivid testimony of the triumphal spirit of those years in the *Relación de lo sucedido durante la prisión del rey Francisco de Francia*, a historical report dating from a few years later when he was back in Santo Domingo.[43] The cornucopian display of American exotica which Oviedo offered to the victorious emperor in the *Sumario* was particularly fitting for such an occasion.

The publication of the *De la Natural Historia* follows the first important wave of books dealing with the New World, which started with the first three *Decades* by Peter Martyr of Anghiera in 1518 and continued with the *Summa de Geographia* by Fernández de Enciso in 1519 and the gradual publication of Hernán Cortés's letters from 1522 to 1525. Oviedo's *Sumario* offered the novelty of being devoted to natural history and of containing the first images of American phenomena to have been portrayed *in situ*. With the introduction of these novel elements Oviedo intended to surpass all previous accounts of America both in the nature of the subject matter—*facta* as well as *res*—and the truthfulness—not only the heard, but also the seen and experienced.

Oviedo chose for the publication of his book the flourishing workshop of Reme Petras in Toledo, which was currently in charge of printing the legal dispositions delivered by the Castilian Cortes.[44] Petras was one of the most innovative printers working in the Iberian peninsula at the time. His workshop was well known for skill in making original woodcuts for book illustrations at a time when the recycling of images was a frequent practice. This was probably a factor which Oviedo considered when choosing Petras's workshop for the publication of his illustrated description of American nature. That same year Petras also produced another landmark of Spanish early printed literature: *Medidas del Romano* by Diego de Sagredo, the first printed treatise on Vitruvian architecture in the vernacular, which, like Oviedo's work, contained images to complement the verbal

[42]Oviedo's *Sumario* is today—as it was in the sixteenth century—the most widely available of his works. In addition to the two well-known modern Spanish editions by Enrique Alvarez López (Oviedo 1942) and Antonio Ballesteros Gaibrois (Oviedo 1986), there is a modern English translation by Sterling A. Stoudemire under the title *Natural History of the West Indies by Gonzalo Fernández de Oviedo* (Chapel Hill 1959). There is also an easily available facsimile edition published in honor of Sterling A. Stoudemire ten years later (Oviedo 1969).

[43]*Relación de lo Sucedido en la Prisión del Rey Francisco de Francia*. National Library of Madrid MS 8756.

[44]For the early printing in Toledo and probably the most insightful account of the general development of printing in Spain, see Jesusa Vega González 1983.

explanations.

Oviedo may well have planned the Italian translation of the *Sumario* soon after the Toledo edition. This follows from Amada López Meneses's hypothesis of a possible meeting between Oviedo and the Venetian ambassador, Andrea Navagero, either in Toledo or Seville sometime during 1525–1526.[45] The correspondence between Navagero and his friend, the Segretario della Serenissima Gianbattista Ramusio, reveals the interest of both Venetian patricians in any information concerning the new Spanish discoveries. Oviedo records having met in that period the ambassador of the marquis of Mantua, who had been given the task of taking to Venice the news about the Indies which Navagero had been collecting in Spain.[46] The diaries of Marin Sanuto record that Navagero possessed a copy of the *Sumario* in Italian when he was forced to leave Spain because of the war between the emperor and Francis I of France, who at that time was allied with the Venetians.[47] In December 1534, Gianbattista Ramusio finally published—very likely with Oviedo's permission—an Italian translation of the *Sumario* which may well be the same one which Navagero had brought from Spain eight years earlier.[48] This Italian translation was the basis of the English version which Richard Eden included in his 1555 edition of Peter Martyr's *Decades* together with a random collection of travel accounts and descriptions of exotica.[49]

The structure of the *Sumario* is initially organized geographically, but this is gradually replaced by a thematic and encyclopedic layout. The work begins with a description of the island of Hispaniola, its geography, the customs of its inhabitants, and their agriculture. The order of the remaining chapters follows roughly the model of Pliny's *Historia Naturalis*: terrestrial animals, birds, insects, reptiles and other small animals, mining, and fishing.

Although Oviedo paid very little attention to the discovery, he announced in the first chapter of the *Sumario* a detailed account of Columbus's voyages which he intended to include in his projected *Historia General y Natural*. The praise of Columbus in chapter 11 has a characteristic classicist flavor which he was to use again in the *Historia General y Natural*.

4. Cathálogo Real de Castilla (y de todos los reyes de las Españas é de Nápoles y Secilia . . .)

In 1532 Oviedo presented to the empress Isabel of Portugal a manuscript volume entitled

[45]See Amada López Meneses 1958.

[46]Andrea Navagero, letter to Gianbattista Ramusio, Granada, 31 May 1526, in Navagero: 326. A testimony of Oviedo's contact with the ambassador of the marquis of Mantua when accompanying his patron the duke of Calabria is found in the *Relación de lo sucedido* . . . Oviedo ca. 1535: fol.19 recto.

[47]"A Spanish book by Oviedo that he translated into Italian as well as a description of things founds in the New World with a picture of that New World and a navigation chart of Spain." Marin Sanuto: vol. 52, col.590, 170. 6,1. Massimo Donatini has defended the direct responsibility of Ramusio in the translation: Donatini 1980. Whoever the translator was he reveals a perfect knowledge of Spanish toponymy since some mistakes found in the Toledo version with regard to "Calpe" and "Avila" (chap. 11, fol. 19 verso) were corrected in the Venetian copy (fol. 14 verso).

[48]Oviedo 1534. By that period Ramusio and Oviedo were already in contact, since Girolamo Fracastoro asked Ramusio in a letter of 10 February 1534 about the constellations of the southern hemisphere: "You could write about these questions to Signor Oviedo, or I could do it myself if you wish" (Fracastoro: 65).

[49]*The Hystorie of the western Indies*, trans. Richard Eden in *The Decades of the Newe Worlde and West Indies. Contayning the navigations and conquestes of the Spaniards* (Oviedo 1555).

Cathálogo Real de Castilla, the first part of a major three-part historical work on the Spanish monarchy which he was currently writing.[50] This first and only surviving section consists of a genealogical history of the Spanish monarchy from its most remote and mythical origins to the reign of John II, father of Queen Isabel. The autograph manuscript of the *Cathálogo Real*—which has been part of the Royal Library ever since—remained practically unnoticed until very recently.

Very much in the tradition of the *Regum Hispaniae Anacephaleosis*, dedicated by Alfonso de Cartagena to John II to defend the antiquity of the Castilian monarchy, the first part of the *Cathálogo Real* is a kind of extended genealogical tree or *Compendio Historial* designed to support Charles's claims to have dynastic primacy in Europe. To this effect, Oviedo displayed at the end of the volume a series of genealogical trees of the royal houses of Castile, Leon, Aragon, Navarre, Naples, Portugal, Burgundy, Flanders, and France. Two further columns were included in order to show the parallel between the imperial line from Julius Caesar and Augustus to Charles V and the papacy from Saint Peter to Clement VII.

This attempt at genealogical legitimization had a direct connection to the historiographical project promoted by Charles's grandfather Fernando three decades earlier. As Oviedo informs us in the opening lines of the *Cathálogo Real*, King Fernando had ordered him to write a similar work in 1505, "which I started compiling in 1505 after Our Lord's birth because I knew that the very serene Catholic king Fernando wanted such a compilation."[51] Oviedo seems to have worked quite intensely on this genealogical project during his stay in Spain after the trip he made to Brussels in 1516. A letter of March 1518 from Oviedo's mentor, the royal secretary Lope Conchillos, states that he had recently received a work of just this kind from his protégé.[52] It was never published but, as was to happen on future occasions, Oviedo's failure to bring one of his works into print did not prevent him from reusing and elaborating the same material fourteen years later when he wrote the *Cathálogo Real*.

The composition of the *Cathálogo Real* involved the systematic compilation, critical selection, and synthesis of Spanish historiography from the earliest chronicles, such as the *Toledano*, the *Tudensis*, and the *Chrónica General* of Alfonso X, to the most recent works of the Trastámara period by Alfonso de Cartagena, Alonso de Palencia, Diego de Valera, Andrés Bernáldez, Antonio de Nebrija, and Lucio Marineo Sículo. This task was all the more valuable after, as Oviedo informs readers, "many of the writings, books, and original privileges of the nobility of Castile had been lost due to the quarrels and passions of the past Comunidades, especially in Burgos were they were kept."[53] Robert Brian Tate

[50]Oviedo 1532. Amador de los Rios was able to see the second part of the work, the so called *Epílogo Real* covering the reigns of the Catholic kings and Charles V until 1517, which is missing today. The manuscript of the *Cathálogo* has been recently published by Evelia Romano de Thuesen as part of her Ph.D. dissertation: Oviedo 1994.

[51]"Lo qual comencé a compilar el año de mill e quinientos y cinco de la natividad del señor consciendo quel sereníssimo rey Catholico don Fernando quinto de tal nombre desseava una compilación semejante" (Oviedo 1532: fol.1 verso).

[52]Otte: 24.

[53]"Averse perdido muchas escripturas y libros y privilegios originales de la nobleza de Castilla por los tumultos y passiones de las comunidades passadas, en especial en la ciudad de Burgos donde estavan" (Oviedo 1532: fol.1 verso). In the *Quinquágenas* Oviedo gives more information about this loss: " Sé que había en

has called attention to the interest of King Fernando in rescuing and compiling the historiography of previous centuries through the actions of his secretaries Alonso de Palencia and Galíndez de Carvajal, who, as Oviedo claimed to have done, made a systematic search for historical codices in monasteries and old archives.[54]

Amador de los Ríos's view of the *Cathálogo Real* as a traditional chronicle bearing a medieval worldview should be reconsidered in the light of contemporary historiographical trends throughout Europe.[55] Oviedo's return to the old genealogical tradition promoted by the Trastámara dynasty a century earlier occurred at a moment in which genealogy and chronology were objects of intense discussion both on the part of the new national monarchies and the religious factions which had emerged during the Reformation.[56] Oviedo's enthusiastic acceptance of the ancient genealogy of the Spanish monarchy drawn by pseudo-Berosus (Annius of Viterbo's creation) was shared by other historians, among them the humanist Antonio de Nebrija, who is not usually accused of naiveté or archaism.[57] Robert Brian Tate has noted how Berosus/Annius's account was generally accepted (with the famous exception of Juan Luis Vives and Antonio Agustín) by many historians up until Scaliger's works on chronology.[58] With the help of Berosus, the *Cathálogo* drew the uninterrupted history of the Spanish kingdom into perfect synchronization with the postdiluvian history of the world—the Isidorian sixth age—a task which Pablo de Santa María had already attempted in his poem *Siete Edades del Mundo* one hundred years earlier.[59] The translation of world chronology in terms of the genealogy of the Spanish monarchy gave Oviedo the chance to present a universal interpretation of the achievements of his compatriots both in the past and the present, at the same time that it allowed him to describe the ongoing Spanish imperial expansion as the outcome of a providential mission. It is not surprising that Oviedo's attempt to map historical time in terms of the Spanish monarchy is contemporary to his endeavor to map the geography and the nature of the whole world in the *Historia General y Natural*. The references to Columbus in the *Cathálogo Real* correspond to this Hispanocentric interpretation of history.

Burgos muchos libros y escritos originales muy importantes para el tesoro y patrimonio real y que Alonso Ruiz de la Mota estaba encargado de su cuidado con un buen sueldo. Se conoce que durante las Comunidades, los comuneros traidores quemaron la casa de Mota con todos los papeles y el dinero que tenía. No me sorprendería que la historia general se destruyera entonces" : *quinquágena* 3, *estancia* 4. Oviedo 1556: National Library MS 2217, fol. 9 recto.

[54]Tate 1983.

[55]José Amador de los Ríos 1851–1855: XC.

[56]On the continuity between chronology and ideology in the sixteenth century, see Barnes 1988 and Vega 1994.

[57]As Robert B. Tate has noted, the *Commentaria super opera auctorum diversorum de antiquitatibus loquentium* which Annius of Viterbo dedicated to the Catholic kings in 1498 including fragments of a supposedly ancient chronicle by Berosus were widely used by Nebrija in both his *Muestra de las Antigüedades de España* and his *Decadas*. See Tate 1970: 186–187. For the impact of the Annius of Viterbo in Spanish historiography see also Tate's essay "Mitología en la Historiografía Española" in Tate 1970: 25–28; and Pérez Vilatela 1993. The political connotations of Annius of Viterbo's construction of Berosus were studied by Anthony Grafton. C. R. Ligota has underlined the non-humanist foundations of Annius's historical method, a fact which illustrates the eclecticism of contemporary European historiographical trends.

[58]Tate 1996.

[59]See Sconza. Robert Brian Tate has followed the development of Pablo de Santa María's arguments in his

5. HISTORIA GENERAL Y NATURAL DE LAS INDIAS

The fifty books of Oviedo's immense *Historia General y Natural de las Indias* are, above all, a celebration of the Spanish conquest of America which for Oviedo was the most important achievement ever accomplished by any nation in the history of humankind. The relevance of this event also applied to the book in which it was recorded, a text that Oviedo even went so far as to compare to the Bible.

According to the terms of his appointment as royal chronicler in 1532, the formal recipients of the *Historia General y Natural* were the king of Castile and Leon and the members of the council of the Indies in his name.[60] However, the actual audience to which Oviedo addressed his writings was by no means restricted to Spanish official circles as this may suggest. Indeed, the *Historia General y Natural* cannot be understood without taking into account the publishing aspect of Oviedo's project. His concern with the reception of his books surpassed contemporary standards of authorial zeal, affecting every step of the process of production: the elaboration of the manuscript, the financial aspects of the printing, the distribution of the book, and its translation into foreign languages. It could be said that Oviedo was as aggressive in the editorial context as he was in the defense of the Spanish supremacy in America. He was in this regard a follower of Gutenberg no less than of Columbus. In spite of his efforts Oviedo was not able to publish the complete three parts of the *Historia General y Natural*. When he died in 1557, only a first version of part 1 and the first book of part 2 had been printed.

Nearly three hundred years after the writing of the *Historia General y Natural*, the "enlightened" members of the Spanish Royal Academy of History, Francisco Cerdá and Juan Bautista Muñoz, rediscovered the manuscripts of Oviedo's complete text when they were in search of a Spanish forerunner of modern science who could match the English and the French in this field. A few decades later, the same concern led to the appointment of a special commission in the Royal Academy of History under the direction of a member of the liberal party, Fernández de Navarrete, in order to publish the by then little-known early-colonial material. Despite repeated attempts, however, the members of the Academy failed to restore Oviedo's contributions to the history of science.[61] Indeed, the recovery of the complete manuscript of the *Historia General y Natural de las Indias* by another member of the Academy, José Amador de los Ríos, in 1851–1855 came from a rather different political position. The portrait of Oviedo which Amador de los Ríos rendered in the introduction to his edition was more a nostalgic celebration of the lost Spanish empire than a vindication of the national scientific legacy in America.[62] Amador's version of Oviedo and his work was the one which, with very few exceptions, modern scholarship either endorsed or rejected until the publication of Antonello Gerbi's *Natura delle Indie Nuove*.

son Alfonso de Cartagena and Rodrigo Sanchez de Arévalo (Tate 1970: 55–105).

[60]See the introduction to Oviedo 1959.

[61]For the institutional efforts of the Royal Academy of History to recover the early Spanish historiography on America, see especially Nava 1985 and 1989. On Juan Bautista Muñoz, see Ballesteros Baretta. On the specific case of Oviedo's work, see Contreras 1988. Fermín del Pino has analyzed the nationalist implications of the enterprise undertaken by Spanish institutions in the eighteenth century. See del Pino 1988 and 1990.

[62]See López-Ocón 1989 and 1992.

5.1 A Chronological Analysis (1535–1549)

According to the introduction of *De la Natural Historia de las Indias*, the so-called *Sumario* of 1526, Oviedo had already written a general draft of the *Historia General y Natural de las Indias* which he left in Santo Domingo on his way to Spain in 1523.[63] This may be partially true, since in January 1526 Oviedo applied for permission to publish this work in Seville.[64] Although Oviedo had probably finished most of the writing at an earlier stage, he was still compiling information for the first edition of part 1 in 1535, the year of its publication in Seville. The printing house chosen by Oviedo was that of Juan Cromberger, the same one which had published two of Hernán Cortés's letters in 1522 and 1523.[65] According to the *carta misiva* to the president of the council included at the end of this edition, Oviedo had paid for the costs of printing and distribution of the book. Clive Griffin interpreted this statement as a proof of Juan Cromberger's reluctance to invest in a genre with no proven demand.[66] In my opinion, however, Oviedo's decision corresponds to a desire to optimize the potential benefits obtained from the sales. In fact, in the aforementioned *carta misiva* there is an explicit reference to the income—even if scarce—that Oviedo expected from the book.[67]

There is evidence in the original manuscripts of Oviedo's frustrated plan to publish part 2 of the *Historia General y Natural* plus an augmented version of part 1 at the beginning of 1541.[68] The cancellation of this first project is probably related to Oviedo's decision to make changes in the general organization of the three parts, which were to be finished in early 1542. According to a letter addressed to the viceroy of New Spain Antonio Mendoza, dated from Santo Domingo in March 1542, Oviedo was ready to depart for Spain to have his manuscript published.[69] As Oviedo described it, the 1542 text consisted of three volumes containing the three complete parts of the *Historia General y Natural de las Indias*.

As Oviedo informs Antonio Mendoza in a subsequent letter, the projected departure

[63]Oviedo 1526: introduction fol. 2 recto.

[64]According to the documents preserved in the Archivo de Protocolos of Seville, first noticed by Manuel Marticorena, by the same date that the *Sumario* was published in Toledo and during his stay in Seville attending the imperial wedding, Oviedo sold the rights of publication of the projected *Historia General y Natural* to Rodrigo de Ayala and his brother Alfonso de Alfaro, booksellers. Also according to Marticorena, some umpublished documents of the Archivo de Indias reveal that the printing of the *Historia General y Natural* had already been authorized in January 1526, a permission which was extended until 1535, when the first part of the work finally appeared in Seville. Manuel Marticorena derived the reference from the Catálogo de los Fondos Americanos del Archivo de Protocolos de Sevilla (vol. 5, n. 1, 1061).

[65]See C. Griffin 1988.

[66]C. Griffin 1988: 139–140.

[67]". . . vine a esta cibdad de Sevilla a la hazer imprimir. En lo qual assi en el tiempo como en la costa desta primera impression yo he trabajado y despendido harto más de lo que el interesse que por tales libros se oviere" (Oviedo 1959: vol. 1.3; Oviedo 1535: fol. 192 recto).

[68]"Y entre tanto que el sol me tura, en este año de la Natividad del Redemptor de mill e quinientos e cuarenta (later deleted), este año o en el siguiente, se reimprima esta primera parte, acrescentada y enmendada, y más ornada que estuvo en la primera impresión. E así mismo se imprimirá la segunda, y yo quedaré continuando la tercera; en la cual no me hará falta voluntad para concluirla, pues que está en grand parte della descripta en minutas": *Historia General y Natural*, book 6, proemio, according to the earlier dates found in the autograph manuscript. This fragment was updated at three different stages in 1545, 1547, and 1548: Huntington Library MS HM.177, vol. 1, fol. 2 recto.

[69]According to the letter to Antonio de Mendoza, viceroy of New Spain, included in bk. 33, chap. 53, by March 1542, when Oviedo was preparing to depart for Spain, he had a manuscript of nearly two thousand folios in three volumes ready for publication (Oviedo 1959: vol. 4.254).

was suspended due to a naval offensive of French corsairs in the Caribbean.[70] Four years later, in 1546, Oviedo was finally given permission to leave for Spain. The text originally finished in 1542 was corrected and quite substantially lengthened during the period when Oviedo had to wait in Santo Domingo (1542–1546). These changes did not affect, however, the general structure of the work which remained as it was in 1542.

According to his own testimony, at the end of 1548 Oviedo finally obtained permission from the council to publish the *Historia General y Natural de las Indias* and, consequently, he decided to go back to his home in Santo Domingo. During the two and a half years which he spent in Spain (1546–1549) Oviedo added to the manuscript a great amount of new information that he obtained both at the royal court and in Seville. Many of the dates which refer to the moment of writing were updated to 1548, the year in which he expected the work to be published. In part because of financial problems and in part because of Bartolomé de las Casas's intervention, Oviedo's plans for printing were delayed and he decided to go back to Santo Domingo.[71] There are a few final additions dating from early 1549 which Oviedo wrote shortly before his departure. According to a letter addressed to Bishop La Gasca in 1550, Oviedo had left the manuscript of the *Historia General y Natural* in a monastery in Seville waiting for a better chance to have it published.[72] According to Oviedo's later description of the manuscript, the three-volume text mentioned in 1542 was one volume longer when it was left in Seville in 1549.[73]

In the introduction to his last work, the *Quinquágenas* of 1555–1556, Oviedo states that the second and third parts of the *Historia General y Natural* were being printed at that moment. The only result of this final attempt at publication is the one volume containing the first book of part 2 which appeared in Valladolid in 1557.[74] In the last page of this edition, the printer informs readers of the interruption of the publication due to the death of the author. There is an undated and partially different copy of book 21 preserved in the Ayer Collection of the Newberry Library which, in my opinion, bears witness to the sudden cancellation of the printing.[75]

[70]Oviedo 1959, bk. 33, chap. 54, vol. 4.258.

[71]As recorded by Francisco López de Gómara 1912: 139–140.

[72]Oviedo 1550.

[73]"La historia natural y general de Yndias Yslas y Tierra Firme del mar océano en tres partes en quatro volúmenes repartida" in Oviedo ca. 1535–1552: *batalla* 2, *quinquágena* 4, *diálogo* 9, University Library of Salamanca MS 359, fol. 617 recto.

[74]Oviedo 1557.

[75]Oviedo ca. 1556–1557. The Ayer copy reproduces exactly the text of bk. 20 of the sixteenth-century manuscript copy preserved in the Library of the Royal Palace of Madrid (MS II/3041). The date of the copy is discussed in Turner 1983. I do not agree with Turner's interpretation. Turner thinks that the Ayer copy was written in 1556 and explains the suspension of the edition as an attempt to update the prologue of the volume which still referred to Queen Juana—the emperor's mother—who had died that year. The interpretation I propose here is that the printer Fernández de Córdoba decided to stop the already started printing of the entire part 2 immediately after he received the news of Oviedo's death in June 1557. He probably prepared a new printing restricted this time to bk. 20, whose type he had already prepared, removing from the original set both the introductory page, where the contents of the original volume were described, and the traces of the beginning of bk. 21 in the verso side of the last folio. Fernández de Córdoba's removal of the last passage of the final chapter of the book (chap. 36, although it shows 35 due an error in numbering), which appears both in the Ayer copy and the manuscript copy of the Royal Palace in Madrid, probably has a financial cause. This passage followed the last stop of the recto side of the folio and occupied the verso in which the following bk. 21 was supposed to start. By eliminating a few lines, Fernández de Córdoba avoided printing one side of the folio. Disregarding these minor changes, the 1557 edition corresponds to the Ayer copy even in the errors in

Oviedo mentions a fifth volume containing the fourth part of the *Historia General y Natural* that he was writing shortly before his death in 1557. There is no trace of this last volume.[76]

5.2 Manuscript sources

In 1851–1855 José Amador de los Ríos finally published a reconstructed version of the complete *Historia General y Natural de las Indias*.[77] Seventy years earlier, the academician and royal cosmographer Juan Bautista Muñoz had made a general survey of the material which Oviedo had left in Seville in 1548—the so-called Monserrate manuscript—which the Royal Academy of History had recently acquired from the Salazar legacy.[78] When Juan Bautista Muñoz had described the first four of the seven files of which the Monserrate manuscript consisted, he had made a detailed account of the important parts which were already missing: books 1 and 2, and the first twelve chapters of book 3 in the first file; book 10, and from the end of book 12 to chapter 9 of book 17 in the second file; books 20 to 28 in the third; and a few folios of the fourth file which contained books 29 to 32.[79]

The manuscript which is preserved today in the library of the Royal Academy of History is not as complete as the one which both Juan Bautista Muñoz and José Amador de los Ríos had the opportunity to study. At the beginning of this century important fragments of the Monserrate manuscript consisting of books 4, 6 to 12, 32, and 37 disappeared in obscure circumstances. These books were later acquired by the Huntington Library of Los Angeles, where they are still today (MS HM 177, 2 vols.), except for book 8 on fruit trees and book 12 on terrestrial animals, which have been missing ever since. The part of the Monserrate manuscript which is still preserved today in the Academy is divided into six separate files containing: the last chapters of book 3 and book 5 (MS 9/551); books 29 to 31 (MS 9/553); book 33, except for chapters 34 to 47 (MS 9/555); book 34 (MS 9/554); books 46 and 47 (MS 9/556); and book 42 from chapter 7, and book 49 from chapter 10, up to chapter 21 of book 50 (MS 9/557).[80]

There are three other important manuscript sources which compensate, to an extent, for both the gaps already noted by Juan Bautista Muñoz and the more recent loss in the twentieth century. The first and most important one is the transcription of Oviedo's original manuscript which the inquisitor, cleric, and schoolmaster of the Cathedral of Seville Andrés Gascó ordered around 1563, known today as the Truxillos manuscript. Andrés Gascó probably received Oviedo's material for the purpose of inquisitorial inspection after the death of its author and because of his personal interest in the matter—he owned a collection of exotic animals and many books about the newly discovered

numbering in chaps. 3 and 8. The differences in punctuation in the last folio, which Clara A. Smith (curator of the Ayer Collection) notes, are easily explainable, since this was the only page that the printer had to change in order to announce the interruption of the edition and to acknowledge Oviedo's death.

[76]Oviedo c.a 1535–1552:*batalla* 2, *quinquágena* 4, *diálogo* 9, University Library of Salamanca MS 359 fol. 617 recto.

[77]Oviedo 1851–1855. It includes a preliminary study by the editor José Amador de los Ríos: "Vida y escritos de Gonzalo Fernandez de Oviedo."

[78]For a first approach to the history of the Monserrate manuscript, see Turner 1985; and Contreras.

[79]Oviedo ca. 1780: unnumbered folio.

[80]These signatures refer to the Salazar Collection of the Library of the Royal Academy of History.

lands—he decided to make a copy before giving it back to the Council of the Indies.[81] Andrés Gascó died in 1566 and it was his nephew Antonio Gascó who finished the transcription of Oviedo's manuscript some time later. The extant parts of this copy are divided into three volumes. Two of them are preserved in the library of the Royal Palace of Madrid (MSS II/3041 and II/3042) containing, respectively, book 17, chapter 21–27; and books 39 through 50. The remaining volume, which consists of books 29–32, is in the Biblioteca Colombina of Seville (MS 83-6-15). For unknown reasons, book 28 of the Truxillos manuscript is today in volume 108 of the Jesuit Collection of the Library of the Royal Academy of History in Madrid. Unfortunately, the Gascó copies do not include the books on natural history (7–15).

The second important manuscript source is volume A/34 of the Juan Bautista Muñoz Collection: Oviedo/Adiciones y enmiendas a los libros 1–19 in the Library of the Royal Academy of History.[82] In this volume Muñoz transcribed both the single passages and the complete chapters which Oviedo added to the Seville edition of the *Historia General y Natural* after 1535. This volume is directly connected to a copy of the 1547 Salamanca reedition of this same work which is also preserved in the Royal Academy of History (4/2959) and which includes the same notes written by Muñoz in A/34, either added on the margins or pasted on the printed page. It is impossible to determine whether these two volumes are related to Juan Bautista Muñoz's ambitious *Historia del Nuevo Mundo* or if they belong to an abortive project to publish the *Historia General y Natural de las Indias*.[83] Be that as it may, Muñoz's copies provide very valuable information about the missing parts of Oviedo's manuscript: They offer a complete transcription of books 8 and 12—today lost—which includes what seem to be accurate copies of Oviedo's illustrations of American flora and fauna; and they have the original index of the whole augmented version of part 1, including the titles of the new chapters of books 10 and 13–16, which were already lost in Muñoz's time.[84]

The most recent of these three manuscript sources is the copy of the complete *Historia General y Natural de las Indias* today at the Hispanic Society of New York, which José Amador de los Ríos made probably around 1855, the date of his printed edition.[85] Amador's copy follows Juan Bautista Muñoz's very closely, except for the fact that it does not contain the illustrations which Muñoz had so carefully reproduced in his own transcription. This obvious resemblance suggests a direct relationship between Amador's edition of 1851–1855 and the transcriptions made by Juan Bautista Muñoz in the previous century.

The passages contained in the present volume correspond to the edition of José Amador de los Ríos as republished by Juan Pérez de Tudela in the Biblioteca de Autores

[81]See Wagner: 159–160. According to a document recorded by José Toribio Medina, the manuscript had been requested from Andrés by a royal order of November 1563; see Wagner: 160.

[82]There are some other volumes of the Muñoz Collection containing partial copies of the *Historia General y Natural* which are not so relevant for our purposes because there are extant original manuscripts available.

[83]On Muñoz's troubled relationship with the Academia and his *Historia del Nuevo Mundo*, see Ballesteros Baretta.

[84]Bk. 10 was seven chapters longer; bk. 13, five; bk. 14, twenty-four; and bk. 15, sixteen.

[85]Oviedo ca. 1850. My gratitude to the librarians of the Hispanic Society of New York for their generous help.

Españoles, volumes 117–121 (Madrid 1959). This edition is more generally accessible than Amador's nineteenth-century original and includes very useful indexes. In all passages taken from the first part of *Historia General y Natural*, I refer to the original text of the 1535 edition. When the 1535 text differs from the Amador/Pérez de Tudela edition, the 1535 version is transcribed in a footnote. In cases where the manuscript source is still available, the precise reference has been added to the quotation of the Amador/Pérez de Tudela edition. When the manuscript sources bear corrections or additions with regard to an earlier version of the text, a transcription is included in a footnote.

6. Batallas y Quinquágenas escriptas por el Capitán Gonzalo Fernández de Oviedo, criado del príncipe don Johan hijo de los Reyes Catholicos y cronista mayor de Indias, del Emperador Carlos V (ca 1535–1552)

The third part of the *Cathálogo Real* as Oviedo described it in 1532 was intended to deal with the "illustrious and generous gentlemen who served under your lordship."[86] Oviedo was thus planning to complete his historiographical program with an account of the lives and achievements of illustrious gentlemen in the fashion inaugurated in Spain the previous century by Pérez de Guzmán with his *Generaciones y Semblanzas* and continued by the royal chronicler Hernando del Pulgar with his *Claros Varones de Castilla*.[87] Whatever reasons Oviedo had to change his original project, the fact is that by 1535 he had already decided to make of this third part an autonomous work with a completely new structure.[88] The result of this change of program was the *Batallas y Quinquágenas*.

As Oviedo informs his readers, he felt obliged to interrupt the writing of the *Batallas* shortly after he became aware of the intentions of the new royal chronicler Florián de Ocampo to include a similar account in the last volume of the general chronicle of Spain which he was currently writing. Oviedo restarted the *Batallas* after his return from Spain in 1549, with the excuse of having given enough time to Florián de Ocampo: "Waiting for the description of arms and lineage which was promised by the learned master Florián de Ocampo in the first printed part of his Cosmography (sic) where he says that it will appear in the last part of that work, I waited for twelve years in order to learn from his work the things I did not know. But as I see that his help is so long in coming, it is reasonable that I finish my dialogues as best I can without him."[89]

The work consists of two large sections or *batallas* which are divided in three *quinquágenas* containing fifty dialogues each of which more than two hundred have

[86]". . . illustres y generosos varones que debaxo de vuestro señorío y serviçio militaron" (Oviedo 1532: fol. 1 verso).

[87]In the introduction of his last work, the *Quinquágenas* of 1556, Oviedo demonstrated his taste for the biographical genre when referring as a main model to the work of Johan Sedeño, *Summa de varones illustres, en la qual se contienen muchos dichos, sentencias y grandes hazañas y cosas memorables de dozientos y veynte y quatro famosos* (Medina del Campo 1551).

[88]". . . y de las de mis diálogos de las casas de España ilustres e de nobles linajes e famosos cavalleros en que ha que escrivo desde el año 1535" (Oviedo 1556: *quinquágena* 3, *estancia* 33, National Library of Madrid MS 2219, fol. 61 verso).

[89]"Y esperando una promesa e aviso de armas e linajes quel dotto maestro Florián de Ocampo prometió en la primera parte que anda impresa de su Cosmographia (sic) que dize que en la última parte de aquella su obra la veremos, he hecho una pausa de doze años que ha que le espero por me avisar arrimado a él de lo que podría ser que yo no se. Pero ya veo que tanto se tarda su socorro ques bien que sin él acabe mis diálogos lo mejor que yo pudiere" (ibid.).

survived. Every dialogue deals with the biography of a Spanish aristocrat, most often Castilian, whom Oviedo had met. The biographical narrative was followed by an account of the ancestry and wealth of these gentlemen in the fashion of Lucio Marineo Sículo's *De Rebus Memorabilibus*: "This is a work which deals with people and the founders of their lineage and households as well as with their genealogy and arms. I shall always start with the gentleman whom I have met from the lineage I am dealing with and in the dialogue I shall give an account of his ancestors and descendants."[90]

The literary framework of the *Batallas* is the fictional dialogue between two characters—the Sereno and the Alcaide, the latter being a personification of Oviedo himself—which they held at the Castle of Santo Domingo in Hispaniola at the end of their lives. The excuse to deliver information about a particular gentleman was the Alcaide's remembrance—at the Sereno's request—of his previous life among Spanish aristocrats and courtiers. As Oviedo confessed, the main motivation behind his use of a dialogical structure was his taste for novelty and originality and his enduring ambition to do the as yet unattempted, which he justified as a natural human tendency: "As you have already said, novelty is the most beloved thing in the world, and although talking and writing about the lives of illustrious gentlemen is not new and many others have done it before, the form in which you and I are doing it in these colloquia and dialogues is new."[91] The "more than one thousand and five hundred pages" which, according to Oviedo, made up his dialogues, offer a unique source for the study of Spanish aristocratic life in the late fifteenth and early sixteenth centuries.

Interestingly enough, there is very little information about individuals who became famous in the New World. None of them, not even Columbus, deserved a dialogue in Oviedo's collection or at least not in the series which is today preserved. Any reference to American issues is either autobiographical or part of a digression.

Juan Bautista Muñoz records having seen the two-volume autograph manuscript of the *Batallas y Quinquágenas* in the library of the Colegio Mayor de Cuenca in Salamanca. One of the volumes remains today in the University Library of Salamanca (MS 359), whereas the other is kept in the Royal Academy of History of Madrid (MS 9/5387). Although some of the dialogues are missing, there are at least four later partial copies: two in the National Library of Madrid (MSS 3134–3135), one in the Royal Academy of History of Madrid (MS 9/4023), and another one in the library of the Royal Palace also in Madrid (MS II-2604). Fragments of this immense work have been partially published on numerous occasions. Juan Pérez de Tudela edited a selection of dialogues which had been previously transcribed by José Amador de los Ríos: *Batallas y Quinquágenas* (Madrid 1983). Juan Bautista Avalle-Arce edited and published the Salamanca volume, which he thought to be the only remaining autograph manuscript of the work: *Batallas y*

[90] "Y es obra en que se tracta de personas e fundadores de sus mayoradgos e casa e de sus genealogías e armas. E comienço siempre en el cavallero que vi e conscí en la casa de que tracto e dialogando tráense a consecuencia los ascendientes e descendientes de los tales" (Oviedo 1556: *quinquágena* 3, *estancia* 33, National Library of Madrid MS 2219, fol. 61 verso).

[91] "La novedad es la cosa más amada del mundo, vos la haveis bien apuntado de susso y aunque no sea nuevo como dezis hablar o escribir en las vidas de los varones illustres, que muchos lo hayan echo, nueva cosa es la forma con que vos y yo lo hacemos en estos colloquios y diálogos" (Oviedo ca. 1535–1552: *batalla* 1, *quinquágena* 2, *diálogo* 2, National Library of Madrid MS 3135, fol. 175 recto).

Quinquágenas (Salamanca 1989). Both editions contain interesting information in their introductions.

7. QUINQUÁGENAS DE LOS GENEROSOS E ILUSTRES E NO MENOS FAMOSOS REYES, PRINCIPES, DUQUES . . . QUE ESCRIBIÓ EL CAPITÁN GONZALO FERNÁNDEZ DE OVIEDO, ALCAIDE DE SUS MAJESTADES DE LA FORTALEZA DE LA CIUDAD E PUERTO DE SANTO DOMINGO

At the beginning of 1556 Oviedo finished the three-volume manuscript of the *Quinquágenas*, a luxuriously bound work in beautiful calligraphy which he planned to send as a gift to Prince Philip of Spain (soon to become Philip II). Although Oviedo's intention was, as he explicitly stated in the prologue, to have his book printed, the material quality of the manuscript exceeds by far what could be expected from a draft for printing. The original manuscript is today in the National Library of Madrid (MSS 2217–2219).

Oviedo probably started the *Quinquágenas* after having abandoned temporarily his other major project—the *Batallas y Quinquágenas*—around 1543 and it took him some twelve years to finish it.[92] Apparently, the *Quinquágenas* was originally conceived as three series—*quinquágenas*—of fifty poems—*estancias*—each dealing with a wide range of topics. Sometime after the work was started, however, Oviedo decided to add a long gloss to each *estancia* which explained the content of his verses in the fashion of his admired Juan de Mena:

> When I gave up writing that work, I decided to dedicate my time to these three *Quinquágenas* which are written in common verse and second rhyme (. . .) which I started some ten years ago; then I decided to add commentaries to my verses, because although they are clear and quite different from those by Juan de Mena, I thought it was a good idea to make explicit their purpose and to tell some good stories which are not generally known.[93]

In this his last work, Oviedo sustains the same skeptical view of human affairs which also appears in the final additions to the *Historia General y Natural de las Indias*. Together with historical information, the *Quinquágenas* offers a random compilation of advice intended to guide individual action in the precarious domain of human existence. The main guidelines for Oviedo's admonitions are total submission to the established religious and civil authorities and training in modes of behavior based upon the need to survive in a chaotic world. Oviedo probably derived this approach from one of his favorite readings during the period: Antonio Brucioli's *Dialoghi*, a collection of dialogues or colloquia in which a character impersonating Machiavelli was one of the participants.[94]

According to a passage of the *Quinquágenas*, civil law—"ley civil o derechos del mundo"—should equal the *patria* in the love and respect owed to them by all indi-

[92]Oviedo 1556: *quinquágena* 3, *estancia* 50, National Library of Madrid, MS 2219, fol. 81 recto.

[93]"Y en este tiempo que, como digo, paré en aquella obra quise ocuparme en aquestas tres Quinquágenas en verso común e segunda rima (. . .) que puede aver diez años que lo començé y después acordé de comentar mis versos, porque aunque son claros y no tales como Johan de Mena, no será mal que el comento declare mi intención y aún algunas historias que no todos las saben" (Oviedo 1556: *Quinquágena* 3, *estancia* 33, National Library of Madrid MS 2219, fol. 61 verso).

[94]Brucioli 1537–1538: especially dialogues 7, "Del Giusto Principe," and 9, "Del Capitano."

viduals.[95] However, the laws imposed by the king, even the just ones, seemed to be most often like spider webs trapping the weak and leaving the crimes of the powerful unpunished.[96] This was the cause of a disjunction between the thoughts and the words of all active gentlemen, who were forced into complex subterfuges so as not to be caught in the invisible but ubiquitous network of surveillance and punishment set up by the monarchy: "The walls have ears (. . .) and from afar the long arms of the king can exact revenge on his subjects without their even seeing his hands."[97] This precarious situation forced individuals constantly to reevaluate their positions vis-à-vis the changing climate at court. Circumstances dictated position with respect both to the law and other members of the community: "There are times when it is necessary to dissimulate with the mighty and even moderate the severity of the law with the less powerful. As it says in Holy Scripture: 'Omnia tempus habet,' there is a time for everything."[98]

Vicente de la Fuente published the first volume of the manuscript in Madrid in 1880 and Juan Bautista Avalle-Arce made an extensive but rather personal selection of the three *Quinquágenas* in an 1974 edition entitled *Las Memorias de Gonzalo Fernández de Oviedo* (2 vols., Chapel Hill).

8. Sources

Oviedo de la Natural Historia de las Indias

The text included is a transcription of the 1526 original printed in Toledo by Reme Petras. Both the spelling and the division of paragraphs have been modernized according to the same criteria (modern Spanish) used in the other texts contained in this volume. The original folio division is marked on the text.

Cathálogo Real e Ịmperial de Castilla

The text is a transcription of the manuscript presented by Fernández Oviedo himself to the empress in 1532. It is preserved in the Library of the Royal Monastery of El Escorial,

[95]"El ombre deve estimar la patria y la ley más que los propios ojos. La ley se entiende aquí por la ley civil o derechos del mundo. Pero dexando aparte la ley cristiana sobre todo, en lo demás la patria y la ley civil se deven mucho estimar" (Oviedo 1556: *quinquágena* 1, *estancia* 30, National Library of Madrid MS 2217, fol. 77 verso).

[96]"A Solón filósofo le preguntaron que cosa son las leyes y el rey, respondio que eran muy semejantes a las telas de araña en las cuales los animales pequeños se revuelven y atan y los grandes las rompen. Esta virtud de las leyes y aun aquellas que en sí son buenas y justas no tienen más rigor y fuerça de quanto son executadas y puestas en efecto" (Oviedo 1556: *quinquágena* 2, *estancia* 1, National Library of Madrid MS 2218, fol. 1 verso).

[97]". . . porque las paredes tienen oidos (. . .) y porque los brazos del rey desde lexos alcançan vengança de sus subditos sin que se les vean las manos": Oviedo 1556: *quinquágena* 1, *estancia* 27, National Library of Madrid MS. 2217, fol. 71 verso. Not only the king, but especially his favorites are the target of this simulation: "ninguna cosa es más necesaria al cortesano que conservarse en la gracia y amistad del que esta favorescido del rey (. . .) y dese tal el que estuviere ausente y que no le pueda ver, visítele con sus cartas y aun sírvale con algunas cosas que parezca que son de la amistad y no para soborno y aunque al no se pida cosa alguna en retorno ni recompensa no dexe de aprovechar adelante y mejor le sera satisfecho porque de ser esquivo y desconversable por bueno que sea el ausente es presto olvidado" (Oviedo 1556: *quinquágena* 1, *estancia* 31, National Library of Madrid MS 2217, fol. 79 verso).

[98]"(. . .) tiempos hay en que conviene disimular con los poderosos y aún con los chicos templar el rigor de la ley, asi mismo. Por lo qual quadra bien aquella autoridad de la Sagrada escritura que dize: 'Omnia tempus habet,' todo tiene su tiempo" (Oviedo 1556: *quinquágena* 2, *estancia* 2, National Library of Madrid MS 2218, fol. 4 verso).

MS h-j-7. Both the spelling and the division of paragraphs have been modernized according to the same criteria used in the other texts contained in this volume. The original folio division is marked in the text.

Historia General y Natural de las Indias
The text included combines the different sources available, both printed and manuscript. The specific source of every passage is identified in a footnote. Both the spelling and the division of paragraphs have been modernized according to the same criteria used in the other texts contained in this volume.

The main source used for the first part of the *Historia General y Natural de las Indias* is the 1535 *Primera Parte de Historia General y Natural de las Indias,* printed in Seville by Juan Cromberger. For book 20 (the only book of the second part to be printed in Oviedo's life) the main source is the 1557 *Libro XX de la segunda parte dela general historia de las Indias. Escripta por el Capitan Gonzalo Fernández de Oviedo y Valdes* . . . printed in Valladolid at Fernández de Córdoba. The original folio division of both editions is marked on the text.

As explained above, a revised and expanded version of the work remained unpublished when Oviedo died. The manuscripts containing this new version—the so-called Monserrate manuscript—are incomplete. The remaining parts are preserved in two different libraries: the Library of the Royal Academy of History of Madrid MSS 9/551, 9/553, 9/555, 9/554, 9/556 & 9/557; and the Huntington Library of Los Angeles MS HM 177, 2 volumes. As the manuscripts were written over a long period of time (1535–1549) during which they were constantly modified, every passage is dated in a footnote according to references, either explicit or implicit, found in the text.

A sixteenth-century manuscript copy (ca. 1565) entitled *Historia General y Natural de las Indias*, 3 volumes (the so-called Truxillos manuscript) has been used whenever the passages in the Monserrate manuscript are missing. Volumes 1 and 3 are in the Library of the Royal Palace of Madrid II/3041-42. Volume 2 is in the Colombina of Seville MS 83-6-15. Book 28 is in volume 108 of the Jesuit Collection of the Library of the Royal Academy of History.

The only modern edition of the whole work is consistently referenced in the footnotes: *Historia General y Natural de las Indias*, edited by Juan Pérez de Tudela in Biblioteca de Autores Españoles 117–121, 5 volumes (Madrid 1959). This is a reedition of the 1851–1855 *Historia General y Natural de las Indias, islas y tierra firme del mar Oceano, por el capitán Gonzalo Fernández de Oviedo y Valdes, primer cronista del Nuevo Mundo*, 4 volumes, edited by J. Amador de los Rios. The division into paragraphs used here largely follows that found in the Amador–Pérez de Tudela edition.

Batallas y Quinquágenas escriptas por el capitán Gonzalo Fernández de Oviedo, criado del príncipe don Johan hijo de los Reyes Catholicos y cronista mayor de Indias, del Emperador Carlos V
The passages of this immense work (1535–1552) included here correspond to different manuscript sources, both original and copied. The original manuscripts are preserved in two volumes at the University Library of Salamanca MS 359 and the Library of the Royal

Academy of History MS 9/5387, respectively. There are at least four later partial copies: Library of the Royal Academy of History of Madrid MS 9/4023; Library of the Royal Palace of Madrid MS II-2604; and National Library of Madrid MSS 3314-15. Both the spelling and the division of paragraphs have been modernized according to the same criteria used in the other texts contained in this volume.

Quinquágenas de los generosos e illustres e no menos famosos reyes, príncipes, duques (...) que escribió el capitán Gonzalo Fernández de Oviedo, alcaide de Sus Majestades de la fortaleza de la ciudad e puerto de Santo Domingo, 1556.
Autograph manuscript in the National Library of Madrid MSS 221-19. Both the spelling and the division of paragraphs have been modernized according to the same criteria used in the other texts contained in this volume.

TRANSLATION

OVIEDO ON COLUMBUS

[1] FROM *THE NATURAL HISTORY OF THE INDIES*

[1.1] Chapter 1: Navigation.

1.1.1. The route commonly taken from Spain to the Indies begins at Seville, where your majesty has his Royal House of Commerce for these regions and officers to license the ships' captains and masters for the voyage. They set out from Sanlúcar de Barrameda, where the Guadalquivir river meets the Ocean Sea, and set their course for the Canary Islands. They generally stop at one or two of the seven islands, either Grand Canary or Gomera. They take on water and firewood, cheeses and meats and other items, whatever they need in addition to the provisions they bring from Spain.

1.1.2.The voyage from Spain to these islands usually takes a week, more or less, for two hundred and fifty leagues. From there the ships sail some twenty-five days until sighting the first land of the islands that are before the one we call Española. The first landfall is usually one of the Todos Santos islands, Maríagalante, La Deseada, Matininó, Dominica, Guadalupe, San Cristóbal, or one of the many others in the area. But sometimes it happens that the ships pass through without seeing land until they reach Puerto Rico, Española, Jamaica, or as far as Cuba—or even Tierra Firme,[1] the continent—but that is only when the pilot is a poor navigator. Making the voyage with skillful sailors (of which there are many to be found), some one of the first-mentioned islands will be sighted, nine hundred or more leagues from the Canaries. From there to the city of Santo Domingo is another one hundred fifty leagues. It is altogether a thousand and three hundred leagues from Spain, but the sailing route covers at least fifteen hundred leagues or more.

1.1.3. The voyage takes usually thirty-five or forty days. That is the normal duration, not taking into account extremely slow or very quick passages, because this is intended to show the normal course of a voyage. The return trip is longer, as much as fifty days, more or less. Notwithstanding, in this very year of 1525 four ships sailed from Española to Sanlúcar in Spain in twenty-five days. But as has been mentioned, we are not dealing with the exceptional case, but rather the common run.

1.1.4. The voyage to the abovementioned island is very safe and often made; from there to Tierra Firme ships cross in five, six, or seven days, or even more, depending on where they are headed, because Tierra Firme is very large and there are many possible routes and destinations. It is the land closest to the island of Española, directly across from the city of Santo Domingo. But these matters are best left to the navigational charts and the new cosmography, unknown to Ptolemy and the ancients. It is not necessary to go into the details here, better suited to the *General History* that I am

[1]South America.

writing about the Indies; I will pass on to other particulars at length.

[1.2] Chapter 3: The native peoples of Santo Domingo and other peculiar circumstances of the island.

1.2.1.The people of this island are somewhat shorter than Spaniards and of moderately dark complexion. They have their own wives and not one of them marries his daughter or his sister, or lies with his mother. They will have intercourse with women of any other degree of relationship, their wives or not. They have broad foreheads, straight black hair, and not one in a thousand has a beard nor any hair anywhere on their bodies, the men no more than the women. They go naked as the day they were born, except for a little loincloth in front, a handbreadth wide, which does not serve to conceal their private parts. But before going farther, I must say something about their diet; it will save time later treating of Tierra Firme, because the food is almost the same in both places.

[1.3] Chapter 11.

1.3.1. No writer ever knew about most of the animals living in those parts, including the ones I mention here, since they are in a region and a land which was unknown until our times and was not mentioned either in Ptolemy's cosmography or any other until the admiral Christopher Columbus made it known to us. Surely this deed is more worthy and without possible comparison, a bigger achievement than Hercules's having opened the Mediterranean Sea to the ocean, because before him, the Greeks did not know about this opening. . . . Your majesty has as a device with that the sentence *plus ultra*. These words are truly worthy of such a great and universal emperor and not suitable for any other prince. . . . It is certain that if Columbus had lived in their times, the ancients would have thought that a gold statue of him was insufficient payment.

[2] FROM *THE ROYAL AND IMPERIAL CATALOG OF SPAIN*

[2.1] The Sixth Age. In praise of Spain.

2.1.1.The sixth and last item, or cause, of the wealth of Spain is the immeasurable quantity of gold and pearls and other jewels, sugar and many different products which regularly come to Spain from the islands and Indies of the Ocean Sea, which belong to Castile. I have served in the Indies from 1514 until the present year of 1532; I served their late Catholic majesties and serve their present majesties, and at present my wife and children are there. I myself have made three round trips, crossing the Ocean Sea six times, and with God's help I intend to return soon to that new homeland of Spaniards and all Christians and people who are in Africa, Asia, and Europe. I shall carry out my duties as inspector of gold smelters. Once I am home, God willing, I mean to put an end to my travels, not only because at my age I do not need more journeys, but because Spain would not suit my health or my humor. There are storms and the inconvenience of summer and winter; these extremes (and others) are lacking in the Indies. I bring this up as his majesty's officer and overseer of the gold smelters in the province of Castilla del Oro of Tierra Firme and a long-term resident, so it will be clear that I know whereof I speak. For if the gold, pearls, and other goods brought form the Indies are uncounted up to now, greater quantities of greater value will follow, because more veins of gold are discovered daily, the men are more skillful and more accustomed to the climate, there are more Christians and more farms, so that all sorts of goods are produced in greater quantity, and the land is ennobled by buildings and churches and much more. The sea-routes are better known and for that reason the voyage is less dangerous. And if the royal share of gold and pearls is so enormous in itself, who shall put a price on the treasure brought to Spain by private individuals?

2.1.2. Never mind the fables of Midas, nor of Perseus and the treasure of the Hesperides. Let us speak of true and authentic history. Never mind rhetoric to enhance the truth: Gonzalo Fernández de Oviedo speaks in plain and simple language of the wealth of the Indies; but the most flowery of historians, even the incomparable Tullius Cicero, could not find words to express the everyday reality I have touched and seen with my own eyes. And I believe the Hesperides are in fact the Indies, according to Solinus, *De Mirabilibus Mundi*, where he says: "The Hesperides islands are beyond the Gorgades (as Sebosus says), at a distance of forty days' sailing into the deepest reaches of the sea." So that, taking Solinus as an authority, remembering that he wrote the above in Italy and that the Gorgades are the islands now called the Cape Verdes, sailing with your eyes closed you would have to end up in the Indies. I suspect, furthermore, that this same authority inspired Christopher Columbus, inventor or discoverer of the Indies, enricher of Spain, to sail with good hope and certainty of success to the New World. Returning to our theme of the wealth of Spain, what province or region of the world is there as rich, prosperous, and exalted as Spain?

[2.2]

On Christopher Columbus, first discoverer of the Indies, islands, and mainland of the Ocean Sea to whom the Spaniards owe the most after Saint James who first brought the Christian faith to Spain, because by having discovered the Indies he was the most useful to everybody.

[2.3]

Spain was populated by Tubal.
James converted it;
And Rodrigo lost it
By God's decision;
And Columbus made it rich.
But Charles V devoted himself
To Spain's immortal fame.

[3] FROM *THE GENERAL AND NATURAL HISTORY OF THE INDIES*

FIRST PART

[3.1] Prologue

3.1.1. For the better understanding of this great, natural, and general history of the Indies, I will differentiate the parts with a prologue at the beginning of each book giving a summary of the principal subjects treated therein. Therefore, I declare that this second book continues the history set forth in the first book, according to the obligation laid on me by his imperial majesty. Also, I shall imitate Pliny and touch briefly on the controversy with regard to the dedication of his *Natural History*. In addition I shall give my own opinion as to whether the ancients were cognizant of these isles as the Hesperides and prove it by weighty authorities. I shall tell of Christopher Columbus, discoverer and admiral of the Indies, and how he came to discover them—when it was, what happened on the first and second voyages, and what his discovered on each—and of the apostolic donation of the Indies made by the pope to their Catholic majesties Fernando and Isabel and their successors to the kingdoms of Castile and León. (Although according to my opinion, in ancient times the Indies belonged to Spain.) I shall tell who were some of the knights and gentlemen first to conquer and pacify this island of Española, and the difficulties of the Christians here when the admiral went to discover Jamaica.

[3.2] Book 2, chapter 1: The theories about to whom Pliny dedicated his *Natural History*; also a partial summary of the matters to be discussed in this second book.

3.2.1. I shall describe Christopher Columbus—his appearance and character; his origins, his first, second, third, and fourth voyages of discovery—and how their Catholic majesties Fernando and Isabel, conquerors of Granada and Naples, etc., granted him the rank and title of perpetual admiral of the Indies for himself and his heirs, with the arms of Castile and León and others combined with his own in a particular form as will be told. He was also made a noble, with the address of *don* for himself and his heirs. It will also be told how he discovered part of Tierra Firme, which I do not believe can be smaller than Asia, Africa, and Europe together.

3.2.2. I will not dwell on these things which are well known. I will mention some of the opinions current today about the discovery and where Columbus first heard of the New World, totally unknown to Ptolemy and other cosmographers. But I will not give more credit in this case (nor so much) to the vulgar opinion that these lands and seas were discovered first by another person, than to the self-evident accomplishments of the admiral. In truth, while a case can be made out of myth and fable to discredit Columbus, it is not plausible. The glory belongs to Columbus; the late Catholic kings, the present king and queen, and those to come owe the glory to him only, under God. And not only the possessions of the king of Spain, but foreign countries may thank Columbus for the great utility of the Indies and the uncountable treasure they have yielded, are yielding, and will yield as long as men live there.

[3.3] Book 2, chapter 2: The origins and personality of the first admiral of the Indies, Christopher Columbus, and how he came to discover the Indies, according to popular report.

3.3.1. Some people say that the New World was known a long time ago and its exact location written down, and all knowledge of it was lost. Then Christopher Columbus, a well-read man and learned in the science of navigation, dared to discover the Indies. Now I do not myself disbelieve this theory, for reasons that will be set forth in the following chapter. However, for contemporaries and posterity I will deal first with the man to whom we owe so much as leader and founder of the great enterprise he began. Christopher Columbus, as I have learned form his compatriots, was born in the province of Liguria, Italy, wherein lie the city and dominion of Genoa. Some say he was from Saona, others say from a little village or hamlet called Nervi on the eastern coast two leagues from Genoa; it seems most likely he was from a place called Cugureo, near Genoa. A decent man of a respectable family, of a good height and appearance, taller than average and strongly built, with a quick eye and regular features. He had red hair, a rather ruddy face and freckles; was well spoken, circumspect, and highly intelligent; a notable Latinist and learned cosmographer; amusing when he wished to be; furious when he was angered.

3.3.2. His ancestors came from Placentia in Lombardy, on the banks of the river Po, of the noble house of Pelestrel. Young Columbus, well-educated and just past adolescence, left his homeland during the life of his father, Domenico. Columbus went east and traveled much, or most, of the Mediterranean, learning the art of navigation by experience. After a few voyages, his spirit rose to wider seas and loftier ideas; he wanted to see the great Ocean Sea, and he want to Portugal. He lived some time in Lisbon in straitened circumstances, but as a grateful son he always sent part of his earnings to his aged father.

3.3.3. The story is told that once a caravel set out from Spain for England with a cargo of wine and foodstuffs and other merchandise the British Isles lack and are accustomed to import. The caravel encountered terrible storms and contrary winds; she ran westwards for so many days she fetched up on one or more of the islands of the Indies, landed, and saw naked people like those here. When the winds abated she took on water and firewood. As the story goes, since the ship's cargo was chiefly foodstuffs and wines, the crew was able to survive the hardships of the long voyage and catch a fair wind for Europe. But the return voyage was long and hard, especially for those who in such fear and peril had been forced to sail for four or five months, or even more. Almost all of the crew died on the voyage home, and only the pilot and some three or four of the sailors disembarked in Portugal; these survivors were so ill they also died a short time later.

3.3.4. It is said that the pilot was a close friend of Christopher Columbus and that he understood something of taking a reading of latitude and had done so for the strange lands he had seen; he told Columbus all this in secret. Columbus begged him to draw a map and mark on it the location of the strange land; it said also that Columbus took the pilot into his house as a friend and got medical attention for him, for he was very ill—but the pilot died like the rest of the sailors. This was how Columbus knew of the Indies and how to get there, and he was the only man in possession of the secret. Some say the pilot was Andalusian; others, that he was Portuguese or Vizcayan. It is also said Columbus was on the island of Madeira, or the Cape Verdes, and that it was there that the caravel made port at last.

3.3.5. No one can now affirm the truth or otherwise of this story, but it is commonly believed. Personally I consider it false, as Augustine says: "Melius est dubitare de occultis, quam litigare de incertis": It is better to doubt what we do not know for sure than to insist on what is uncertain.

[3.4] Book 2, chapter 3: The author of this *Natural and General History of the Indies* gives his opinion as to whether the ancients knew and wrote of the whereabouts of the Indies, and proves it by references.

3.4.1. In the previous chapter the common theory with regard to the discovery of the Indies was aired; now I will say what I think the truth of the matter is and why Columbus, a wise, learned and daring man, undertook his famous voyage of discovery. He knew that these lands were, in truth, forgotten. But he found written evidence of their existence, and I myself do not doubt that the Indies were known in ancient times to the kings of Spain and belonged to them.

3.4.2. . . . So that, as Spain and Italy and that city said to be in Mauritania were called Hesperidas and Hesperide, after Hespero, twelfth king of Spain, the islands called the Hesperides by Sebosus and Solinus and Pliny and Isidore of Seville must of necessity be the Indies, which undoubtedly belonged to Spain since the time of Hespero, twelfth king of Spain, in the year one thousand six hundred and fifty-eight years before the birth of Christ, according to Berosus. Since at present it has been one thousand five hundred and thirty-eight years since the glorious birth of Christ, it follows that three thousand one hundred and ninety-three years ago Spain and her king Hespero ruled over these islands, or Indies Hesperides. With such an ancient right, and because of the fame I mentioned—or will mention, when I recount the voyages of Columbus—God returned the sovereignty of the Indies to Spain after so many centuries. Since the Indies belonged to Spain, divine justice returned them and wills that they be perpetually Spanish possessions for the sake of the blessed Fernando and Isabel who conquered Granada and Naples, etc., in whose reign the admiral discovered the New World, or a great part of it, forgotten by the universe. Afterward, in the reign of his imperial majesty, these lands have been further discovered and explored, to augment his dominions.

3.4.3. Therefore, all the above authors mention the Indies; so I believe that Columbus, following these authorities or others he may have known, set out to look for what he found, braving certain danger and a long voyage. Whatever his inspiration, with or without the aforementioned authorities, he undertook what no one before him had dared.

[3.5] Book 2, chapter 4: How Columbus taught the Spaniards to navigate by latitude and the magnetic north, and how he went to Portugal and other parts looking for someone who could help him discover the Indies; how Fernando and Isabel, who commissioned the discovery, heard about him.

3.5.1. It is the general opinion, and it stands to reason, that Christopher Columbus was the first to teach the Spaniards to navigate the ocean by means of latitude and magnetic north, and applied the knowledge, because before him, although celestial navigation could be studied in books, few or none dared rely on it at sea, because the science cannot be completely mastered without experience in waters out of sight of land. Sailors and navigators until then practiced their trade according to their best judgment, but did not attain the exactitude with which we now sail the ocean. They clung to the coasts of the Mediterranean, Spain and Flanders, Europe and Africa and all parts of the world that could be reached without sailing far from land. But to sail in search of provinces as distant from Spain as these Indies are, and to navigate by means of the quadrant, seas of great latitude and longitude are required, like from here to Europe or to the Especiería [2] to the west of Tierra Firme of these Indies.

3.5.2. Columbus, therefore, either because he wished to prove his mastery of the art of navigation or because he had the secret of the hidden lands from the aforementioned pilot in Portugal or in the islands (if the story be true), or because of the authors cited in the previous chapter, or for whatever reason, worked to find a sponsor for his projected voyage. Through his brother Bartolomé he approached the king of England Henry VII (father of Henry VIII, who reigns now), offering much treasure and the extension of his dominions. The king's counselors and other persons consulted about the project advised him not to take Columbus's proposal seriously. Columbus, undiscouraged by the English king's refusal, made the same proposals to João II of Portugal. The king of Portugal put no credence in him either, although Columbus was married in Portugal and therefore a naturalized subject of the king. But that made no difference, the king refused to help him in any manner. Therefore Columbus determined to go to Spain. When he arrived in Seville, he consulted with the illustrious and valorous don Enrique de Guzmán, duke of Medina Sidonia, but to no avail. He presented his project at length to the very illustrious don Luis de la Cerda, first duke of Medinaceli, who also dismissed him as a liar—although some people say the duke was willing to outfit Columbus in his town of Puerto de Santa María but their Catholic majesties refused him permission to do so. Therefore Columbus went to the court of their serene and Catholic majesties Fernando and Isabel; he was there for some time, poor and misunderstood, seeking the favor of the monarchs to outfit a few caravels and discover the New World in their name.

3.5.3. However, no one could comprehend or believe in this project but Columbus himself. For seven years he persisted, offering enormous wealth and dominions to the crown of Castile. Added to the sheer incredibility of a plan proposed by an unknown foreigner with no patron, his obvious poverty induced people to consider him a liar and a dreamer.

3.5.4. Well may it be said that God took care to bestow the Indies on whom he did! Offered to England and Portugal, and the aforesaid dukes, God saw to it that neither powerful king nor wealthy duke should advance the small sum Columbus asked, so that he might go in search of the king and queen of Castile, currently occupied with the conquest of Granada.

[2] "Land of Spices," or Indonesia.

3.5.5. It is no wonder that the very Catholic king and queen, looking more for souls to save than kingdoms and wealth to trouble themselves with, decided to support the enterprise of the discovery. Let no one call it good fortune, for no eye has seen, nor ear has heard, nor heart imagined such things as God prepares for those who love him. This and many other blessings came to those good monarchs of ours, because they were true servants of Jesus Christ and promoted his sacred worship. Therefore, it was by divine will that Christopher Columbus came to their notice, for God sees all things under heaven even to the ends of the earth.

3.5.6. When at last the long negotiations concluded, these were the terms settled which were settled on. When Columbus, as I have said, was frequenting the court, he used to go to the home of Alonso de Quintanilla, chief accountant of their Catholic majesties and a prominent and loyal servitor. Quintanilla took pity on Columbus's poverty, providing him with food and other necessities. This friend introduced him to the illustrious reverend cardinal of Spain and archbishop of Toledo, don Pedro González de Mendoza; the cardinal gave audiences to the sailor and discovered he was both learned and well spoken in explaining the reasons behind his proposals. Seeing Columbus as a man of great ability and ingenuity, the cardinal formed a good opinion of him and decided to advance his cause with the king and queen. Thus Columbus had the ear of their majesties, and his petitions began to attract some attention. The business was concluded while their Catholic majesties laid siege to the great and famous city of Granada in 1492. From the royal camp at the town Santa Fe that they founded amid their armies, they dispatched Columbus; there, as it may be said, in the very holy faith of their royal hearts the discovery began.

3.5.7. The sainted rulers were not content with the holy conquest they had in hand of all the Moors in Spain (who had been in occupation in spite of the Christians since the year 720, as many authors agree); besides bringing all Spain to the Catholic religion, they decided to look for new worlds to evangelize without losing an hour from the service of God. With this sainted purpose they sent Columbus, with their orders and royal credentials, to Andalusia for three caravels, manned and provisioned for the voyage. The most certain thing about such a long voyage was the zeal and holy purpose of those most Christian rulers by whose order the great enterprise was begun. Money was lacking for the expedition, because of the war, so the royal secretary Luis de Santángel loaned the necessary sum for the first voyage. The king and queen made the first capitulation with Columbus in Santa Fe, the royal camp, on the eighteenth of April in 1492; this took place in the presence of the secretary Juan de Coloma. It was confirmed by a royal privilege he received thirteen days later, granted on the thirtieth of April in the city of Granada in the same year. With this Columbus departed and went to Palos de Moguer, where he prepared for the voyage.

[3.6] Book 2, chapter 5: The first voyage of discovery to the Indies made by Christopher Columbus, first discoverer, for which he was rightly made perpetual admiral of the seas and the empire of the Indies.

3.6.1. You have heard how and why Columbus came to the attention of Fernando and Isabel, during the siege of Granada, and how they made an agreement with him and gave him royal authorization, and he went to Palos de Moguer to begin his voyage. You must also know that he started out with three caravels: the biggest was called the *Gallega*,[3] and the other two were from Palos; and all were provisioned and equipped with everything necessary. According to the capitulation with Columbus, Columbus had a tenth of the royal revenues from whatever he discovered, which was paid to him until he died, and afterwards to his son don Diego, the second admiral, and now to don Luis, his grandson and the third admiral to enjoy the title and estate.

3.6.2. Before weighing anchor, Columbus had some long consultations with a religious known as Fray Juan Pérez, a Franciscan and his confessor, in the monastery of La Rábida, half a league from Palos. This friar was the only person to whom Columbus communicated his secrets; and even today it is said he received useful information, because the friar was a great cosmographer. Columbus spent some time with him at La Rábida, and Fray Juan sent him to the royal pavilion in Granada, where the terms of the contract were finalized. After that Columbus returned to the monastery and told the friar about his journey, put his temporal and spiritual affairs in order, and, like a good Catholic, put himself and his enterprise in the hands of God—as befits a faithful Christian, and in God's own interest, since he proposed to greatly enlarge the republic of Christian souls. After confession he received the Eucharist and set sail on the first voyage of discovery the same day. In the name of Jesus he left the port of Palos by the Saltés river to the Ocean Sea with three caravels, Friday, 3 August 1492. He was successful, achieving this great undertaking by the will of God, who chose to make him the agent for such a venture.

3.6.3. The *Gallega* was the flagship of the three caravels in which Columbus sailed. The others were the *Pinta*, commanded by Martín Alonso Pinzón, and the *Niña*, commanded by Francisco Martín Pinzón, in which Vicente Yáñez Pinzón sailed. The three of them were brothers, pilots from Palos. All in all, the crew numbered 120 men; they set a course for the Canary Islands, which the ancients called the Fortunate Isles.

3.6.4. For a long time no one had visited these islands, nor knew how to get there, until the minority of Juan II of Castile, in the regency of his mother doña Catalina. By their command and license the islands were found again and conquered, as is told in more detail in the *Chronicle* of the same king Juan II. Many years afterwards a noble gentleman of Jerez de la Frontera called Pedro de Vera, and Miguel de Móxica conquered Grand Canary in the name of their Catholic majesties Fernando and Isabel, and all the other islands except La Palma and Tenerife. The last two were conquered by Alonso de Lugo, whom Fernando and Isabel made governor of Tenerife.

3.6.5. The people of the Canaries were robust, almost naked, and so primitive it was said they did not have fire and did not have it until the Christians conquered the islands. Their weapons were sticks and stones, with which they killed many Christians, until they were subjugated and put under the government of Castile. The nearest islands are two hundred leagues from Spain, and the farthest, Lanzarote and Hierro, are two hundred and forty leagues: they occupy a space of fifty or sixty leagues. The islands are located from twenty-seven to twenty-nine degrees from the equator, in the

[3]The *Santa María* had been built in the Galician shipyards; hence the alternate name.

northern hemisphere; the westernmost island is parallel with Cape Bojador in Africa at a distance of sixty-five leagues. These islands are all fertile and abundant with the necessities for human life, and of a temperate climate. Few of the native people who were there when the islands were conquered remain, but there is a large population of Christians.

3.6.6. And there, an appropriate place and useful for journey, Columbus arrived on his voyage of discovery with his three caravels; he took on water and firewood, meat and fish and other provisions to continue the voyage. When the fleet was watered and victualled, they left from Gomera on 6 September 1492 and then sailed across the great Ocean Sea for many days, so many that the crew grew faint-hearted and wanted to turn back. They murmured behind Columbus's back, criticizing his navigation and his daring, fearful of the voyage ahead. The captains and crew mutinied, as each day their fear increased and their hope of seeing the land they sought lessened. Finally, they told him openly and without shame that he had deceived them and they were lost; the king and queen were wrong and cruel to send them with such a man, trusting in a foreigner who did not know what he was talking about. They went so far as to assure him if he did not turn back they would force him to, or throw him in the sea. They thought him crazy and they said they did not want to be and that they did not believe that he could finish what he had started and therefore they all agreed not to follow him.

3.6.7. At this juncture they came upon what looked like huge pastures of grass on the sea; thinking they had come to drowned continents and they were lost, the men redoubled their complaints. And for those who had never seen such a thing doubtless it was a fearful sight. But the alarm was short-lived, seeing there was no danger in the weed called sargasso which floats on the surface of the water according to the winds and currents, east or west, north or south, in mid-ocean or closer to shore. On some voyages the ships encounter little or no sargasso; sometimes there is so much it looks like vast green, yellow, and gold meadows.

3.6.8. Once out and free from concern and fear of the grass, the three captains and the crews were determined to turn back, debating only whether or not to throw Columbus overboard for having deceived them. But he was wise enough to guess what they were saying and prudent enough to soothe the men with many encouraging words. He begged them not to throw away the time and trouble they had already invested; he reminded them what glory and profit their perseverance would gain them; he promised a quick end to their trials and the voyage, great and certain prosperity; and at last he told them they would find the land they were seeking within three days. So they must go bravely on, for in three days he would show them a New World, their troubles would be over, and they would see he had told the truth, both to them and to the king and queen. If it were not so, they could do as they liked—but he was absolutely sure of what he was telling them.

3.6.9. This raised the faltering spirits of those who were tending towards a shameful act of cowardice, especially the three brothers and captains mentioned before. They agreed to do as he asked and sail for three days and no more, turning back to Spain if no land was sighted. They in fact expected to turn back, because not one of them thought there could be any land along that parallel, and would not sail an hour farther, because the provisions and water they had left would hardly get them back to Spain without great privation, however carefully they were rationed.

3.6.10. So as they sailed on, the fearful crew never ceased to complain, threatening the commander in chief. Nor did he rest for a moment, encouraging and raising the spirits of all the men; the more fearful he saw them, the more cheerful a face he put on. That same day, Columbus realized by the cloud formations that they really were close to land. He advised the pilots that if the ships became separated, to set such-and-such a course in order to rejoin the convoy. Night fell; he ordered sail shortened and the fleet went on with only the foresails set. Then a sailor on the flagship, a man from Lepe, cried: "Light! Land!" A servant of Columbus's, called Salcedo, answered, saying, "My lord the admiral told you so." Then said Columbus quickly, "I said it a good while ago; I saw the light on land." So it was that, on Thursday at two in the morning, the admiral called for Escobedo, chamberlain to his majesty, and told him he saw a light. The next morning at daybreak, at the time Columbus had predicted the day before, the island the Indians call Guanahaní was visible to the north of the flagship. Rodrigo de Triana first sighted land, at daybreak, 11 October 1492.

3.6.11. The admiral predicted the landfall so accurately it gave credence to the suspicion that he had been informed by the pilot said to have died in his house, as was mentioned above. It might also be the case that he simply trusted in God that they would see land before the three days were up and the crew turned back.

3.6.12. Going back to the history: that first island was one of the Lucayos. And the sailor who first saw the bonfires on shore felt he was unappreciated on his return to Spain and went over to Africa and abjured his faith. This man, I heard from Vicente Pinzón and Hernán Pérez Mateos, was from Lepe, as I mentioned before.

3.6.13. As soon as the admiral saw land, he knelt and wept tears of joy, saying as did Ambrose and Augustine, "Te Deum laudamus, Te Dominum confitemur," and so on. Thus, giving thanks to God with all his men, they were indescribably joyful. Some embraced the admiral and some kissed his hands; others begged his pardon for their lack of confidence. Others begged favors and pledged themselves to him. In short, there was such rejoicing at the successful conclusion of the voyage they were almost beside themselves. I find it easy to believe, because even now when the voyage between Spain and the Indies is certain and sure, there is no pleasure to compare with sighting land after a long time at sea. How much more might the sailors rejoice seeing land after such a doubtful trip.

3.6.14. However, I must point out that there is a contrary opinion: some say the opposite of Columbus's courage and even affirm that he would have turned back if the Pinzón brothers had not insisted on continuing and that they were really the ones responsible for the discovery, not Columbus. This matter is best left to the lawsuit pending between Columbus and the crown, with all the charges and countercharges. I do not want to get into that, as it is a question of law, and the law will decide. I have given both sides of the argument; the reader must use his own good judgment.

3.6.15. It took the admiral thirty-three days from the Canary Islands to the first landfall; he arrived in October of 1492.

[3.7] Book 2, chapter 6: How the admiral discovered this island of Española and left thirty-eight Christians in the territory of the cacique Guacanagarí while he carried the news of the discovery safely home to Spain.

3.7.1. On the island of Guanahaní the admiral and his companions saw Indians and naked people, who told him of the island of Cuba. Then they found many islets clustered around Guanahaní, which they called the Islas Blancas because of the white sand; but Columbus named them the Princessas, because they had been the first sighting of the Indies. He sailed by these islands, between Guanahaní and another called Caicos; but according to the pilot Hernán Pérez Mateos, resident at this time in this city of Santo Domingo, who says he was there, they did not land on any of them. On the other hand, I have heard many people say that the admiral landed on Guanahaní and named it San Salvador and took possession of it, which is the more likely story and worthy of credit. From there he came to Baracoa, a northern port of Cuba, twelve leagues west of the point called Maicí. There he encountered people from Cuba itself and from the many other islands whose overall name is the Lucayos, although they all have names: Guanahaní, Caicos, Jumeto, Yabaque, Mayaguana, Samaná, Guanima, Yuma, Curateo, Ciguateo, Bahama (the largest), Yucayo, Necua, Habacoa, and many more.

3.7.2. To return to our history: the admiral, as I said, landed in Cuba with some of his men and asked the Indians where Cipangu was located. They answered him with signs and signaled that it was the island of Haiti, which we now call Española. The Indians, thinking that Columbus did not have the name right, said, "Cibao! Cibao!" thinking that they had said "Cipangu" for "Cibao," because Cibao is where on the island of Española the richest mines with the finest gold are located. Several Indians volunteered to board the ships and guide them, so the three caravels left Baracoa de Cuba and came to the island of Haiti, now Española, anchoring in a very good harbor on the north coast. They called it Puerto Real. But at the entrance to the harbor the flagship *Gallega* ran aground and stove in her hull. There was no danger, and it was widely believed that Columbus cleverly did it on purpose to have an excuse to leave some men ashore. The admiral and all the men disembarked. Soon some peaceful Indians came to talk with them on behalf of the king Guacanagarí (their word for "king" is "cacique"), with whom the Christians easily entered into a pact of peace and amity. The cacique visited the Spaniards continually with the utmost civility; he was given some trifles that the Indians found wonderful, such as bells, pins and needles, and some colored glass beads. In return the Indians supplied the Christians with food and other necessities.

3.7.3. When the admiral saw how civil these people were, it seemed that he could certainly leave some Spaniards there to learn the language and customs while he returned to Spain. Therefore on a sandy spot on the coast near the port, he had a square stockade built with the timbers of the *Gallega*, bundles of faggots, and earth. He ordered thirty-eight men to stay there and told them what to do while he took the great news of the discovery to their Catholic majesties and returned with rewards for all—especially for those who stayed behind. He appointed captain a gentleman called Rodrigo de Arana, who was from Córdoba, and ordered them all to obey him in the way that they would the admiral himself. He selected also two alternates in case Arana should die before he returned. He also left a surgeon with them, master Juan, a good fellow. Columbus admonished the men not to explore the interior of the island, nor disobey the captain, nor separate, nor take women, nor annoy the Indians in any way, as far as possible.

3.7.4. Since the flagship was lost, the admiral embarked on the *Niña* with Francisco Martín and Vicente Yáñez Pinzón. Their brother Martín Alonso Pinzón, captain of the *Pinta*, was not pleased at leaving the other men on the island and contradicted Columbus at every point. He said it was a crime to leave so few Christians so far from Spain; with no provisions to sustain them, they would perish. He said more on the subject, which angered the admiral; Martín Alonso feared he would be arrested, so he weighed anchor and took the *Pinta* to the harbor of Gracia twenty leagues east of Puerto Real.

3.7.5. While the admiral was engaged in constructing the stockade, he heard from the Indians where Martín Alonso and the caravel had got to. The other two Pinzón brothers, who were still with the admiral, effected a reconciliation and Martín Alonso was finally pardoned. Columbus did it for many reasons, not least among them the fact that most of his seamen were relatives and friends of the Pinzón family, from the same town, and considered them leaders. So he wrote Martín Alonso as generous a letter as the case demanded, and ordered that the bay he fled to be called Puerto de Gracia, which is its name to this day. The Indians who took the letter returned with Martín Alonso's answer, thanking the admiral for his pardon. It was agreed that on a certain day Martín Alonso with one ship and Columbus with the other would meet at La Isabela, some eighteen leagues or so east of Puerto Real. They all landed there in perfect harmony.

3.7.6. The Indians were astonished at how the Christians communicated by letter; the messengers carried the letters in a cleft stick, regarding them with fear and trembling as the abode of spirits who spike like men by supernatural arts.

3.7.7. So then the admiral and all his men, except the thirty-eight who were left behind, took on water, wood, and such provision as the land afforded to eke out the stores they had brought from Spain; they sailed from La Isabela, named in honor of the Catholic queen by Columbus. From there they went to Puerto de Plata (as the admiral named it) and then to the port of Samaná (as the Indians called it). From Samaná, on the north coast of Española, the two caravels set their course joyfully for Spain, commending themselves to God and the merits of their Catholic majesties of Spain, who awaited the great news with more confidence in the mercy of God than the skill of the admiral.

3.7.8. He took along nine or ten Indians as witnesses of his success, to kiss the royal hands and see the land of the Christians and learn the language; when they returned here, they and the Christians who stayed with Guacanagarí at Puerto Real could be interpreters for the conquest, pacification, and conversion of these people.

3.7.9. Since it was the will of God that these lands be discovered, just as the first voyage was rapid and prosperous, so was the return voyage; and the discoverer was carried safely from the Indies to Spain. The Azores were sighted, and on 4 March 1493 Columbus sailed into Lisbon and from there to the port of Palos from whence he had started.

3.7.10. The whole voyage took only fifty days from this island to Castile. But a storm separated the two caravels near Europe and the admiral ran to Lisbon while Martín Alonso made for Bayona in Galicia. Then each ship made its way to the Saltés river and by chance entered the same day, the admiral in the morning and the other ship in the afternoon. Martín Alonso suspected the admiral might order him arrested, because of what had happened; he secretly put off in a boat as the ship sailed into harbor and went into hiding. Meanwhile, the admiral set out for court with his great tidings. When Martín Alonso heard of his departure he himself went home to Palos, where he died in his own house a few days later, for his was very ill.

3.7.11. It took Columbus almost three months from when he first left Spain to landfall in the Lucayos, as I have said; the time he spent here, and the return home, another three months; so the whole voyage took six months, give or take ten days.

3.7.12. Returning to the history: Columbus arrived at Palos with the Indians he had taken from these islands, except for one who died at sea. He left in Palos two or three of them who were sick and took the six healthy ones to the royal court with him to announce to the monarchs how the prosperity and extent of their dominions was augmented. No one expected the news so soon, because it was truly extraordinary, given the usual duration of the round trip from Spain to the Indies, until it was better understood. Even today, that would be good time for two ships; since, as I have said, the route is well known now, and then they had to sail by guesswork, lead, and line to take soundings in hand, shortening sail at night; with great caution, like wise and prudent pilots in unknown waters.

[3.8] Book 2, chapter 7: Four remarkable events of the year 1492: the arrival of Christopher Columbus at the court of their Catholic majesties Fernando and Isabel, and the favors granted him after he returned to Spain from the first voyage of discovery to the Indies; and the reasons why it it is likely that the apostles, or one of them, preached the gospel in these lands.

3.8.1. One who speaks of things he has heard merits less credit than an eyewitness. Saint Gregory says as much about the fourteenth and fifteenth chapter of Job. But I do not quote him only on account of those authors in Spain who write about the Indies, but because here I will speak of events in Spain while I am in the Indies, for I also saw what happened in Spain, even though I live in the Indies.

3.8.2. Since it is relevant to my purpose, I will say 1492 was a very notable year in Spain. On 2 January Fernando and Isabel took the great and famous city of Granada. The same year, at the end of July, they expelled the Jews from their dominions. The same year, Friday 7 December in Barcelona, a peasant from the village of Remensa in Catalonia, named Juan de Cañamares, stabbed the Catholic king in the neck. It was a dangerous wound and the king almost died; exemplary justice was done on the perpetrator, in spite of the fact he was evidently mad and always said if he killed Fernando, he would be king himself. That same year Columbus discovered these Indies and arrived in Barcelona in April of 1492 to find the king very thin but out of danger.

3.8.3. These remarkable events are recalled to illustrate the era in which Columbus arrived at court. I speak as an eyewitness, because I was there at the siege of Granada as a boy. I was a page, and I saw Santa Fe founded by the army, and afterwards saw their Catholic majesties enter Granada when it yielded. I saw the Jews expelled from Castile; and I was in Barcelona when the king was wounded as I have said; and there I saw the admiral Christopher Columbus come, with the first Indians of the discovery. So I do not speak from hearsay of any of these events, but as an eyewitness, even though I am now writing here—or rather, referring to my memoirs in which these matters were written down at the time. Let us return to the history.

3.8.4. When Columbus reached Barcelona with the first Indians to travel from here to Spain, some samples of gold, many parrots, and other things people here use, he was kindly and graciously received by the king and queen. After he had related in detail and at great length everything that had occurred during his voyage, the grateful rulers granted him many royal boons and began to treat him as a distinguished and prominent person—which he fully merited.

3.8.5. However, I think (as I mentioned in the prologue to book 1) that it is only right to insist that in these our Indies the gospel was proclaimed; first in our Spain by the apostle Saint James the Greater, and afterwards the apostle Paul, as Saint Gregory writes. And if from our Castile the holy gospel was cultivated and transplanted in these times, that does not mean that these savage peoples did not know, from apostolic times, of the redemption and the blood of Christ spilled for humankind. It must rather be believed that these generations and the Indians of these parts had forgotten, since "in omnem terram exivit sonus eorum, et in fines orbis terrae verba eorum," in agreement with the psalmist David. Saint Gregory says, with reference to the sixteenth chapter of Job, these words: Holy church has already preached the mystery of our redemption in all parts of the world. So these Indians must have been informed of the gospel and they can't feign ignorance in this case; let the matter be left to the theologians, as it is their province. But even though the ancestors of these Indians must have known of our holy Catholic faith, the people have forgotten it. So it was a great service their Catholic majesties did for God, discovering the Indies. Our nation acquired enormous merit by finding these provinces and kingdoms full of lost souls and idolaters, owing to the diligence of the admiral Christopher Columbus, in company with him and under his guidance. Thus in these countries so far from Europe, where Hell swallowed so many millions of souls, the sacred Passion and the commandments of God and the Catholic Church were reintroduced and cultivated; idolatries and diabolical sacrifices and rites devoted to Satan for centuries ceased; and the practice of abominable crimes and sins against nature were forgotten.

3.8.6. Many books of history would not suffice to tell the holy zeal of Fernando and Isabel and their successors for the conversion of these people. The royal will, royal command, and constant care have been directed to the good of the Indians' souls and kind treatment for them. If there has been any lack of the latter, it is the fault of the ministers, men who come here as governors or prelates and neglect their duty. But the abuses last only until they come to the attention of the emperor or of his royal Council of the Indies, at which time immediate attention is given to correcting whatever may be wrong.

3.8.7. I myself am inclined to attribute the principal cause of any failures, or less than the expected success in this case, not to the officials who undertake the pious and holy work of teaching doctrine to this generation of Indians, but to the Indians' own incapacity and evil tendencies. For it is true there are few—very few—of the multitude who persevere in the faith. Most slip away like hail from a lance point. God will have to take a hand, so that the teachers and the pupils make more progress than they have to date. I shall return to the history.

3.8.8. Six Indians went to court with the admiral, to Barcelona, as I have said. Of their own free will, acting on advice, they asked to be baptized; their Catholic majesties in their mercy granted the favor and stood their godparents along with the prince and heir don Juan. The leader of the Indians, a native of Española and a relation of the cacique Guacanagarí, received the name don Fernando de Aragón; another became don Juan de Castilla; the others also received Christian names according to their own wish or the decision of their sponsors. Prince Juan adopted Don Juan de Castilla and took him into the royal household, to be honored and treated as if he were the son of a prominent gentleman and favorite. The prince had his steward Patiño indoctrinate the Indian in all the matters of our holy faith; I met him when he spoke Castilian very well. Two years afterwards he died.

3.8.9. The other Indians returned to this island on Columbus's second voyage. Columbus himself received many favors from the king and queen, and his privileges were confirmed in Barcelona, 28 May 1493. Among them, he received the patent of nobility and the title of perpetual admiral of the Indies with the right of inheritance and primogeniture, the title of *don* for his whole family, including his brothers, and the royal arms of Castile and León, conjoined with newly-conceded arms and the confirmation of some old arms of his lineage. From all these a new and handsome coat of arms with his crest and device was formed in this manner, as may be seen:

3.8.10. A shield with a golden castle on a heraldic red field with blue doors and windows and a purple or violet lion rampant on a silver field with a golden crown and its tongue sticking out, like the royal lion of the kingdoms of Castile and León. The castle and lion are in the upper quadrants, the castle on the right and the lion on the left. The two remaining quadrants are divided; on the right, a sea in memory of the great Ocean Sea: the water in natural blue and white with the Tierra Firme of the Indies occupying almost the total circumference of this quadrant, leaving the upper part open, so that the extremes of this large landmass appear to occupy the southern and northern regions; the lower part, that signifies the west, is indicated by land continuing from one side to the other; and within this configuration the sea is filled with many large and small islands of different shapes, so that this figure, according to the way it is emblazoned in this quadrant, can signify the Indies. The land and islands must be very green, with trees and palms, because here leaves do not fall from the trees, or very seldom; and Tierra Firme must have much gilding to signify the innumerable rich gold mines in these lands. By this illustration, if the reader did not understand clearly the size and location of Tierra Firme described in the first chapter of book 2, he will see it now. And I will go back to the coat of arms I was describing. In the remaining left quadrant of the shield are five golden anchors on a field of blue, appropriate for the office and title of perpetual admiral of the Indies; in the lower part of the shield are the family arms of Columbus, the upper part in heraldic red and below it a blue band on a field of gold. Above the shield is a helmet in natural color,[4] with eight openings, a scroll, and blue and gold dependencies; the crest of the helmet is a globe with a red cross above it and the Indies and Tierra Firme are painted on the globe. Below the shield this motto is inscribed in black letters on white: "For Castile and León, Columbus found a new world."

3.8.11. As a compliment to the admiral, their Catholic majesties also made his brother Bartolomé governor of Española and granted many other privileges which in order to avoid prolixity I will omit here, but which appear in the royal decree which I have seen several times.

[3.9] Book 2, chapter 8: The second voyage which the first admiral, Christopher Columbus, made from Spain to this island of Haiti or Española; how he found that all the Christians he had left behind in the king Guacanagarí's land were dead; and Pope Alexander VI's concession of the Indies to Fernando and Isabel and their heirs in Castile and León. Also the discovery of the islands of the Indians armed with bows and arrows, called Caribs, and other remarkable things.

3.9.1. Who does not know that the Lord created earthly things for our use, and the souls of men for his own, as Saint Gregory reminds us? Therefore, the blessed monarchs Fernando and Isabel, desiring to win the souls of these Indians for God, sent the admiral back to Haiti (or Española) with a goodly fleet and many gentlemen and knights of the royal household and other noble and well-born men who wanted to see the New World and its marvels.

3.9.2. These blessed princes had first got the pope's concession of the Indies, to justify their holy purpose (which was to extend the Christian religion as faithful servants of God); although they needed no permission, they asked for license of Christ's vicar to whom their hearts were always faithful. Also, these lands and seas belong by conquest to the crown of Castile, and only their Catholic majesties were concerned in this memorable and holy undertaking; and finally, as I said, many centuries ago the Indies were part of the dominions of the kings of Spain.

3.9.3. Therefore the pope awarded the Indies and the rest to the king and queen and their successors in the kingdoms of Castile and León. He made a line from pole to pole, stretching from a hundred leagues before the Azores and the Cape Verdes as far west as the world goes, giving Spain all the lands not already in possession of some Christian prince.

3.9.4. Afterwards Spain and Portugal agreed to draw the line three hundred and sixty leagues to the west of the pope's line, and give Portugal the difference between the two. From this the Portuguese argue that all the east is theirs, but they deceive themselves. The papal bull or donation to Castile and her kings comprised all the islands of the Especiería and of the Moluccas and Brunei (where cinnamon is harvested) with all of the Especiería and the rest of the world east to the first line of demarcation

[4]A "baúl" or a "yelmo baúl de torneo" is a type of jousting helmet.

a hundred leagues from the Azores and Cape Verde Islands. All this, as I have said, is included in the part of the world conceded to their Catholic majesties of glorious memory and belongs to the crown of Castile.

3.9.5. Since these matters have been approved by the vicar of God and of the holy church, it is necessary to say only that I have seen an authorized, signed copy of the papal bull, dated as follows: "Datis Romae apud Sanctus Petrum, anno Incarnationis Domini millesimo quadrigentessimo nonagessimo tertio, quarto nonas maii, pontificatus nostri anno primo."

3.9.6. As directed by the holy father in the bull, with regard to the care which must be taken as to the conversion of the Indians, many religious came, persons of exemplary and holy life and letters. Especially chosen was Fray Buyl of the Order of Saint Benedict, from Catalonia; the holy father gave him full authority to administer the church in these parts, as head of the clerics and religious which at this time came here to celebrate divine worship and convert these Indians. They brought all the ornaments and crosses and chalices and images, everything necessary for the churches and temples to be built. The pope also directed the king and queen by their holy obedience to send to the Indies good, God-fearing men, learned and expert, to teach and instruct the inhabitants of these new lands in the Catholic faith and good habits, with all the diligence the case requires.

3.9.7. Therefore, in obedience to the pope, with holy zeal to fulfill their duty to the utmost, their Catholic majesties searched their kingdoms for such ecclesiastics and laymen to carry out the task set them. That same year a handsome equipage, and a brilliant and noble company, went with the admiral from court in Barcelona to Seville in Andalusia; men and ships for the fleet were collected in the bay of Cádiz.

3.9.8. The ships passed in review, each captain and sailing master and pilot received his course and his orders. Then from Cádiz the fleet set sail with a fair wind, Wednesday 25 September 1493. At dawn the flagship hoisted sail, and all the other ships followed: there were in all seventeen sails, a force of fifteen hundred good men well-equipped and armed, provisioned with everything necessary, paid by the crown. Religious, gentlemen, knights, and worthy men traveled in the fleet, men fit to colonize new lands and cultivate both the spiritual and temporal aspects in a true and godly fashion. There were also many royal servitors, as was to be expected of such exceedingly Christian rulers. I knew personally most of the more important expeditionaries, some of whom are alive to this day here in the Indies and in Spain—although there are few left now.

3.9.9. Returning to the history of the second voyage: the admiral, having profited like an expert navigator by the experience of the first voyage, set a more direct course this time. The first landfall was an island that he named La Deseada as soon as he saw it, because he and all the fleet desired to see land. Then they sighted another island and the admiral named Maríagalante, because that was the name of the admiral's flagship. He named all the other islands in the reach, from north to south as follows: first and nearest, Guadalupe, Barbada, Aguja, Sombrero, and others. Nearer still, Anegada, and the many small Virgin Islands to the west of it, and farther on the isle of Boriquén, now called San Juan. This island is very rich and one of the most important ones, as will be explained when I come to it. To the south of La Deseada the nearest island is Dominica, so-called because the admiral first saw it on a Sunday. Then Todos Santos; still more to the south, Matininó, to which some chroniclers have attributed a population of Amazons, and other fables; all untrue as those of us who have seen the island and others in the area have found out. It is not true that the island is entirely populated by women, either, nor was that ever the case, as far as is known.

3.9.10. There are other islands, Santa Lucía, San Cristóbal, the Barbados, and many small and unimportant islets. But when I relate the discovery of Tierra Firme, I will name the rest, between Barbados and the coast of Tierra Firme, such as Libuqueira, which the Christians call Santa Cruz and the chronicler Peter Martyr calls Ayay.

3.9.11. All the islands near this one, or most of them, are populated by Indians who use bow and arrow, called Caribs, which in the Indian language means fierce and daring. They have a deadly arrow poison, for which there is no cure; wounded men die raving, biting their hands and their own flesh because the pain drives them mad. If anyone survives, it must be by means of the most assiduous application of antidotes—which we have not seen many of here. Really, the only time anyone survives is when the venom is old or lacking some of the poisonous ingredients (which I will explain later), for the Indians of different regions have different recipes. In these islands they eat human flesh, except in Boriquén; also in many parts of Tierra Firme, as will be seen. Pliny says the same of the anthropophages of Scythia; besides eating human flesh, they drink from the skulls of dead men and wear necklaces of their teeth and hair. I have seen just such necklaces in Tierra Firme.

3.9.12. Let us return to the history of the voyage, for the criminal customs of the Indians will be described at length in the proper place. Therefore I will say that having sighted La Deseada and nearby islands, the fleet sailed on among them, as soon as it had watered, and came to Boriquén (now called San Juan, as I said before). This is the biggest island in that area and the most important. Farther on I will make a particular point of describing where it is, how big, what it is like, and what kind of people live there, how far from Spain and from the other islands. Let the reader not think for a moment that all the islands I have mentioned were discovered on this voyage, as some authors have mistakenly asserted; no, the admiral saw La Deseada, and nearby islands he necessarily had to see as well, because they are so close together; but the others were discovered and conquered by different captains, in time, as these seas were explored.

3.9.13. Returning to the history, I say that after the fleet passed Boriquén (or San Juan), it came to Haiti, which we call Española; in December of the same year it sailed into the northern harbor of Puerto de Plata, then down the west coast to La Isabela. From there it went to Monte Cristo, dominion of the king Guacanagarí, now know as Puerto Real. This province was ruled by a brother of the king, and that was where the admiral had left thirty-eight men on the first voyage. The Indians had killed all of them, because the Indians couldn't tolerate their abuses: they took the women and had their will of them, and committed other crimes, like a lawless rabble. They had scattered, one by one and two by two, three or four together at the most, and strayed to the interior, wherever they liked, in total disorder. Seeing them quarreling and separated, the Indians decided to kill them; thinking the admiral would never return and they would never again see any Christians, they finished off these scattered few who had injured them. These people are naturally feckless and never think of the future, which was also a factor.

3.9.14. The thirty-eight Christians died (as the Indians themselves said) for the reasons cited above and because they would not stay where the admiral had told them to. The admiral, when he learned the truth, went back to La Isabela to found a settlement, which he did, with the men he brought (some fifteen hundred, as has been mentioned). He called the town Isabela after her serene majesty the Catholic queen.

3.9.15. This was the second Christian settlement in the Indies—the first being the thirty-eight men left on the first voyage—here on the island of Haiti (now called Española), and it lasted until 1498. From La Isabela the colony moved to this city, Santo Domingo, as I will tell. . . .

[3.10] Book 2, chapter 9: The voyage from Spain to the Indies, route and navigation; and the marvelous tree of the island Hierro, one of the Fortunate Isles, now called the Canaries.

3.10.1. . . . I shall only say in this case, that whosoever wishes to sail to the coast of Tierra Firme and the great river Marañón from the aforementioned island of Hierro (one of the Fortunate Isles, or Canaries, famous for its water) must sail six hundred leagues or less; he will understand better if he consults modern charts of the Indies, because Ptolemy, the great ancient cosmographer, never said anything about Tierra Firme; and while it was mentioned in the second chapter of this book that Aristotle and Solinus and Pliny and Isidore of Seville speak of the islands of the Hesperides, they do not have anything to say about Tierra Firme. From which I conclude (with the pardon of those who may have read something else) that the admiral did not go off on a wild goose chase to discover the Indies but knew on the best authority where he was going. . . .

[3.11] Book 2, chapter 12: What the admiral Christopher Columbus did after he learned the Indians had killed the Christians he had left on this island of Española on the first voyage; how he founded the city of La Isabela and the fort of Santo Tomás; how he discovered the island of Jamaica, and explored the coast of Cuba; also about the first samples of mined gold sent to Spain.

3.11.1. The first and second voyages of the admiral Christopher Columbus to the Indies have been related; and how, on the first voyage, he left thirty-eight men in the lands of the king or cacique Guacanagarí. He chose those men he thought were the most careful and diligent. But as he was also aware of the element of human frailty, he left many men to ensure some would survive until his return, and also so they could look after each other and keep each other out of trouble. He did not leave more men because he needed the rest to sail the ships back to Spain, and in any case the Indians seemed gentle and peaceful. The men were not left there to fight; nor did the admiral have any idea the peaceable-seeming Indians would do such a thing, or he would not have left the men. But to learn the language and keep the peace they were too many, for ten or twelve would have done better. Or two hundred should have been left, which the admiral did not have. Finally, the error was less his than theirs, in that they failed to maintain discipline. The admiral had given them many warnings and told them how they should behave among savages. Promising many rewards, he shared out the provisions and supplies with them. He left weapons as well, with strict instructions not to use them except as a last resort, in self-defense. He commended the men warmly to the lord of the country Guacanagarí, to whom he gave many gifts so he would favor the Spaniards and treat them well. The captain of the group, as I have said, was a good gentleman of Córdoba, called Rodrigo de Arana; there was another worthy man with them, master Juan, an excellent surgeon. But most of the group were sailors, who act nothing like landsmen, no more is their calling like any other. Few or none of them were able to do what the admiral expected, that is, behave themselves properly among the Indians, learn their language and customs, and tolerate whatever defects and bestiality they might encounter. But the truth of the matter is, leaving out the seamen who are decent people (and there are such), I am of the opinion that sailors in general are unfit for land. Besides being ignorant and low people, they are greedy and inclined to vices like gluttony, lust, and rapine; and they are quick to anger. Those Columbus left on this island had not a particle of prudence or shame to restrain them, nor did they obey his wise precepts, nor did they stay where he left them. They made a poor showing—or rather, did not show up at all when the admiral returned.

3.11.2. Afterwards it was known that the Christians committed all manner of crimes against the Indians, taking their wives and daughters and anything they had, just as they pleased. Even so, they might have survived had they stayed together under their leader; but they disobeyed the captain and scattered into the interior of the island, so they were killed to the last man. It was also known that the selection of two alternates to substitute for the captain was a factor, since according to the Indians each of the alternates wanted to lead. As soon as the admiral left for Spain, it was every man for himself. As Livy says, majority rule is not much use for war. Thus did they court their destruction, scattering by twos and threes with no thought for the Indians who could no longer tolerate their outrages and who caught them asleep, or disarmed them, however they could, and killed every one.

3.11.3. Among the Indians who returned from Spain with Columbus was one called Diego Colón, who had learned the most Spanish and spoke it fairly well. Through him the admiral was thoroughly informed by many Indians and Guacanagarí himself about exactly what had happened; the chief showed much regret. But the admiral was full of remorse; as soon as he had found out everything, a few days after he arrived at Puerto Real, he moved to another part of this island and founded the town of La Isabela.

3.11.4. From there he set out exploring with two caravels, leaving as lieutenant and governor of Española don Diego his brother until such time as his other brother don Bartolomé should arrive; he had stayed in Spain and was sailing from England to join the admiral. He left Pedro Margarit as warden of the fortress at the mines of Cibao (the richest on this island, near the Janico river). The admiral ordered this fort built as soon as he heard of the mines; Spaniards mined a few grains of gold there, because the Indians only knew how to pick up gold on the surface of the ground. The Spaniards themselves did not have the mining experience of the ancient Asturians, Lusitanians, and Galicians, from whose provinces the Romans took so much treasure.

3.11.5. The fort was the second on this island, and the commander Pedro Margarit was the first warden of it. It was called Santo Tomás, because they were doubtful about the gold and wanted to see it to believe it, so the admiral named the fort for Doubting Thomas. At the beginning only a little gold was produced, which the admiral sent with Captain Corvalán. This gentleman took the news of rich gold mines of Cibao to Fernando and Isabel, who rewarded him. Some people say it was the captain Antonio de Torres, brother of the housekeeper of the prince Juan of glorious memory, whom Columbus sent to Spain with the first samples of gold.

3.11.6. At any rate, after the discovery of gold, the admiral left La Isabela with such gentlemen as he needed for two well-loaded and provisioned caravels. While he was away exploring, the Christians who stayed here suffered many trials and tribulation, as will be told. That same year of 1493 four ships were lost off La Isabela, including the flagship *Maríagalante*.

3.11.7. Meanwhile the admiral discovered the island of Jamaica, now called Santiago, which is twenty-five leagues from point Tiburón, the westernmost part of this island. Actually, the admiral named the eastern end of this island cape San Rafael, and the western end cape San Miguel, although the ignorant now refer to the latter as cape Tiburón.

3.11.8. Getting back to Jamaica, the island is located sixteen degrees from the equator and is some fifty leagues long and twenty-five leagues wide. Before the admiral discovered it, he went to Cuba and explored the coast farther than he had on the first voyage; the island is now named after the memory of his serene highness King Fernando of glorious memory. I believe this is also the island Peter Martyr sometimes calls Alfa, and sometimes Juana; but there are no such islands in all the Indies. I have no idea why he would call Cuba by these names. However, as these islands will be discussed more specifically later on, this will do for the moment.

[3.12] Book 2, chapter 13: The troubles and wars of the Christians under don Diego and don Bartolomé in the town of La Isabela, during the time that the admiral was exploring; what happened to Pedro Margarit, warden of the fort of Santo Tomás, with certain turtledoves; and the founding and colonizing of this city of Santo Domingo, to which the admiral returned after discovering Jamaica and other things, etc.

3.12.1. When the admiral left La Isabela he appointed his brother don Diego lieutenant and governor of this island until the governor don Bartolomé should arrive—which he did.

3.12.2. First it must be understood that when the city was laid out, the admiral distributed the parcels for each Spaniard to build his house and marked out the landholdings. The Indians, seeing their neighbors were settling in permanently, resented them. To drive them away the Indians thought of a low trick, which resulted in the deaths of more than half the Spaniards and innumerable Indians. It was impossible to prevent, because the Christians were newcomers and did not realize the implications of what was happening: the Indians all decided not to plant their crops at the proper time.

When there was no corn, they ate yucca, as these are the two grains and principal foodstuffs that are here. The Christians ate up their provisions; when they looked for indigenous foodstuff, there was none for them nor for anyone. Men fell dead of hunger in the city; half the garrison of the fort Santo Tomás under Pedro Margarit starved to death; Indians died everywhere. The stench was terrible; many other illnesses besides hunger came upon the Christians. So the Indians' evil wish was fulfilled, that the Christians should go away for lack of food or stay and die of the same cause. The Indians who survived fled into the interior and shunned our men, both to do them more harm and to find food for themselves in other parts of the island.

3.12.3. In this time of great need, the Christians ate the native dogs, which were mute and could not bark. They also ate the dogs they had brought from Spain and all the hutias they could catch, all the *quemis* and other animals called *mohuy* and *corís*, which are like small rabbits. These four kinds of animals they hunted with their Spanish dogs, which they also ate, in payment for their services, after they had eaten the native dogs. They not only finished off these five kinds of four-footed animals, all that there were on the island, but also a sort of snake with four feet, called an iguana, a horrible-looking creature to anyone not used to it. They did pardon lizards, large or small, nor any of the various snakes, none of which are poisonous. In order to live, they ate anything and everything; whatever they caught, they cooked, either boiled or roasted, and had plenty of appetite for the ugliest creatures. Between the diet and the dampness of the island, the survivors suffered many serious and incurable illnesses. So it was that the first Spaniards to return to Spain from here went back as yellow as the gold they came to seek, but not as lustrous. They looked like citrons, saffron-colored and jaundiced, so sick they soon died, either because of their hardships here or because Spanish bread and food is harder to digest than the herbs and bad rations here, and the air is thinner and colder than here. Although they got back to Castile, their lives there were soon ended.

3.12.4. The first settlers in this island were bothered by chiggers[5] and suffered greatly from buboes,[6] for they originated in the Indies. And well I may say "the Indies" for the land to which this contagion is endemic and also to the Indian women, who very possibly infected some of the first Spaniards who came with the admiral to these lands. These Spaniards spread the disease to Spain on their return, and thence to Italy and other countries, as I will relate later, not forgetting to explain with particular attention the eleven remarkable phenomena mentioned in this chapter: the five four-footed animals—dog, hutia, *quemi*, *mohuy*, and *corí*—and the iguana, a four-footed serpent. The large and small lizards and snakes must not be left out; and I will tell of how disagreeable the chigger is and the dreadful disease of buboes, which will make up the list of eleven phenomena.

3.12.5. Therefore, to fulfill my promise at the beginning of this chapter 13, I will relate that while the Christians in La Isabela were suffering such trials and tribulations as I have told, besides other privations I do not have time to go into, Pedro Margarit

[5]"Las Niguas": the *sarcopsylla penetrans*.
[6]A reference to syphilis.

with as many as thirty men held the fort of Santo Tomás at the Cibao mines. They suffered as much as La Isabela, from hunger and disease and the usual problems of the first settlers in distant and savage lands, hostile to strangers. So the garrison grew smaller and smaller each day. They were too few to leave the fort; they should not abandon their post; the warden's loyalty was firm; the admiral was not there, away exploring as I said; the inhabitants of La Isabela under the governor don Bartolomé could hardly help themselves; the Indians had fled to the interior to escape the famine. The garrison being in these dire straits, one day an Indian arrived at the fort. He said the warden seemed to him like a good man, one who did no wrong to the Indians native to the island nor permitted others to wrong them, so he brought him a pair of live turtledoves. The warden invited the Indian up into the tower, accepted the turtledoves with many thanks, and gave him some glass beads (which the Indians valued highly at that time) to wear around his neck. When the Indian had left, happy with his string of beads, the warden told the Christians with him in the fort that two doves were not enough to feed all of them, but would satisfy him for the day. The men said he was right, that two doves were nothing among so many, and as the warden was the sickest of any, he should have them. Then the warden said, "God forbid I should do as you say. You have all shared famine and trouble with me until now, and I will share your fortune alive or dead until God wills we starve to death or in his mercy delivers us." Saying this, he let the doves go, and they flew away out of the window of the tower.

3.12.6. With this the men were as cheerful and content as though each of them had been given the doves and felt such loyalty to the warden not one deserted him or the fort no matter how hard it was. The Christians being in such sore trouble, for the hardships they had to endure continued and increased, so that nothing should be lacking to their cup of misery the north winds (called "cierzo" in Castile) began to blow. Those are unhealthy winds in the islands; not only Christians but native Indians died.

3.12.7. They had no help but God's mercy; his remedy turned out to be a new location for the city of La Isabela. It happened in this fashion: a young Aragonese named Miguel Díaz quarreled with another Spaniard and stabbed him several times. The man did not die, but since he was one of the governor's men, Díaz did not dare stay in the settlement for fear of punishment. He left in the company of five or six other Christians; some came because they were implicated in the crime and some came for friendship's sake. Fleeing La Isabela, they went along the coast to the east, then around the coast south to where the city of Santo Domingo is now. Here they stopped because they found a village of Indians. Miguel Díaz became friendly with a female cacique, who was afterwards called Catalina and bore him two children. But almost as soon as the Spaniards arrived, this female cacique took a liking to Miguel Díaz and tolerated the others for his sake. She told him about the mines located seven leagues from this city and begged him to bring his friends from La Isabela to this beautiful fertile land with a fine river and harbor. She would see to it they had all the support they needed. So to please this cacique, and even more because he thought that if he took news of a fine and abundant land to sickly and barren La Isabela, the governor would pardon him, and also, and principally, because it was the will of God that it should be so and that the remaining Christians should not perish—for all these reasons, Miguel Díaz agreed to go to the governor and, with his companions, made his way overland to La Isabela, guided by Indians this cacique sent with them. The distance was about fifty leagues, more or less. There Díaz spoke secretly with some of his friends and discovered that the wounded man had recovered. Therefore he dared to present himself before the governor, his superior, and sue for pardon, alleging both his past service and the present news of good land and gold mines. The governor received him graciously, pardoned him, and reconciled the erstwhile combatants. When he had heard all the particulars about the province and river valley, he decided to come in person and see it with a party of selected men. Everything Miguel Díaz had said turned out to be true. The governor even went down the Ozama river (which runs through this city) in an Indian dugout; he sounded the depth, reconnoitered the depth of the channel at the harbor entrance, and was more than satisfied. He went to the mines for two days, and found gold. From there he returned to La Isabela, where the news was received with great joy. Then the governor gave orders that all the inhabitants should travel overland to the new site, and the two caravels they had should take their belongings by sea. They arrived, it is said, on Sunday, feast day of the glorious Santo Domingo, 5 August 1494. The governor don Bartolomé founded this city across the river, opposite where it now is, on the coast, because the chieftainess Catalina's village was on this site. However, I wished to know for sure why this city was called Santo Domingo and after inquiries I heard it said that not only was it founded on Sunday and the feast of Santo Domingo, but the father of the admiral and the governor was Domenico and the city was named for him.

3.12.8. Two and a half months later, more or less, the admiral and his men returned from exploring. As soon as he arrived in this city he sent to see if Pedro Margarit was still alive, and if so to come with all the garrison to Santo Domingo and leave the fort with the captain Alonso de Ojeda. This was done; Ojeda was the second warden, and the garrison recovered health in the abundant and fertile lands here.

3.12.9. But once all the Spaniards were together again, the Devil, who never ceases to tempt and persecute the faithful, sowed discord among them. The admiral and Fray Buyl had many disagreements arising from the admiral's unaccustomed severity; he hanged several men, among them one Gaspar Ferriz, an Aragonese. Of course he should have reasonably expect to be obeyed, and no doubt he heeded the sentence of the emperor Otto, "Pereunte obsequio imperium quoque intercidit," which says if there is no obedience there is no rule. But Solomon also says, "Universa delicta operit charitas." Now if charity covers a multitude of sins, as the sage says in the proverb, mercy is advisable especially in these new lands; since no one can be spared from such a small company, it is well to pass over things that in other circumstances should be punished. A prudent captain should take this into account more than anyone else, for it is written: "Others made you a leader; do not attempt to exalt yourself, but be among them as one of them." The authors of these sacred words are Solomon and Saint Paul. At any rate, Fray Buyl considered the admiral cruel, and it was his duty by papal authority to stop him. So when Columbus imposed justice the friar considered unjust, he declared an interdict and the divine offices ceased. Then the admiral ordered that rations to the friar and his household should cease, and no one should give them anything to eat.

3.12.10. Pedro Margarit and others managed to reconcile them, but not for long; as soon as the admiral did something cruel, the priest suspended the canonical hours and holy offices, and the admiral suspended rations to the friar, all the other priests, and their servants. Glorious Saint Gregory says, "Concord can never be obtained except by patience; in human affairs motives for discord are always arising."

3.12.11. There was more than one opinion on this sorry state of affairs, although not publicly expressed; still, each side found ways of making its views known in Spain. Receiving contradictory reports, their Catholic majesties decided to send a servitor of theirs, Juan Aguado (now a resident of Seville). He came as captain of four caravels, with a royal letter patent I have seen. It was signed by their Catholic majesties, dated in Madrid, 5 May 1495. Another letter patent ordered the inhabitants of the Indies to give faith and credence to the said Juan Aguado. It went like this: "The king, the queen; knights and squires, the other persons resident in the Indies by our command, we send you Juan Aguado, our royal steward, who will make our wishes known to you. We command you to give him faith and credence. Madrid, 9 April 1495. I the king. I the queen." It was countersigned by Fernán Alvarez, secretary.

3.12.12. This captain made public the royal letter patent in the island of Española and all the Spaniards declared themselves completely at the service of the rulers. Therefore, a few days later Juan Aguado told the admiral to prepare to leave for Spain. Columbus took this very hard; he dressed in drab colors like a friar and let his beard grow.

3.12.13. The admiral's return to Spain was in the year of 1496, since he was not arrested. Fray Buyl and Pedro Margarit were also summoned and went back to Spain with the same fleet. Also went the commanders Gallego and Arroyo, the treasurer Bernal de Pisa, Rodrigo Abarca, master Girao, and Pedro Navarro; all servants of the royal household. When they all arrived in Spain, each went separately to kiss the hands of their Catholic majesties. Although the rulers had heard in letters from here, and afterwards in person there, the complaints of Fray Buyl and others about the (possibly exaggerated) sins of the admiral, after they heard him and took into account his great services to the crown, they not only pardoned him out of their royal clemency, they sent him back as governor of these lands. These exceedingly Christian monarchs commanded him to continue exploring the rest of the Indies, to treat their Spanish vassals and the Indians well, and to be more moderate and less severe, as was reasonable. The admiral promised, although most of those who went from here spoke ill of him. That does not surprise me, though the fault be none of his own; for many of those who come here are badly affected by the atmosphere peculiar to the Indies, which incites them to discord and to do things that would never have occurred to them at home. And of course the Indians and native inhabitants are always at odds, for good reason, as on account of this sin and many other sins common among them, God forgot these people for so many centuries.

3.12.14. However, the Spanish temperament was the cause of much of the dissension in the early years of the settlement; Spaniards are naturally more inclined to war than to idleness. If they have no outside enemies, they fight among themselves, as

Justinus observes; their talent and quickness frequently lead to impatience. Also, the great variety of people who have come here is a factor; although they are all vassals of the kings of Spain, who shall reconcile the Catalonian with the Vizcayan, who speak different languages and come from different provinces? How can an Andalusian get along with a Valencian, or a man from Perpignan with one from Córdoba, an Aragonese with a Basque, a Galician with a Castilian (who suspects he is Portuguese), an Asturian or a man from Santander with a Navarrese, and so forth? By no means do all the vassals of the Castilian crown have the same customs or speak the same language. And in those early days, for every nobleman of pure blood who came to the Indies, there were ten uncouth fellows of low breeding who ended up quarreling.

3.12.15. But the conquest of the Indies has been such a great enterprise, scions of noble houses, knights, and gentlemen have always left their province in Spain to come; especially to this city, first Christian outpost in the Indies, as will be told later.

3.12.16. However, lest I be accused of carelessness in failing to mention two new plagues (among those cited and many more omitted) from which the Christians suffered on the second voyage, I will discuss them in the next chapter. These ills were notorious and dangerous; one was carried to Spain on Columbus's return and from there to all parts of the world, it is believed.

[3.13] Book 2, chapter 14: The two famous and dangerous scourges or plagues which the Christians and settlers in the Indies suffered, and some still suffer today; the diseases are native to the Indies, and one of them spread to Spain and from there to the rest of the world.

3.13.1. Just as so much of the gold of the Indies has gone to France and Italy and even to the Moors and enemies of Spain throughout the world, it is only fair that those who got the profit of our labor should share in our pains, so that one way or another they should remember to thank God. They should embrace either pain or pleasure with the patience of blessed Job, who when he was rich was not proud, nor impatient when he was poor and sick, but always gave thanks to our Lord.

3.13.2. Many times in Italy I had occasion to laugh up my sleeve hearing the Italians speak of the French disease and the French referring to the disease of Naples; they should both have called it the disease of the Indies, and they would be right. The truth of this will be seen in this chapter and through the history of *guayacán*,[7] the best remedy for the terrible malady of buboes. For God's mercy is so great that wherever he permits us to suffer for our sins, there also is found the remedy. More will be said about medicinal trees in book 10, chapter 2; at this time, let it be known how the buboes went to Spain along with the samples of gold from this island of Haiti or Española.

3.13.3. In the previous chapter I told how Columbus returned to Spain in 1496, as was the case. After his return I spoke with some of the men who went with him, such as Pedro Margarit and the knight commanders Arroyo and Gallego, with Gabriel de León and Juan de la Vega; also Pedro Navarro, gentleman of the bedchamber of

[7]Lignum vitae.

Prince Juan, my master. In fact I knew most of those I named as royal servitors who went on the second voyage of discovery. From them I heard a great deal about this island, what they saw and suffered and learned on the second voyage. In addition I heard about the first voyage from Vicente Yáñez Pinzón, pilot, one of the Pinzón brothers mentioned before, a friend of mine until his death in 1514; from the pilot Hernán Pérez Mateos, currently a resident of this city, who was on Columbus's first and third voyages; and from two gentlemen who came here on the second voyage and live here still, Juan de Rojas and Alonso de Valencia; and from many other eyewitnesses of events on this island who told me about them in great detail. But more than anyone else I rely on the account of Pedro Margarit, a distinguished courtier much esteemed by King Fernando.

3.13.4. It was he whom the king and queen chiefly believed in the matter of what happened here on the second voyage, as has been told. This gentleman was so ill and complained so much I believe he suffered from the buboes, though I never saw them. A few months later, in 1496, other courtiers fell ill with the same symptoms. At first the disease was confined to lowly persons, and it was believed they got it frequenting prostitutes; but afterwards it spread to the highest in the land.

3.13.5. This caused great consternation, because the disease was terrible and contagious, and many died of it. No one had any idea what to do about it, as it was new, and the doctors did not understand how to treat it or cure it.

3.13.6. Subsequently their Catholic majesties sent the grand captain Gonzalo Fernández de Córdoba to Italy with a huge fleet, as their general in chief. He was to support King Ferdinand II of Naples against Charles of France, called the Thickhead. Among the Spaniards were some infected with the disease, and by means of prostitutes it spread to the Italian and French armies. Since they had never seen anything like it before, the French called it the Neapolitan disease, thinking it originated there; and the Neapolitans, thinking the French brought it, called it the French disease. And so it is called still all over Italy, because before King Charles came there, there was no such scourge in those lands.

3.13.7. But the truth of the matter is that from this isle of Haiti or Española the scourge spread to Europe, as it is said; it is very common among the Indians and they know how to treat it; there are excellent herbs and medicinal trees and plants for this and other illnesses, like lignum vitae, which some people say is ebony, and will be discussed in the section on trees.

3.13.8. Therefore, of the two dangerous plagues of the Indies still affecting Christians and new settlers, the buboes is one; it spread to Spain and the rest of the world without diminishing the incidence of it here. So, continuing the subject of the disadvantages of the Indies, let the other scourge, chiggers, be mentioned.

3.13.9. In this island and all the Indies and Tierra Firme, there are buboes and chiggers. Chiggers are not a disease, but just as bad, a tiny live parasite smaller than the smallest flea. It is a sort of flea, because it jumps, although it is so small. This insect lives in dust and can only be controlled by frequently sweeping the house. It gets into the feet and other parts of the body, particularly the toes, and the victim does not feel it until it is under the skin and starts to eat into the flesh like ringworm, only more so.

The longer it stays the worse it gets. The victim scratches, but the parasite hastens to reproduce itself; it makes a nest, or cyst, under the skin, the size of a lentil or even a chickpea, full of nits which grow into many chiggers. If they are not removed with a pin or needle, like ringworm, they are serious; especially when they breed and itch the most, for the victim scratches and spreads the chiggers so he never gets rid of them if he does not know how to treat them.

3.13.10. Since the Christians did not know this either, just as they did not know a treatment for buboes, many of them lost their feet or at least a few toes, because they became inflamed and full of pus and had to be cauterized or cut. But it is easy to get rid of the chiggers at the beginning; however, for novice black slaves they are dangerous—either because the Negroes are so thin or because they are so ignorant that they do not know how to keep clean or to speak up in time—and they end up lame, as do many others. I have had chiggers in my feet, in these islands and Tierra Firme both, and I do not think it is something for a sensible man to fear, though it is a nuisance; it is easy to take out the chiggers in the beginning. I have discovered, and other people with experience agree, that it is necessary to be careful to kill the chigger; because sometimes when the pin or needle uncovers it, the animal jumps like a flea. This happens if it burrowed into the foot fairly recently, and it is believed it may go out again the same way, leaving its eggs, to do more damage elsewhere, as it may when it is taken out, after leaving in the foot innumerable generations more of chiggers.

[3.14] Here begins the third book of the *Natural General History of the Indies*: Prologue

3.14.1. In this third book will be discussed the war that the Christians and Captain Alonso de Ojeda, in the name of the admiral Christopher Columbus, had with the king Caonabó, and the latter's imprisonment and death. Also the victories of the governor don Bartolomé, brother of the admiral, over king Guarionex and fourteen other caciques or kings allied with him; and how Roldán Jiménez, with a few others of his same opinion, rebelled against the admiral and the governor. And also the third voyage of discovery of the first admiral when he found and explored part of the coast of Tierra Firme and the island of pearls, called Cubagua, will be told. And also the admiral's government, and what kings and great lords there were on that island; and of the great lake of Xaraguá, and another lake in the highest mountains of the island. And how the Indians fought, with what weapons, and who the Caribs and bowmen are. And the miraculous and devout cross of la Vega will be described. Also the coming of the knight commander Francisco de Bobadilla, who sent the admiral and his brothers home to Spain in chains. And why all the many Indians there were on Española died. And the coming of the supreme commander of Alcántara, don Nicolás de Ovando, and the departure of the knight commander Bobadilla, who was drowned at sea with many ships and men and much gold, and how well the supreme commander governed. And how the old first admiral, Christopher Columbus, made his fourth voyage of discovery to these Indies, finding Veragua and other provinces of Tierra Firme; and about his death in Spain afterwards. And how this city of Santo Domingo came to be situated where it is now. And about the nobility and particulars of this city and this isle, and about the towns and settlements, and other matters concerning this project of the *Natural History*, as will be treated in detail in the following chapters.

[3.15] Book 3, chapter 1: The war Captain Alonso de Ojeda had with the cacique Caonabó, his imprisonment, and death.

3.15.1. In the second book it was told how after Commander Pedro Margarit left the fort of Santo Tomás, the admiral put it in charge of Captain Alonso de Ojeda as warden, with a garrison of fifty men; the fort was strategically important both for its proximity to the gold mines and in order to uphold the reputation and strength of the Christians.

3.15.2. But as the admiral had left for Spain, the Indians became arrogant (especially the Caonabó, the authority in that province) and were not happy with the proximity of the fort and the new authority. Caonabó and the Ciguayas (Indians who used bow and arrow, from the north coast of this island) decided to burn the fort or raze it, if they could. With five or six thousand armed men they surrounded the fort and besieged it for a month, not letting a single man go out. But the warden was a bold and wily warrior, and he resisted so long the Indians abandoned camp like the undisciplined savages they were, laying themselves open to condign retaliation. Being not only wily but foresighted, the warden continued the war by any means in his power, sometimes by fighting and sometimes by the tricks and traps veteran captains know. Although some Christians died in the course of the war, they killed a great many Indians and at last took Caonabó and most of his leaders prisoners. It was said Ojeda violated the safe-conduct the cacique said he was promised; or possibly Caonabó misunderstood him.

3.15.3. The imprisonment of Caonabó resulted in the pacification of the whole island. But Caonabó had a brother, a bold man and well-liked by the Indians, who flocked to his leadership. He was not unmindful of his brother's plight, and resolved to ransom him by force of arms. He proposed to take as many Christian prisoners as possible and then exchange them for the liberty of Caonabó and other Indian leaders. He mustered more than seven thousand men, most of them archers, and advanced on the Spaniards with five battalions. The Spanish captain, Alonso de Ojeda, had some cavalry and what few man could be spared from the defense of the fort, and a few more the governor don Bartolomé sent to aid him: not three hundred men in all, to fight the Indians. But God favored our cause and gave us the victory, for they had never seen men fight on horseback before. So they had many losses, and the leader, Caonabó's brother, was taken prisoner with many other Indians. That day Ojeda showed himself a brave soldier, a bold cavalryman, and, no less, a prudent captain.

3.15.4. The governor decided to send Caonabó, his brother, and some of the other prisoners to Spain, thinking that would be much more convenient than trying to keep Caonabó on the island, since he was not only the chief but also a troublemaker, daring and wise in warfare. So in two caravels which were about to weigh anchor for Spain, the governor ordered them sent. But Caonabó's brother died soon after learning that they had to go to the Catholic king and queen; and Caonabó died as well, after a few days at sea. So the lands of Caonabó were pacified by the Christians. His wife

Anacaona, sister of the cacique Behechio (lord of the west end of this island) went to live with her brother in the province they call Xaraguá, where she was honored and obeyed. More will be said of her later, for she was a great lady, held in high esteem in these parts for her courage, spirit and intelligence; she was a remarkable woman for good and evil both, as will be set down in the proper order.

[3.16] Book 3, chapter 2. The victorious battle the governor waged against king Guarionex and fourteen other caciques or kings, and how Roldán Jiménez rebelled against the governor and the admiral.

3.16.1. At about the same time as Caonabó had surrounded Captain Ojeda (as some say), or after the siege was lifted (as others affirm), the cacique Guarionex called up all the Indians and chiefs he could, to the number of more than fifteen thousand men. He planned to attack the governor don Bartolomé and the Christians with him in the city of La Vega and that area. The reasons for this were, as I have said, that the Indians were angry at the continued presence of the Christians and did not want them on the island; they feared losing their autonomy (as appeared to be happening); and also because the Christians disapproved of their rites, ceremonies, and amusements and said so. The moment seemed to have come for their evil purpose: few Christians were left, what with sickness and hardship, and they could be exterminated before the newcomers arrived with the admiral (who was expected any day). The old hands by now knew something of the country; they would advise and help the newcomers, to the disadvantage of the Indians. Therefore, they mustered an army and advanced on the Christians.

3.16.2. The governor, when he found out, did not lose time trying to fortify the little town, which might be surrounded or set on fire by night; like a good knight and an experienced captain he set out across country and marched into the night. In the second watch, almost at midnight, he drew near Guarionex's camp. With barely five hundred men (some of them sick), he attacked on both flanks with such force and fury that the Indians broke and scattered. Since they were savages, without weapons or skills in warfare to match the Christians, many were killed and all who did not escape under cover of night were taken prisoner. Guarionex himself and fourteen more leaders were taken, all who were in the battle, near where the town of Bonao was founded.

3.16.3. This great victory established the Christians' reputation in the minds of the Indians and had the very desirable result of making them cease their rebellions and uprisings. They became more civilized, treated with the Christians, and gave up the idea of war. In truth, the people of this island are the least warlike in all the Indies and Tierra Firme, of the most pacific and quiet habits; although as I have said there were always some feuds and disagreements among them, these were neither so bloody nor so constant as in other lands.

3.16.4. To return to the history: after the governor won the victory, it seemed to him that it would tend to promote peace and amity between Christians and Indians if he set Guarionex at liberty on the best terms the cacique would understand, and so he ordered it done. Guarionex thereafter welcomed and treated well any Christians who entered his territory or passed through it. Others say that Guarionex was not in the battle and that his tribe had fought under the direction of the cacique Mayobanex, who had actually been captured and released, and that the war had continued until the wife of Guarionex had been captured and he had made peace with the Christians in order to get her back.

3.16.5. After these victories the governor's personality changed. He became very severe with the Christians from then on, more than some of them would bear, especially Roldán Jiménez, who was the magistrate for the admiral. The governor gave him neither the courtesy nor the deference he felt was his due; nor did Roldán intend to let the governor administer justice just as he pleased. There were heated words, and the governor insulted Roldán and, according to some people, laid hands on him, or tried to. Roldán's indignation was such that he marched off to the interior with seventy men, eschewing the company of Christians and proclaiming everywhere the wrongs done by the governor and the admiral—or the wrongs he imputed to them in anger. Determined not to rebel against their Catholic majesties, he made these statements to escape the rule of the governor and the admiral for good; he never obeyed them again, but went to the province of Xaraguá, territory of the king Behechio, and stayed there until the commander Francisco de Bobadilla came to govern this island, as will be told.

[3.17] Book 3, chapter 3: What happened on this island while the admiral went to Spain. The third voyage of discovery he made, finding the coast (and much of the unknown territory) called in general Tierra Firme, including great kingdoms and provinces. How he also discovered the island of Cubagua—the rich pearl fishery—and other new islands; the end result and other matters pertaining to the history.

3.17.1. After the admiral had been a few days at the court of their Catholic majesties, answering the charges brought against him by Fray Buyl and others, he was heard and pardoned, as was told in the second book. They then gave him leave to come back and govern these lands and ordered him to continue exploring. Therefore in March of 1496 (although some say it was 1497) he set sail from Cádiz with six well-loaded caravels, well-provided with supplies all that was necessary for the voyage. When he arrived in the Canaries, he sent three caravels with provisions and men to Española, while with the other three ships he sailed on around the islands commonly called the islands of Antonio, now the Cape Verdes, the same the ancients called the Gorgades. From there he ran southeast a good hundred and fifty leagues. A great storm came up and they were forced to cut the mizzenmasts and jettison much of the cargo, finding themselves in great danger. The pilot Hernán Pérez Mateos, resident today in this city of Santo Domingo, tells of this storm. But according to the admiral's son Fernando, who was there, they were becalmed in such heat that the casks split and the wheat rotted. They had to retreat from the equator, and they sailed west by northwest and sighted the island of Trinidad. The admiral named it that because he had already decided to call the first landfall Trinidad; when he first sighted land he saw three hills close together and called it Trinidad. He sailed into the channel called Boca del

Drago,[8] and saw much of the coast of Tierra Firme. However, because the coast and the island are inhabited by fierce Caribs, who shoot arrows with deadly poison, they could not speak with the Indians, although they saw many of them in their dugout canoes (of which more will be said later) as well as on land.

3.17.2. This island lies nine degrees from our north pole, from the south coast, and ten degrees from the north coast. It is eighteen or twenty leagues wide, more or less, and twenty-five or more long.

3.17.3. The south coast of this island faces El Palmar on Tierra Firme, so called for the many large groves of palms. To the east is the Salado river, so called because when the sailors tried to fill the water casks they found its water to be brackish, so the admiral gave it that name. Between this point and Tierra Firme—although the point itself is part of the continent—lies a gulf the admiral called Boca del Drago (because it looks something like the open mouth of a dragon), with many islets.

3.17.4. From Salinas point, which lies ten degrees from the equator, the admiral sailed west along the coast and sighted the islands he called Los Testigos and another called La Generosa. And he saw many more islands there. Farther on he discovered the rich island of Cubagua, which we now call the Isla de las Perlas because it is the best pearl fishery in the Indies. There is a much bigger island next to it, which the admiral called La Margarita. Cubagua lies almost fifty leagues west of Salinas point. It is a small island, about three leagues around, four leagues from the province of Tierra Firme called Araya. There he discovered the archipelago of Los Testigos, the Isla de Pájaros, and many others. Still sailing west with his three caravels along the coast, the admiral discovered the island of Poregari, twenty-seven or thirty leagues from Cubagua. Farther on he discovered more islands called Los Roques and the island La Orchila, called Yaruma, where it is said that there are great quantities of orchil. The island is twelve leagues from another, called Corazao, that the admiral discovered to the west. In this way he discovered many more islands and archipelagos, until he reached Cabo de la Vela on Tierra Firme. He called it that because they saw a great dugout canoe under sail there. From this cape to Salinas point and the Boca del Drago it is about one hundred and eighty leagues. From Cabo de la Vela he sailed across the channel to Española and came to this city, which at the time was located on the other side of the river. Cabo de la Vela is directly south of Beata, an islet thirty-five leagues to the west of Haiti, or Española.

3.17.5. This, then, was the third voyage of discovery made by the admiral of the Indies. However, since it was mentioned that on Cubagua he found the pearl fishery, and that is such a rich and remarkable thing, it will be told how he found out about the pearls when we discuss that island in particular.

[3.18] Book 3, chapter 4: What the governor don Bartolomé did when the admiral was in Spain and when he was discovering part Tierra Firme before returning to this city. About the admiral's government until he was imprisoned, and about the kings or lords there were on this island.

[8]Mouth of the Dragon

3.18.1. In the previous chapter the third voyage of admiral Christopher Columbus was related up to when he returned to this city of Santo Domingo. During the whole period he was in Spain and discovering part of the coast of Tierra Firme and the islands mentioned in the previous chapter, no ships came from Spain nor sailed for Spain. The men who had gone back to Spain with the admiral (and before him) had endured the hardships I have described; they were thin and sick and looked like dead men, thus giving the Indies a bad reputation so that no one could be found who wanted to come here.

3.18.2. I myself saw many of those who returned to Castile at that time, in such condition that I think if the king had offered to give me the Indies, I would have refused. It was no wonder the men returned in such bad shape; indeed, it was surprising that any of them survived, moving to lands so far from where they were born and raised, leaving the familiar foodstuffs of their childhood, exiled from family and friends, lacking medical treatment, and all the other privations it would take too long to list.

3.18.3. Since there were few survivors, and everyone went back to Spain except those who were not able to, or could not get a boat, and the admiral's return was uncertain, this land was considered a dead loss and the inhabitants were in great fear. And they would have been lost without the timely arrival of the three caravels from Spain which Columbus (as I said) sent from the Canaries. In addition to the crews, there were three hundred convicts exiled to this island; together with the few earlier settlers, they were sufficient to maintain the colony. The Christians had not dared to leave the city, even to cross the river; now with reinforcements they had a new lease on life and the island was saved, for there were brave men and notable persons among them.

3.18.4. The Indians abandoned the siege of Concepción de la Vega and of this city and fortress (in its first location on the other side of the river) and lost all hope of ever seeing the land free of Christians. The more so, as a short while later the admiral with three more caravels and good men put into the harbor. He had discovered the islands and part of Tierra Firme and the Las Perlas, as was told in the previous chapter. When he reached this city (which, as I have said, was located first on the other side of the river, across from where it is now), he found the governor, his brother, and the other Christians who were on good terms with him; but many were not very happy with the departure of Roldán Jiménez. There was also an undercurrent of dissent, as was usual in this country, still infected with dissension from the time of Fray Buyl. But everyone received the admiral with apparent joy and did homage to him as viceroy and governor in the name of their Catholic majesties.

3.18.5. Exercising his office to the best of his ability, the admiral never lacked for detractors; if he favored or helped some people, others considered themselves injured. Only an angelic governor could make everyone happy; he would have to be superhuman, because some men are inclined to vice and others to virtue; some to work hard, others not; some to spend, some to save; some to one thing and others to the opposite. No governor can please everyone, because some do not want to settle the land, but only want to fight and steal and go back to where they have friends and expect to spend the rest of their lives. Others who would like to settle and put down roots do not get the help that they need. So it is clear that men have such diverse and difficult to understand purposes that in order to be loved, governors need the special favor of God. This is not to say that the governor does not have a good deal to do with whether he is popular or not with his subjects. But even a disagreeable governor is satisfactory if he will but be just, generous, and without greed. Let us return to the history.

3.18.6. At this time the order was given to found, or rather reform, the city of Concepción de la Vega and the towns of Santiago and Bonao. These three settlements were founded by the admiral Christopher Columbus on this island: the first of all was La Isabela; then the people moved to this city of Santo Domingo, as was told in the second book. Matters being in this state, Columbus went back to Spain. Their Catholic majesties were much pleased with him and reconfirmed his privileges in Burgos, 23 April 1497.

3.18.7. With reference to matters that will be taken up in this history, it is important to establish which kings or princes ruled this island of Haiti or Española. According to eyewitnesses, and the notes I took when I was in Barcelona in 1493 at the court of their Catholic majesties and saw the first Indians who accompanied Columbus, there were five chiefs or kings, whom the Indians call caciques, over all the island. They were obeyed by the Indians in their territory or sovereignty, who followed them in peace or war as the caciques commanded. The five were named: Guarionex, Caonabó, Behechio, Guacanagarí, and Cayacoa.

3.18.8. Guarionex ruled the plains, more than sixty leagues in the center of the island. Behechio held the west end, the province of Xaraguá where lies the great lake, of which more will be said. The cacique or king Guacanagarí's territory was the northern part, where the admiral left the thirty-eight Christians on his first voyage. Coyacoa had the eastern end of the island as far as this city and the Haina river, and almost to the mouth of the Yuna river. He was one of the greatest chiefs of the island, and his people the most bellicose because they were closest to the Caribs. He died shortly after hostilities broke out. His wife inherited his position and afterwards converted to Christianity with the name of Inés de Cayacoa. The king Caonabó ruled in the mountains, and he was a great lord of a large territory. He had an under-chief as captain of the territory, called Uxmatex, who was cross-eyed and such a fierce man all the other Indians and caciques on the island feared him. Caonabó married Anacaona, sister of Behechio; he had been a leader among the Caribs, came to this island as a raider, and won the princess by his personal merits. His capital was where the village of San Juan de la Maguana is today, and he ruled the whole province.

3.18.9. The Indians of this island fought for three reasons only: boundary disputes, fishing rights, or invasions by the Caribs from other islands. When an invasion took place, or was rumored, the caciques of this island buried their differences and allied themselves against the common foe.

[3.19] Book 3, chapter 6: The coming of the commander Francisco de Bobadilla to govern this island of Española, and how he sent the admiral Christopher Columbus and his brothers don Bartolomé and don Diego home in chains. And about the many

Indians there were on this island and the reasons that they died and that there are hardly any of them left.

3.19.1. The admiral governed until 1499, when their Catholic majesties Fernando and Isabel became very angry at the reports they heard of what was happening on this island and how the Columbus brothers were governing. They decided to send a new governor, an old servitor of the royal household and an honest and religious man called Francisco de Bobadilla, knight of the military order of Calatrava. As soon as Bobadilla arrived in this city, he arrested the admiral and his brothers Bartolomé and Diego and sent them off in separate caravels. They were taken to Spain in irons and put in the custody of the military governor of Cádiz until such time as their Catholic majesties should make their will known. Some people say Bobadilla had not been ordered to arrest the admiral, but only to make a judicial investigation of the rebellion of Roldán and his cohorts; but the fact was, with or without orders, he did have the admiral and his brothers taken and sent to Spain. He remained to govern this island and did so in peace and justice until 1502, when he was relieved of duty and allowed to return to Spain; fortune, however, did not allow him to reach Castile.

3.19.2. Shortly after Bobadilla's arrival on this island, Roldán wrote to him, and came to him with all the Christians who had been with Roldán in the province of Xaraguá to resume their service as loyal vassals of their Catholic majesties. Bobadilla sent to Spain a great many complaints and reports against the admiral and his brothers relating to his reasons for arresting them. But most of the truth never came out, because the king and queen wanted to see Columbus reformed rather than punished. But I will disclose the charges some people brought against him. They said he tried to keep secret the discovery of pearls and did not report it until he heard that it was already known in Spain and that certain mariners by the name of Niño had visited Cubagua. He did this with a view towards making a new contract for himself. It was also said he was autocratic and despotic, treating the royal servitors badly, and that he only obeyed such royal orders as he liked, ignoring the rest and doing as he pleased.

3.19.3. Other people tell the story differently, saying that he sent a sample of the first pearls that were found to their Catholic majesties with a gentleman named Arroyal. The one certain thing is that the world is full of envy and backbiting. And since these lands are far from their king, and those who come here are from different provinces and have opposing opinions and wants, they look at things differently. Some people, zealous in the service of God and the king, although they thought that the admiral usurped power in the king's name, wanted to see him dealt with less severely. Others, with purposes of their own, painted him so black in their letters that by God's will he and his brothers were imprisoned and taken to Spain, as I have said. The admiral's impatience, unpopularity, and bombast had much to do with it.

3.19.4. As soon as the king and queen heard that he had arrived in Spain, they sent orders that he and his brothers were to be freed and were to come to court. Immediately the admiral went to kiss the hands of the king and the queen, tearfully making his excuses as best he could. When they heard him, in their mercy they said such consoling words to him he became a little happier. And since his services were so notable, although he had gotten somewhat out of hand, it was not consonant with royal gratitude to maltreat the admiral. Therefore they ordered all his rents and royalties, which had been sequestered while he was a prisoner, restored to him. But they never let him govern again.

3.19.5. Now, Columbus was a prudent man. When he had arrived in Spain with the first news of the discovery, he begged a boon of their Catholic majesties: that his sons might be received as pages to the prince Juan. The sons were Diego Colón, oldest and legitimate son of the admiral, and his other son Fernando Colón, who lives to this day. Fernando Colón is a virtuous gentleman, affable and noble and pleasant company; he is learned in various branches of science, especially cosmography. His Catholic majesty values him as much on his own merits as a faithful servitor as for the great deeds of his father the admiral. Prince Juan treated the two sons well and favored them, and they formed part of his household until God took him to glory in the city of Salamanca in 1493.

3.19.6. Returning to the history: After pardoning him, the king and queen treated Columbus as well as at first. As he was a wise man, he endeavored by all means to get himself back into their good graces and obtain permission to return to the Indies. But there had been so many complaints against him he did not succeed immediately. Meanwhile Commander Bobadilla governed this island until 1502, as I have said. During this period much gold was produced from the island, because there were many Indians mining for the Christian settlers and for the crown, which had also estates and farms in the royal name.

3.19.7. All the Indians on this island were divided up and parceled out by the admiral to the settlers who came to these lands to live. The general opinion of those who were here and saw it is that when the admiral discovered these islands there were a million Indians, old and young, men and women and children. Of this original number and their descendants, in this year of 1548 it is believed hardly five hundred remain. Most of the present Indian population was brought from other islands or from Tierra Firme to serve the Christians. Since the mines were very rich, and man's greed insatiable, some of the Indians were worked too hard and others not fed well enough; and also, these people are naturally idle and pleasure-loving, lazy, melancholy and cowardly, vile and disposed to evil, liars, who are forgetful and lacking in perseverance. Many of them, for their own amusement, took poison to avoid working; others strangled themselves with their own hands, and others sickened and died, especially as a result of a smallpox plague that spread over the whole island. In a short time there were no more Indians.

[3.20] Book 3, chapter 7: The coming of the supreme commander of Alcántara, Nicolás de Ovando, governor of this island, and the departure of the commander Francisco de Bobadilla, who was lost at sea with the whole fleet and much gold. And how the admiral, being weather-wise, warned Ovando not to let the fleet sail from that port, and how, because the commander did not believe the admiral or allow him to enter port, the fleet and many men were lost.

3.20.1. At the time the commander of Jerez, Nicolás de Ovando of the military order of Alcántara, came to this city and island, he was not yet supreme commander.

That office fell vacant on the death of don Alonso de Santillán, and the Catholic king sent the title and appointment to Ovando, who had already been here several years. But I will refer to him as supreme commander throughout. He came to this island by order of the Catholic king and queen with a handsome fleet of thirty well-loaded ships and caravels. Many knights and gentlemen came with him from different parts of the kingdoms of Castile and León. During the life of the Catholic queen, only her subjects and vassals were allowed to go to the Indies, since the discovery belonged to them and not to Aragonese, nor Catalonians, nor Valencians nor subjects of the Catholic king. Only by special dispensation were any non-Castilians, servitors of the royal household, licensed to come. For since these Indies belong to the crown of Castile by conquest, her serene majesty wanted only these vassals and no others, save special exceptions, to come here. This was so until the end of 1504 when God took her to his glory. But after that the Catholic king, ruling as regent for his daughter our queen Juana, allowed the Aragonese and any of his vassals he pleased to come to these parts, with official positions. Later still the emperor extended the privilege to all his possessions and his subjects.

3.20.2. The supreme commander, then, sailed from Spain in 1502 and arrived in Santo Domingo on 15 April of that year, when the city was still located the other side of the Ozama river. He was received as governor, and Commander Bobadilla, the former governor, made haste to leave, because their Catholic majesties had relieved him and given permission for him to return to Spain. They were well-pleased with him, for he had carried out all his duties well and honestly like a good gentleman. So he left for Spain with the same fleet that brought Ovando. Now, as a great deal of gold had been mined, the fleet carried on that voyage more than 100,000 *pesos* in gold bars and some huge unrefined nuggets to display in Spain. Gold had been shipped before, for their Catholic majesties and for private persons, but never so much, both refined and in nuggets. Among the latter was a nugget weighing 3,600 *pesos* of gold; in the opinion of experts, that included less than three pounds of ore-bearing rock, or equivalently six marks equaling 300 *pesos*. So, discounting the rock, the gold amounted to 3,300 *pesos*, and the nugget was the size of a loaf of Utrera bread. In the memorial I wrote in Toledo in 1525, I said the nugget weighed 3,200 *pesos*; but that was without my notes, and I need to correct several points. Now I can state, with the confirmation of many eyewitnesses still alive here, that the nugget weighed something over 3,600, as I said above, of gold and ore. An Indian woman belonging to Miguel Díaz found it; they say that was the reason this city was moved across the river. Díaz was in partnership with Francisco de Garay, so the nugget belonged to both of them; the value of it over and above the royal fifth, after taxes, was paid to them and the nugget was sent to their Catholic majesties and lost with the fleet. The nugget was so big that when the Indian woman who found it showed it to the Christian miners, they were very happy and decided to have a suckling pig for lunch. One of them said, "For a long time I have hoped to eat from plates of gold, and since this nugget would make many plates, I am going to carve the suckling pig on it." And he did; and they ate it on the nugget, on which the whole piglet fit, because it was as big, as I have said.

3.20.3. To return to the history: Commander Bobadilla departed at an unfortunate moment, and with him Antonio de Torres, brother of the prince's nurse, who was commodore of the fleet. One or two days before the fleet was to weigh anchor, the admiral Christopher Columbus arrived with four caravels; he had orders from their Catholic majesties to explore and had his younger son Fernando with him. When he was still a league from Santo Domingo, Ovando sent a ship with certain sailors to him. It must be believed he knew of Columbus's arrival and had been warned not to let him enter this port. The admiral resented this and sent to tell Ovando that since he was not welcome in the lands he himself had discovered, so be it; he did not think their Catholic majesties would be pleased. But he begged Ovando not to let the fleet sail from Santo Domingo, for he thought a storm was brewing and he himself was going to look for a safe harbor to ride it out. Therefore he took his caravels to Puerto Escondido, ten leagues from Santo Domingo on the southwest coast, and anchored there until the storm blew itself out, as I will relate. Afterwards, he sailed to the coast of Tierra Firme, and what he discovered will be related in due time. Other people say he went to Azúa to ride out the storm.

[3.21] Book 3, chapter 8: What the captains Alonso de Ojeda and Rodrigo de Bastidas discovered off the coast of Tierra Firme.

3.21.1. While the admiral was in Spain, it happened that the captain Alonso de Ojeda, with permission from Bishop Juan Rodríguez de Fonseca (principal official in charge of the affairs of the Indies) came to discover the coast of Tierra Firme. He set a course to explore below the mouth of the Marañón river and landed eight leagues from where the settlement of the Santa Marta is now, a province called Cinta. The cacique there was one Ayaro, who swore peace and friendship with the Christians; as soon as he had done so he was taken prisoner by means of trickery by another captain named Cristóbal Guerra. This was the year 1501.

3.21.2. But these were not the only expeditions, because Captain Rodrigo de Bastidas sailed west from Cabo de la Vela (which was as far as the admiral had gotten discovering the coast of Tierra Firme), as will be told. I cannot justify omitting noteworthy deeds done in these parts that come to my attention, so I will relate how Rodrigo de Bastidas set out from Cádiz in 1502 with two caravels, at his own expense and that of Juan de Ledesma and other friends. Their first landfall was an island so cool and thickly-forested they called it Isla Verde; it lies between Guadalupe and Tierra Firme, near other islands in the channel. From there they sailed along the coast of Tierra Firme; trading with the Indians along the way, they collected as much as forty marks in gold. They kept on west past the harbor of Santa Marta, from Cabo de la Vela past the Grande river. Farther on Bastidas discovered the harbor of Zamba and the Coronados, a land where all the Indians wear huge crowns. Farther west he discovered the harbor of Cartagena, the isles of San Bernardo and Baru, and the ones called the Arenas, near Cartagena and facing it. From there he sailed on and discovered Isla Fuerte, which is flat, two leagues from the coast of Tierra Firme and where they make much good salt. Farther on is the island of Tortuga, very small and uninhabited. Farther on he discovered the harbor of Cení and Caribana point, at the mouth of the gulf of Urabá. He sailed into the gulf and saw islets and rocks close to the shore in the province of Darién. When he arrived there he had explored the hundred and thirty leagues, more or less, from Cabo de la Vela to the gulf of Urabá. He found the water was fresh at low tide, at four fathoms where he anchored, so he called it Dulce, and later it was named the gulf of Urabá. He missed seeing the San Juan river, also called the Grande, which empties into the gulf by seven channels and turns seawater fresh in an area of twelve leagues wide by forty-five or forty-six leagues long, from shore to shore on the gulf of Urabá. I will relate more particulars of the gulf and the river later, because I was for some years in that territory. On that voyage I sailed with Juan de la Cosa as head pilot, an excellent seaman.

3.21.3. The fleet stayed in the gulf several days. The ships were riddled with shipworm and leaking, so they decided to turn back to Jamaica, where they refreshed themselves. From there they sailed to the gulf of Xaraguá, where they lost the ships, which could not longer stay afloat. By land they reached the city of Santo Domingo, where they found Commander Bobadilla. He had already arrested Columbus, and he arrested Bastidas also, for trading with the Indians of Española, and he sent them to Spain on the same ship. But the king and queen ordered Bastidas freed and rewarded his great service (made at his own and his friends' expense, as I have said) with 50,000 *maravedis* of income for life from the province of Darién.

3.21.4. All that Bastidas discovered on this voyage, to point Caribana, is inhabited by the fiercest people of Tierra Firme from Cabo de la Vela east to Salinas point and the Boca del Drago and all the territory the admiral discovered. They shoot arrows tipped with deadly poison, and if there is an antidote, it is unknown to Christians. In the proper place it will be explained how and with what materials the Indians make their arrow poison, but for the moment I will return to the admiral and his discoveries.

[3.22] Book 3, chapter 9: How the fleet was lost with Commander Bobadilla; the last voyage of discovery made by the admiral Christopher Columbus to Tierra Firme.

3.22.1. I have related in chapter 7 of this book how the admiral approached the port of this city; he was coming from Spain to make his last explorations of Tierra Firme, looking for the passage to the Southern Ocean (in which matter he was deceived, because there is no passage by water, but an isthmus, as will be related in due time). But Ovando would not let him enter the port of Santo Domingo. Therefore, the admiral sent word that the weather appeared threatening, and he thought Bobadilla and the fleet for Spain should on no account depart from the harbor. But he was not believed, and the result of that I will now describe. The admiral, like a cautious seaman, put into Puerto Escondido, and after the storm he went on to explore Tierra Firme. Since he had already heard of Rodrigo de Bastidas's voyage as far as the gulf of Urabá (point Caribana, at the mouth of the gulf, lies at nine and a half degrees), he planned to explore farther west along the coast of Tierra Firme. All this will be told in this chapter, but I do not want to forget the death of Commander Bobadilla, the captain of the fleet, and Antonio de Torres (brother of the prince's nurse), which happened in this way.

3.22.2. Against the admiral's advice, these gentlemen sailed out of the harbor of this city of Santo Domingo. Eight or ten leagues out to sea, they met such a terrible storm that of thirty ships not more than four or five escaped. The rest were driven on reefs, and many sank, and the ocean swallowed them without a trace. More than five hundred men drowned, among them the leaders I mentioned, as well as Roldán Jiménez, who had rebelled against the admiral and his brother. Many other fine men, gentlemen and good folk, were drowned as well. And the great gold nugget I told of, that weighed 3,600 *pesos*, along with more than 100,000 *pesos* of gold and many other treasures, was lost. That was an evil day and a great loss.

3.22.3. The admiral, who understood the weather, put into Puerto Escondido, which he had named. From there, as soon as the storm passed, he made the passage to Tierra Firme with no danger, beyond the point reached by Bastidas. He subsequently discovered the following, according to what I heard from the pilots Pedro de Umbría, Diego Martín Cabrera, and Martín de los Reyes, who were with him. The admiral reconnoitered the island of Jamaica, and Cabo de las Higueras and the Guanajes islands (one of which is called Guanaja); he went to Puerto de Honduras, calling the surrounding area Punta de Cajines, and from there to Cabo Gracias a Dios; he turned east up the coast of the continent and discovered the province and river of Veragua; farther east he came to another big river which he named Belén. This river is a league from the one the Indians call Yebra, which is actually the Veragua, believed to be one of the richest places discovered. From there, still sailing east up the coast, he came to a great river he called the Lagartos. This is the one Christians now call Chagre, which rises near the Southern Ocean, passes four leagues from Panama, and empties into the Northern Ocean. From there he sailed to an island near the coast, which he named Bastimentos, and to Puerto Bello. From there he passed on to the harbor of Nombre de Dios (named by Captain Diego de Nicuesa, as will be related in due course). Columbus went on to the Francisca river and Retrete harbor, and from there to the gulf of Secativa, which he named the gulf of San Blas. He sailed up the coast to the Pocorosa islands and called that point cape Mármol. On this last voyage to the Indies, the admiral discovered a hundred and ninety or two hundred leagues of the coast of Tierra Firme, more or less.

3.22.4. From there he crossed to the island of Jamaica, a hundred leagues northwest of Cabo Gracias a Dios. There he lost the last two ships, which were riddled with shipworm and badly weathered. Of the four he started with, one was abandoned at the Yebra river (in Veragua), the other was abandoned at sea, because it could no longer keep afloat. On the coasts of Tierra Firme, since there are many great rivers, there is much shipworm and ships do not last long. But in the thirty days of the crossing, Columbus reconnoitered Omohaya at the end of the south coast of Cuba, where the village of Trinidad is now. From there he made Jamaica, where, as I said, he lost the other two ships, running them aground at the place on the coast now called Sevilla la Nueva. He sent word to Ovando in Santo Domingo by his servant Diego Méndez in an Indian canoe. Méndez is an honorable gentleman, a resident of this city, and lives to this day. It was a bold venture of his, because the canoe was small and could easily capsize; no one who values his life would put out to sea in one. They are for inshore and coastal waters. But Méndez, like a brave man and a good servant, seeing his master in such difficulties, set forth bravely and crossed the sea from that island to this with letters from the admiral asking Ovando to rescue the castaways. For this service (worthy of the highest praise), the admiral always loved him and favored him. When the Catholic king heard of it, he granted Méndez a coat of arms with a canoe on it, for his exemplary loyalty. There is no doubt that putting to sea with enemies who are expert swimmers, in an unstable boat for a dangerous passage, was an extraordinary deed of courage, loyalty and love for his master.

3.22.5. When Ovando saw the admiral's letters, he sent a caravel to see what the situation was, not to bring the men off. But Diego Méndez bought a ship with the admiral's money and provisioned it, then sent it to rescue the admiral while he went on to Spain to report to their Catholic majesties what the admiral had accomplished on this voyage.

3.22.6. It would not be right to leave out what happened to the admiral on that island, after sending Diego Méndez to this one for help; it is a remarkable story I will relate, worth remembering. Naturally, after so many hardships of the long voyage, bad food, and lack of sleep, many of the shipwrecked men were sick. The sound ones mutinied against the admiral; this action was instigated by two brothers: Francisco de Porras, ship captain, and Diego de Porras, purser of the fleet. They took all the Indians' canoes and said the admiral was not trying to get them home to Castile, because he had told them to wait for Diego Méndez with the answer and ships to take them all. The mutineers ill-advisedly disobeyed the admiral and put out to sea, thinking to reach Española. Although they tried many times, they succeeded only in getting some of themselves drowned. Therefore, they agreed to go back to the admiral and seize whatever ships came for him. But meanwhile the sick sailors that had been left with the admiral had recovered, although there were but few of them. Don Bartolomé, by the admiral's order, took the field with these men as soon as he understood the evil intentions of the mutineers. He fought them, killing three or four and wounding many others, and defeated them. This was the first battle known to occur between Christians in this part of the Indies. The Porras brothers were taken prisoner.

3.22.7. Before the battle took place, the Indians had seen the Christians who were healthy go away, leaving the admiral and a few sick men, so they refused to give the latter food or anything else. Thereupon the admiral called many Indians together and told them if they did not bring food, they could be sure that soon a pestilence would come upon them and that not an Indian among them would escape. As a sign of the plague and bloodshed to come, on such-and-such a day (which he told them), at such-and-such an hour, they would see the moon turn to blood. He said this because, as a skilled astrologer, he knew there was to be an eclipse of the moon on the date he told them. The date arrived; when the Indians saw the eclipse they believed what the admiral had told them, and many of them went to him, crying out and weeping, to ask pardon and beg him not to be angry with them. And they brought food and everything necessary to maintain him and his men and served them very well.

3.22.8. In this laborious manner the admiral and his men lived for a year, sleeping in the ships. They were aground and awash to the decks near the shore, in the bay where Sevilla la Nueva is now, the chief settlement of that island. Near there the battle took place, and the bay is called Santa Gloria.

3.22.9. After all this had occurred, the caravel sent by Diego Méndez arrived for the admiral; when he embarked, the Indians wept at his departure, because they thought he and the other Christians were celestial beings.

3.22.10. When the admiral arrived in this city of Santo Domingo he rested a few days. Ovando made much of him and kept him in his house until the admiral left on the first ships bound for Spain. He went to report to the Catholic king what he had done on the last voyage of discovery to Tierra Firme. But on the way, after he had reached Castile, already old and sick and suffering greatly from gout, he died in Valladolid. It was in the month of May, 1506, while the Catholic king was in Villafranca de Valcázar and his serene highness King Philip I and her serene highness Queen Juana were on their way to reign in Castile.

3.22.11. After his death, the admiral's body was taken to Seville, to the Cuevas monastery of the Carthusians, and left in deposit. May it please God to grant him his glory! . . . besides his service to the crown, all Spaniards owe him a great debt. Although many have perished and died in the conquest and pacification of these Indies, many others have made their fortune. And the best of all is that, in these lands so remote from Europe where the Devil was worshiped and served, he has been cast out; our sacred Catholic faith and the church of God has been implanted and exercised in such remote and strange lands, in such great kingdoms and dominions, by the industry and agency of the admiral Christopher Columbus. And besides, there is all the treasure of gold, silver, pearls, and many other precious things which has been shipped to Spain and which will continue. For these reasons no right-thinking Spaniard will forget the numerous benefits his country receives and has received, God willing, by the hand of the first admiral of the Indies.

3.22.12. His son don Diego succeeded to the title, house, and estate; he married doña María de Toledo, niece of the illustrious don Fadrique de Toledo, supreme commander of León in the military Order of Santiago. With her, the admiral don Diego Colón had his son the admiral don Luis Colón—who afterwards was his heir and enjoys the title and estate at present—and other children.

[3.23] Book 3, chapter 11

3.21.1. I do not deny any of those things or any of the many others which could be said in praise of both Sicily and England; but the reader should consider that all those things support my argument, because for many years those islands have been inhabited by rational people and two of them have had very famous courts with princes and kings. For this reason our island (La Española) should be valued all the more, since it had always been controlled by savage and bestial people, and its beginning can be counted from the year 1492, when the first Christians arrived here together with the first admiral Christopher Columbus (which makes fifty-five years until this year 1547). The fact that in such a short time this island has become as it is described above should be much admired and ascribed only to God's mercy, to the good fortune of our princes the Catholic kings of Spain and their grandson, the unvanquished emperor Charles, and to the virtue and diligence of their soldiers and Castilian vassals whose work and weapons have populated this land which, God willing, will become more and more noble.

[3.24] Book 4, chapter 1: The coming of the second admiral don Diego Colón to this city of Santo Domingo, port of the island of Española, and the changes there have been in the government and other matters.

3.24.1. What her serene highness Queen Isabel said was this: after the first admiral, Christopher Columbus, had discovered these Indies, one day he was explaining to the king and queen some peculiarities of these lands. For example, the trees, no matter how tall, have roots which lie just under the surface, not deep in the earth.

3.24.2. This is true; very few trees extend their roots below the layer of topsoil (half an *estado*, or a little more), because the earth becomes drier and hotter the deeper they go. The top layer is damp, and sustains the trees; their roots spread out like the branches above, because they do not go deep. It is also true that the cassia tree's roots go down to water, the only tree for which this is true; but Columbus never saw one, and there were not any of the medicinal cassia, although wild cassia grows through most of the Indies, as will be told later.

3.24.3. Returning to the history, when the queen heard what the admiral said, she asked him why he thought the trees had shallow roots instead of deep. And he replied that it rains a great deal in the Indies, cooling the surface of the ground so that the trees spread their roots out instead of down into the heat of the earth; it must of necessity be the case in that clime that the earth gets hot enough in the depths to burn the roots. The trees, feeling this, naturally spread out by instinct to where they will find nourishment. The queen seemed sorry to have heard this, and said, "In that land where trees do not have deep roots, little truth and less constancy will be found in men."

Surely, any knowledgeable person cannot deny that the Catholic queen spoke about what I just said like the most learned natural philosopher, not just guessing, but telling the truth and saying what actually happens, for the Indians of this generation are liars and as inconstant as children of six or seven, or even more so.

[3.25] Book 5, chapter 3: Marriage among the Indians, how many wives they have, what degree of kinship constitutes incest, and their vices and lust; with what religiosity they collected gold, their idolatry and other remarkable facts.

3.25.1. The admiral Christopher Columbus, first discoverer of these lands, was a Catholic leader and a good governor. When he heard of the mines of Cibao and saw how the Indians picked up gold in streams and rivers, without digging, with the religious ceremonies described above, he would not allow the Christians to go gold-hunting without confessing and taking communion first. Since the bestial Indians spent twenty days apart form their wives (and other women), fasting, because otherwise they would find no gold, said the admiral, so much more it behooved Christians to eschew sin and confess their lapses. When they were in a state of grace our Lord would be more disposed to grant them both temporal and spiritual goods. This sanctimoniousness did not please everyone. They pointed out that those of them who had wives in Spain were much farther away from them than were the Indians from their wives. As to fasting, many Christians were dying of hunger and eating roots and other unwholesome food and drinking water. And as for confession, since the church only required it once a year at Easter, they confessed then, and some of them made their confessions even more often. Since God asked no more, the admiral should be satisfied and let them make a living without harassing them with his scruples. Thus did they attribute to the admiral a hidden purpose which probably never crossed his mind. But those who confessed and took communion were allowed to go and look for gold; the rest were not, and he punished them if they went without his express permission.

[3.26] Book 6, chapter 8: The metals and gold mines there are on this island of Española, and which is divided into eleven paragraphs or sections. The method of mining gold will be related, and other important details pertinent to the history.

3.26.1. I wish to remind my listener to conclude from this chapter and its contents, like a prudent reader, what an enormous treasure of pure virgin gold must have been sent to Spain from this island and the others inhabited by Christians, and from Tierra Firme, since the discovery, without having previously entered any other nation. And this treasure was not only for the crown (proprietor of this empire and wealthy dominion), but also for the vassals and subjects in even greater quantities. The king takes only one fifth in royalties; and in some provinces, to favor his subjects, he takes a tenth or less. Besides, there are many hundred-weight of silver from Peru and New Spain, to say nothing of uncountable marks of pearls, or of the enormous and important profit there is in these lands, offering advantages to the whole world.

3.26.2. Christopher Columbus, first discoverer and inventor of these Indies and first admiral of them in our time, deserves a much better statue even than that statue called Holosphiraton, and the other one of Leoninus, who was the first man to have a statue of solid gold in the temple of Delphi in the seventieth Olympiad. Columbus does not merit a solid gold likeness on the basis of his oratory, like Leoninus, but rather because he was a daring and wise navigator and a valorous captain who showed us the New World, which is so full of gold, that thousands such statues might have been made from the gold constantly being sent to Spain. And yet Columbus is more worthy of fame and glory for bringing the Catholic faith here where we are, to all the Indians who, by the grace of God, daily augment the Christian religion. What fame attaches to the name and immortality to the soul of that man whose diligence was the cause of such a benefit!

[3.27] Book 6, chapter 43: The diversity of languages of these Indies, islands, and Tierra Firme of the Ocean Sea.

3.27.1. The first language Christopher Columbus, the discoverer, encountered, was that of the Lucayos islands; the second one was that of Cuba; and the third language was that of Haiti or Española. They are mutually unintelligible. This was on the first and second voyages the admiral made to the Indies. Afterwards, when he explored the huge coast of Tierra Firme, he encountered many other languages, all very different, such as that of the Caribs, and other nations differing so much in language, rites and ceremonies, beliefs and customs, that it is impossible to relate all of them given the present state of knowledge. What remains to be encountered and known is infinitely more, so that future historians will have to write a great deal more than I have been able to understand of these matters.

[3.28] Book 6, chapter 46: Concerning a noteworthy and most remarkable phenomenon: the change of climate in this city of Santo Domingo of Española, and even in other parts of the Indies inhabited by Christians.

3.28.1. It is only fifty-six years since Christians have set foot in the Indies; I saw Columbus, the discoverer, and most of the first settlers, that is, the principal men who came here first, and those who have come since with government positions. All those who have been in the Indies for any length of time agree that these parts are much changed, and changing more each day, in the matter of hot and cold seasons; as time passes, the climate grows steadily cooler, or not so hot. Everyone, generally Spaniards who have lived here for some time, says so.

[3.29] Book 9, prologue.

3.29.1. Although it has been only a few years since the first Christians came to these parts—I saw with my own eyes and recognized the pioneers: I saw Christopher Columbus, his brother the governor Bartolomé Colón, the pilot Vicente Yáñez, and other shipmates on the first voyage of discovery, many times—I do not wonder at what has not been accomplished, but rather at how much has been done in such a short time.

[3.30] Book 12, prologue.

3.30.1.The number twelve is beautiful and holy and no Catholic should forget it, and it goes very well with the book on animals. Because these people of the Indies, although they are rational and descended from the family of Noah, had become irrational and bestial with their idolatries and infernal ceremonies and sacrifices, so the Devil had control of their souls for centuries. By means of the crown of Castile and the blessed Fernando V of that name and Isabel of glorious memory, and his imperial majesty the emperor Charles, their grandson and our king, and by the doctrine and arms of the fearless Spaniards (both religious and laymen), the gospel of the twelve apostles was brought to these lands with the guidance of the Holy Spirit, whose minister and captain was the famous Christopher Columbus, first explorer of the Indies.

[3.31] Book 12, chapter 10. The animals of the Indies which the Spaniards call tigers and which the Indians call by different names, according to the language of each province.

3.31.1. I have already said what I think about whether the *ochis* are tigers or not. Whether they belong to the list of those animals with spotted skins, or are a new animal, not recorded in the lists, is the question; of the many animals there are in Tierra Firme, those I will mention here (or most of them) are not recorded by any writer of antiquity, since the provinces they inhabit were unknown in the cosmography of Ptolemy until Christopher Columbus showed them to us. That was certainly a greater and more memorable deed than the labor of Hercules in opening the Mediterranean Sea to the Ocean. The Greeks before that time did not know it, hence the fable that the mountains Calpe, in Spain, and Abyla, in Africa, which face each other across the straits of Gibraltar, were together and that Hercules opened them and made an entrance to the ocean and placed his pillars in Cádiz and Seville. The emperor deservedly bears those pillars on his coat of arms with the motto *plus ultra*, applicable only to a universal emperor whose arms have reached farther than those of Hercules (or any other prince). Hercules only sailed from Greece to Cádiz, and the poets and historians said that was making a door to the ocean; how incomparably greater is the achievement of Columbus!

[3.32] Book 17, prologue.

3.32.1. As I have said, on the first voyage of discovery the first land Columbus saw were the Islas Blancas, so-called for their white sands. But he commanded they should be called the Princessas, as they were the first land sighted of the Indies. He put into Guanahaní, in the middle of the islands, in November of 1492. The Indians call the islands the Lucayos, and they lie north of Cuba and parallel to it. From there he went to Cuba, sixty leagues away.

[3.33] Book 18, chapter 20.

3.33.1. But later on, Gonzalo de Guzmán himself went back to the same government and office, in the name of the admiral Luis Colón, until 1537, when the long lawsuit between the admiral and the royal fisc was finally settled. And our lord the emperor, being a very grateful prince, agreed to finish the lawsuit regarding the services of the first admiral Christopher Columbus.

[3.34] Book 19, prologue.

3.34.1. In this book 19 I shall speak of the island of Cubagua, which is tiny and barren, without a drop of water from river, spring, lake, or pond. Despite this and other disadvantages, having no arable land to plant or harvest any crop, nor grazing for livestock, it is inhabited: there is a splendid settlement called the new city of Cádiz. Nowhere in the Indies is there a Christian settlement so profitable. Yet the island is only three leagues in circumference, more or less. Many people who ought to know say that since 1496, when Columbus discovered it, the abundance of pearls and baroque pearls, the royalties and profits to private persons from the fishery is enormous. It produces daily. But since the story has a certain chronological order I will first describe what I have heard and found out about the discovery of this island.

[3.35] Book 19, chapter 1: The discovery of the island of Cubagua, where pearls were first seen in the Indies, and how the Spaniards knew about them.

3.35.1. The third voyage of discovery Columbus made in 1496, setting sail from Cádiz in March with six well-loaded caravels, as was told in book 3. En route he sent three of the caravels to Española, and continued his explorations with the remaining three. With this fleet the admiral put into the Canary Islands in a few days, took on wood and water and other provisions, and from there sailed to the islands of Antón, or the Cape Verdes, those which the ancient cosmographers call the Gorgades. Some people say those islands are the Hesperides, but I refute them, on the basis of those authorities I cite in book 2, chapter 3, wherein it is sufficiently proved that the Hesperides are these islands of our Indies. But let us leave that aside.

3.35.2. Returning to the point at issue, from the Cape Verdes the admiral sailed southwest a hundred and fifty leagues (according to the pilot Hernán Pérez Mateos, alive and resident in this city to this day); there was a storm which forced them to strike the masts and jettison much of the cargo. They were in such peril they thought they were lost, and ran north by northwest until they sighted the island of Trinidad. But this storm, which the pilot Hernán Pérez tells of, is contradicted by Fernando Colón, son of the admiral, who was on the voyage with his father. He told me the problem was that they were becalmed in such heat that the casks opened and the wheat rotted, and they had to retreat from the equator.

Anyone who hears they retreated from the equator because of the heat, may think that proves the false theory of the ancients, who said the Torrid Zone (the equator) is uninhabitable because of the excessive heat of the sun. Later, speaking of the Southern Ocean, I will explain that on each side of the equator the Torrid Zone is inhabited, since our Spaniards daily pass from one tropic to the other. So I say that Fernando Colón was correct, because at sea, close to the equator on whichever side, there is no doubt it is very hot; so they might well, as he said, retreat from it. But on land, along the very line of the equator, all-provident God took care to put mountains; because of the mountains and the winds, provinces and regions in the Torrid Zone are temperate. There is even ice and much snow in some places in and near this zone. This is what the ancients did not understand, so naturally they thought the equator must be uninhabitable because of the strength of the sun.

3.35.3. Let us return to the history, because when we come to the equator what our Spaniards see daily will be discussed at length. Therefore Fernando says that the admiral, reconnoitering the island of Trinidad, called it that because he already intended to name the first land after the Trinity, and it happened that they saw three hills close together, so the island was named Trinidad. He sailed through the channel and called it Boca del Drago, and saw Tierra Firme afterwards and a great part of the coast, as I have related in more detail in another section. From point Salinas on Tierra Firme (where Boca del Drago lies, ten degrees north of the equator) the admiral sailed west along the coast and discovered more islands, as I have said in book 3. From there he went on to discover the rich island of Cubagua (of which we speak), that the Christians now call Las Perlas. After a few years Nueva Cádiz was founded where the pearl fishery is. Next to this island is a larger one, called La Margarita, because that is what the admiral named it.

3.35.4. This little island of Cubagua is fifty leagues west of point Salinas; it is, as I said, some three leagues in circumference, one and a half leagues long, and a scant league wide. It lies four leagues from the great coast of Tierra Firme, the province known as Araya. And because (as was said in the prologue) there is no water, those who live on Cubagua go to Tierra Firme for water, seven laborious leagues from Nueva Cádiz to the river called Cumaná. But in the interest of high profits, men put up with these inconveniences.

3.35.5. Cubagua lies almost ten and a half degrees from the equator on our horizon. From the isle to this city of Santo Domingo of Española the distance might be a hundred and seventy or eighty leagues, more or less. It lies on a north-south line with the island of Santa Cruz, inhabited by Caribs, a hundred and ten leagues to the north. To the south is Tierra Firme, four leagues away at the nearest point, and the island of Poregari is twenty-five leagues to the west. This is the description of the location of the island, its limits and surroundings; but the nearest land is the island La Margarita, which I have said lies a league to the north.

3.35.6. Everything else the admiral discovered on this third voyage was described in book 3 of this first part, and it is not necessary to repeat it here except what concerns these two islands, Cubagua and La Margarita, and how the pearls came to be discovered.

3.35.7. When the admiral drew abreast of Cubagua with his three caravels, he sent a few sailors off in a boat to intercept a canoe that was fishing for pearls. The canoe, seeing the Christians approaching, fled back to the island. Among the Indians the sailors saw a woman with many strings of baroque pearls around her neck. (The Indians do not bother with seed pearls, nor do they have the skill nor the delicate tools to pierce them.) Then one of the sailors took an elaborately decorated ceramic plate from Valencia (also known as Málaga ware), broke it in pieces, and traded the fragments for several strings of large baroque pearls. They took the pearls to the admiral; understanding better than they the value of the business, he tried to hide his enthusiasm, but did not succeed. He said, "I tell you, you are in the richest land there is in the world; God be thanked for it." He then sent the boat to shore again with other sailors to trade for as many pearls as would fit in a bowl in exchange for another broken plate like the first one and some hawk bells. Landing on the island, they traded with the pearl fishermen for as much as five or six marks of pearls, all mixed as they were taken, baroque and perfect pearls, large and small. The admiral kept them to take or send to Spain to their Catholic majesties Fernando and Isabel of glorious memory. He did not wish to linger for fear of provoking the men's greed for pearls, thinking to keep the matter secret for a more convenient occasion. If he had wished to, he could have traded for three-quarters of a bushel of pearls, according to the pilot Hernán Pérez Mateos, resident here. He says he saw that many pearls, or more, but the admiral refused to trade any more.

3.35.8. But there are few secrets among sailors. When some of them returned to Spain, they talked about it in Palos, the hometown of most of the sailors who navigated these waters at that time. It became known in Moguer, and some inhabitants by the name of Niño, privateers, heard of it. One of them was Peralonso Niño. They set out in a ship, signing on some of the admiral's crew who had seen the discovery of the pearls, went to the island, and bartered for many pearls. They would have returned to Spain rich if they had been able to get away with it. In truth, Peralonso had a license to explore the Indies; but it was given on condition he not go within fifty leagues of places the admiral had already discovered, a condition which he did not heed. They set out directly to the pearl fisheries they had heard of and did their trading. When they returned to Europe they put into Galicia, where Hernando de Vega, lord of Grajal, was viceroy. He was afterwards commander of Castile of the military and knightly Order of Santiago. Peralonso's crew had some differences of opinion with him and said he had not shared out the pearls fairly, nor given the king the royal fifth, as was his due. This came to the attention of the viceroy. He ordered Peralonso arrested, and impounded the pearls and the ship for violating the license. Peralonso and some of the others were sent to court as prisoners, where they regained their liberty with much difficulty. From then on the island was well-guarded.

3.35.9. Some say the admiral was guilty of breach of trust and authority in this matter of the pearls and Cubagua, since they say it was known in Spain from sailors' gossip and from the letters of private persons before he reported it. Others deny this.

[4] FROM *THE GENERAL AND NATURAL HISTORY OF THE INDIES*

SECOND PART, DEDICATED TO THE EMPEROR

[4.1]

4.4.1. Let us leave these matters and return to the main thread of this history. Goths and Spaniards are those who found these our Indies, vassals of your majesty and of the royal crown of Castile, guided by the skill of that famous first admiral of the Indies, Christopher Columbus, whose memory will never grow dim. Although every word written and to be written in the world be lost, the famous tale will be told in Heaven, where God rewards the good and preserves it to the praise and glory of such a great man.

4.1.2. It seems to me right that your sacred majesty and the kings of Castile should keep perpetually in memory the heirs of the admiral, to honor, gratify, and conserve the line of succession of his house, sustain it and amplify it and value it as a jewel and ornament of the kingdom. For Columbus was the cause of so many good things, particularly the reimplanting of the Catholic faith of Christ in these Indies, forgotten since time immemorial in such far-flung regions. And also that such uncountable wealth has flowed into the royal coffers, to be used by your majesty in the service of God, to fight the infidel and for other holy and pious works; all this may be said better by your elegant historians who work near the presence of your majesty, than by one so far away who can only speak fully on matters pertaining to these Indies.

[4.2] Book 20, prologue.

4.2.1. My conscience incites me to begin this second volume of the history (concerning Tierra Firme) with Christopher Columbus, the discoverer, author, and founder of exploration in the Indies, islands and Tierra Firme of the Ocean Sea. This praise and glory is his and his alone. But chronology requires me to begin with Captain Ferdinand Magellan, who discovered the great and famous strait to the south of Tierra Firme. . . . In order not to leave out the admiral or anyone else, so no one can complain of me, I will relate punctually what captains and private persons followed the laudable discoverer, and when and what discoveries each one made. So the admiral keeps the preeminence and superiority of first discoverer of undying memory, and the rest receive their due.

[4.3] Book 20, chapter 1: A description of Captain Ferdinand Magellan and the famous southern passage he discovered around Tierra Firme, and his voyage to the Especiería and the Moluccas, and the ship *Victory*, which circumnavigated the globe, etc.

4.3.1. What Magellan wanted to do was sail due west until, circumnavigating the globe, he arrived at the Orient. This was a difficult, not to say impossible, proposal; it was not so much the distance in air miles, but the question of whether nature had disposed matters so as to permit a ship to sail through Tierra Firme from the west to reach the east. Many have looked for such a passage from sea to sea through the interior of Tierra Firme, because Columbus said there was one and even drew it on some maps of the Indies; but there is no such passage known to this day through the interior of Tierra

Firme. So the reader can better understand what I call the interior, be advised it comprised all that lies between Labrador and Cabo San Augustín.

[4.4] Book 21, chapter 5: The equator, and what it is.

4.4.1.The first and principal discoverer, who showed the way to all his emulators in our time, was the first admiral of the Indies, Christopher Columbus. That honor is chiefly his, although the other captains who followed his lead also deserve praise and fame for their accomplishments and their high aspirations, as long as they recognize Columbus as their master and teacher from whom they took inspiration and guidance and without whom they would never have started.

[4.5] Book 21, chapter 6: Continuation of the description of the geography of Tierra Firme, that which lies coast to coast between the line of the equator or promontory called Cabo Blanco where the line crosses land, to the gulf of Urabá and the Farallones.

4.5.1. The body of water between the Boca del Drago and Trinidad and Tierra Firme was discovered by the admiral on his third voyage, in 1496, as is told in more detail in the third book of the first part of this *General History of the Indies*. He saw first the island of Trinidad and called it that because of the three hills visible at once. He entered the channel which he called the Boca del Drago and did not treat with the many Indians he saw in great dugout canoes. because they are fierce people and bowmen. The southern part of the island lies at eight and two-thirds degrees; it is thirty or more leagues long and twenty-five wide. South of it is the part of Tierra Firme called El Palmar, named by the admiral. Salinas point on Tierra Firme, in the Boca del Drago or the channel between Salinas and the island, was the first sight Christians had of Tierra Firme. It is now called the point of Paria, because the small gulf between the island and Tierra Firme is called the gulf of Paria.

4.5.2. The cartographers who draw navigational charts put down what the sailors tell them and daily change or take away names almost at random; this is great foolishness, and not keeping the original names confuses everything. What the map calls Corazante, the Indians call Corazao, and the admiral who discovered it kept that name. What he called Poregari, now they call Yaruma or La Orchila. Let us proceed. From Cabo de los Monjes forty leagues east to west is Cabo de la Vela; the admiral called it this because he saw there a great Indian canoe under sail.

[4.6] Book 21, chapter 7: Continuation of the description of the geography of Tierra Firme, that which lies coast to coast between the three Farallones of Darién, in the gulf of Urabá, to the end of the gulf called Higueras.

4.6.1. Here the history must return to the author of these discoveries, admiral of the Indies Christopher Columbus, and relate his further exploration of Tierra Firme on his fourth and last voyage. He sailed from Spain to the harbor of Santo Domingo on Española; the supreme commander of Alcántara Nicolás de Ovando, governor, would not let him enter the harbor, as was told in book 3 of the first part of this *General History*. Therefore he proceeded immediately to explore with the four caravels he had, piloted by Pedro de Umbría, Diego Martín Cabrera, and Martín de los Reyes. He went to Jamaica, and from there to Tierra Firme, where he reconnoitered Cabo de las Higueras and the Guanajes islands, one of which is called Guanaja. He went into the harbor of Honduras, and called the point Cajines; on the modern map the name is different, but I heard it from the pilots, as will be told.

4.6.2. From there he went to Cabo Gracias a Dios, turning up the coast to the east, and discovered the rich province of Veragua. Last year, 1536, the emperor granted to the admiral don Luis Colón the titles of duke of Veragua and marquis of Jamaica, plus 10,000 *escudos* in gold each year from the royalties of this island of Española, and the office of chief constable of this city of Santo Domingo with a vote in the municipal council of this rich community. All the above belongs indivisibly to him and his successors, with the title of admiral of the Indies (explored and unexplored) confirmed in perpetuity. This was the action of a grateful prince with regard to the great and notable services of don Luis's grandfather Christopher Columbus, deservedly mentioned here. And in truth, those deeds were far above the common run by which men acquire their estate. If we remember the origin and beginnings of the houses of the grandees of Spain and other nations, we find that for remarkable service to the crown, or a particular relationship, kings made great lords and gave incomes and titles and dignities to whomever deserved such or to whomever they pleased. But you will find none of those so favored ever gave his king a kingdom, like Columbus. What he discovered not only gave the crown of Castile and León and their Catholic majesties of immortal memory and their heirs a kingdom, or rather two or three very large kingdoms; he gave them half the whole world, greater than the three parts which are Asia, Africa, and Europe and which the ancients thought constituted the world. For in these our Indies there are more kingdoms and empires than were known to any author ancient or modern, until Columbus showed us all. That this may be believed, turn back and read what I said in chapter 5 about Pliny, who writes that of the five parts of the world, three are uninhabited; we see, in defiance of his opinion, the national flag and rule of Castile in the Torrid Zone, by the labor of Columbus; we cross back and forth from one tropic to the other in spite of the obstacles to human habitation cited by Pliny and others.

4.6.3. Let now leave off praising and discussing the meritorious deeds of Columbus, for my pen cannot do them justice, and there can hardly be anyone so ignorant or so stupid as to be unaware of them. Let us get back to our way.

4.6.4. So Columbus discovered Veragua and went on to another big river to the east, which he called Belén, a league from another river the Indians call Yebra, which is the same river of Veragua. Farther east he found another powerful river which he called Lagartos, because there are many very large lizards in it—that is to say, cockatrices. The Indians call this river the Chagre, and Christians call it the same; it rises two leagues from the Southern Ocean, passes four leagues from the city of Panama in the province of Cueva (which is now called Castilla del Oro), and falls into the Northern Ocean, where the admiral named this river Lagartos. He went on to an island near the coast which he called Bastimentos, because on it were cultivated corn and cassava, yams and sweet potatoes; he named it Puerto Bello. From there he continued up the coast, past the harbor known as Nombre de Dios, but did not see it. He came to the Francisca river, so called because there they picked up an Indian woman who wanted to become a Christian, and they baptized her Francisca. Farther on he found a harbor called El Retrete and sailed up it to the gulf of Secativa, a great bay in that coast full of islets. He called it the gulf of San Blas, because they arrived on the third of February, the feast of the bishop and martyr. From there they continued to the islands of Pocacosi, and the admiral named the headland Mármol, and from there turned to Jamaica.

4.6.5. These were the parts of Tierra Firme the admiral discovered on the fourth voyage. He returned to Spain and died in Valladolid the year 1506, a few days after disembarking in La Coruña in Galicia. Their serene highnesses King Philip I and Queen Juana, our sovereigns and the parents of his imperial majesty the king and emperor Charles, were on their way to reign in Castile.

4.6.6. Now that the coast of Tierra Firme is well known and there are accurate navigational charts, with past reports it is possible to conclude that Columbus on his last voyage explored as much as two hundred leagues of the coast, more or less; for that reason some people do not believe he got below cape Honduras, because if he reached the gulf of Las Higueras it would be more like three hundred leagues he explored. I will not dwell further on details of this voyage, nor on how the ships were lost, because in the third book of this *General History* the admiral's course is set down. You may have noticed, reader, he sailed from west to east, the opposite way I have reached the gulf of Urabá, because that is the way the admiral did it and the order in which he explored.

[4.7] Book 21, chapter 8: Continuation of the description of the location and geography of Tierra Firme from the gulf of Higueras down Yucatán to the coast of Nueva España as far as the Pánuco river; which is the northern boundary of Nueva España; what there is from there to the Ancón Baja, etc, will be related.

4.7.1. I shall continue from where I left off in the previous chapter, with the gulf of Higueras, which some people say was discovered by Christopher Columbus. But it is not so: it was discovered by the pilots Vicente Yáñez Pinzón and Juan Díaz de Solís and Pedro de Ledesma with three caravels—before Vicente Yañez discovered the Marañón River and Solís the Río de la Plata.

[4.8] Book 23, chapter 11: How Alvar Núñez Cabeza de Vaca was sent as governor and captain general by order of the emperor to the Río de la Plata, also called Paranaguazú, with a good fleet and with the title of *adelantado* [governor].

4.8.1. The only thing I dislike is the title of *adelantado*, because the fact is that such an honor is bad luck in the Indies, and many who bore the title came to a bad end. For example, don Bartolomé, brother of Columbus, was the first *adelantado* in the Indies, and he left no heir and nothing of himself.

[4.9] Book 27, chapter 1: The voyage of discovery the captain and pilot Juan de la Cosa made along the coast of Tierra Firme and in the province of Cartagena and other places.

4.9.1. Columbus was the first discoverer of these Indies, and in fact the others cannot really be called discoverers, but rather followers and continuers of the enterprise Columbus began. Some of the later explorers might better be termed destroyers of the lands, since they came to serve neither God nor the king, only to steal, as is evident from the many deaths there were. However, there was one Juan de la Cosa, a native of Puerto de Santa María, an expert seaman and a bold man, who made his fortune as a pilot in these parts.

[4.10] Book 28, chapter 1: The incident concerning Diego de Nicuesa, the first governor of Veragua and of other provinces: what occurred and the way that he was badly used by the captain Lope de Olano, who changed his direction and deserted him, leaving him lost.

4.10.1. A gentleman, a relative of Nicuesa himself, called Cueto stayed as his lieutenant and captain together with five hundred and fifty men who agreed to wait there for him, for he was going with some of the pilots whom the old admiral Christopher Columbus had taken with him when he had discovered Veragua. . . . They arrived at Puerto Bello, which is one of the best ports on that coast and was named by Christopher Columbus who discovered it. . . . Heading to the west, he met the captain Lope de Olano, who was returning in the brigantine in which he had accompanied the governor Diego de Nicuesa and then had abandoned him and had left him lost, for a pilot who was in Lope de Olano's brigantine said, when he was passing through Veragua, "This is Veragua; I came here with the admiral Christopher Columbus when he discovered this land. . . ." This disloyal captain Lope de Olano, with evil intentions, reversed his direction and went to the east in order to look for the people who had stayed with Captain Cueto. He recognized Veragua and passed by, encountering at sea the other pilot mentioned above, whose name was Pedro de Umbría, whom Cueto had sent to search for the governor because he knew the coast well and he was one of the old admiral's pilots . . . ; and Lope de Olano settled on the river of Belén, which had been named by the first admiral, and founded a village.

[4.11] Book 28, chapter 4: How a long time after what has been related, Felipe Gutiérrez was the governor and captain general of the province of Veragua; the unfortunate outcome of his government and post.

4.11.1. To continue with Veragua, in my opinion this province was discovered by the first admiral Christopher Columbus. Because this land was said to be very rich, as it truly is, and because Castilla del Oro, which is on the east of Veragua on the coast of mainland, has already been settled by Christians and because there are provinces located to the west on the same coast, our lord the emperor wished that the area in the middle, being very rich as it has been said, should be settled and that both the conversion of the Indians and the settlement by Christians should continue. For this reason he asked the vice-queen of the Indies, María de Toledo, mother of the admiral Luis Colón, who was at the court, to order that the province be settled and to send somebody to do it, as Veragua was governed by her son the admiral, because it had been discovered by his grandfather Christopher Columbus.

[4.12] Book 29, chapter 30: The gold mines, pearls, and riches in the province of Cueva and Castilla del Oro, and the voyage to the Especiería, from Panama to the Moluccas and the Puente Admirable, and other matters pertaining to the chronology of the history.

4.12.1. But we were speaking of the mines of Darién. It will be necessary to correct anyone who might have believed the chronicler Lucius Marinus in his work *Memorable Things of Spain*, book 19, the chapter where he tried to describe these Indies, never having seen them. He did not content himself with writing so much misinformation about Spain, in particular, some genealogies in which he departed entirely from the truth. He also had to visit the Indies in dreams; I say in his dreams, because even talking in his sleep he could not have produced just the opposite of the truth. Anyone who writes about what he has not seen, must take great care form whom he gets his information.

4.12.2. He says their Catholic majesties sent Pedro Colón with thirty-five ships and many men to discover other islands, much bigger than the Canaries, with rich and copious gold mines. And he sailed sixty days, arriving at last at lands far from Spain, the Antipodes, underneath our hemisphere. As to all these errors: I say it was not Pedro, but Christopher Columbus; there were three ships; and I wrote about the voyage in the first part of this *General History of the Indies*.

4.12.3. Columbus and other modern cosmographers believed there must be a strait from what we call the Northern Ocean to the Southern Ocean, in the coast of Tierra Firme. The only passage was discovered by Magellan, as was related in book I, chapter 2 of this second part, which is book 20 of the *General History of the Indies*. But here, on this coast of Tierra Firme, there is only an isthmus, no passage by water; the route goes from Nombre de Dios to Panama, or from Careta to Acla, to the gulf of San Miguel, the place from where Vasco Núñez de Balboa discovered the Southern Ocean.

[5] *From The General and Natural History of the Indies*

THIRD PART

[5.1] Book 49, chapter 16: The chronicler concludes this book and notes seven services done for the emperor our sovereign and for the crown of Castile, in the Indies; these are the following:

5.5.1. Among the most noteworthy things I find in this *General History* are seven worth remembering forever, never to be forgotten by present nor future generations.

5.1.2. The first and most important is attributed to Christopher Columbus, who discovered these Indies; nothing can compare to that, nor could a greater service be done for the Crown and their Catholic majesties of Castile, Fernando and Isabel, in whose time the discovery took place, nor for their successors present and future.

[5.2] Book 50, chapter 30: A concluding statement and excuse which the author of these histories makes to his readers in defense of his work; they should know that in Spain, among Latinists and important persons of no little authority, it was discussed whether the writer of such new and strange works ought to write them in Latin. Some blamed him and some excused him, and someone wrote to him in the Indies, telling him what was being said for and against in Spain. He responded with a letter the gist of which you have here, reader, so you can form your own opinion as to which side is right; if you calmly and charitably entertain his excuse with a tranquil mind, taking in your hands the scales of justice and the author's justification, giving truth her due to rightly consider, ponder, and decide the question in the light of what he says.

5.2.1. I did not come to these parts with the first Spaniards who saw them; but I was at the court of their Catholic majesties Fernando and Isabel of immortal memory, in the royal encampment at the siege of Granada, when he who so mightily strove to accomplish this enterprise was sent out to commence it, the year I have said. I met him and saw him many times, both himself and the other leaders concerned in it, as in the course of these essays I have said. I have attained such an age that I almost pass seventy years, and I will keep on writing history in this manner as long as God is pleased to grant me eyesight, breath, hand, and inclination to write what comes to my mind.

[6]

[6.1] FROM THE DIÁLOGO ON ALONSO DE CÓRDOBA, ALMIRANTE DE VALENCIA

6.1.1. His wife's name was [illegible]; he had with her a son and heir don Santiago, admiral of the kingdom of Valencia and marquis of Lista, who is worthy of his father and very like him, who married the illustrious lady doña María Colón, marchioness of Guadalete, daughter of the illustrious gentleman Diego Colón, second admiral of the Indies, and of his wife doña María de Toledo, vice-queen of the Indies. The marchioness is the granddaughter of that famous and illustrious Christopher Columbus, first admiral and discoverer of the new world or second empire and of countless seas and kingdoms . . . through whose work they came under our rule, making the royal scepter of Castile great and powerful.

[6.2] FROM THE DIÁLOGO ON PEDRO GONZÁLEZ DE MENDOZA, ARCHBISHOP OF TOLEDO

6.1.2. You can be sure that the discovery of the Indies would have not been concluded without the participation of the cardinal, for Christopher Columbus, their first admiral, did not trust in the other means he had sought to make his voyage and his wishes were only heard by the cardinal. And the result of the favor that this prelate made to Spain and its kings was the abundant treasure that we all know and have seen with out own eyes. And by means of the cardinal, the Catholic king and the queen received Columbus, dealt with him, and equipped him for his voyage.

[7] FROM *FIFTY STANZAS ON THE NOBILITY OF SPAIN*

Written by the captain Gonzalo Fernández de Oviedo, their highnesses governor at the fort of the city and port of Santo Domingo.

[7.1] Quinquágena 2, stanza 25.

7.1.1. Saint Jerome says the memory recalls what the eye has seen better than what the ear has heard, and all men can bear testimony to the truth of this. By the same token, things seen are better understood than those heard or read of. Before I saw the Indies with my own eyes, I never understood what they are really like. I had heard Columbus himself; the pilot Vicente Yáñez Pinzón, who accompanied him on the first voyage; Fray Buyl, the first religious in the Indies; Pedro Margarit, knight of Santiago; and other gentlemen in the service of their Catholic majesties who went on the second voyage—but still I saw and see the Indies very differently now that I have been here.

[7.2] Quinquágena 3, stanza 4.

Let us not leave out Columbus,
Who discovered the Indies.

7.2.1. It is right and proper that the first admiral of the Indies should be named among the illustrious men, for it was he who undertook such a vast enterprise and carried it out, discovering a new world unknown to any before him. For it is the general opinion that the cosmographers never wrote of this hemisphere, nor did any ships sail these seas or visit the kingdoms of this western empire. So said the admiral himself in these lines: "For Castile and León, Columbus found the New World." Not because it was newer or older than the parts Ptolemy çalled Asia, Africa, and Europe—but because those three had been considered the whole world, and the Indies belong to the world too, and it is all one world. But the Old World (I mean what the ancients called the world) is made up of three continents which are different from each other, and the Old World is not the same as the New, nor the New World the same as the Old. The Old World had these boundaries: from the strait of Gibraltar between Calpe and Abyla to the Nile river; from the mouth of the Nile running leftwards to the Danube, looking east, all that is Asia. From the Nile back to Gibraltar, coast to coast stretching south and east (excluding the southern lands to the right of the Nile), everything in the middle is called Africa. From the Danube to the strait of Gibraltar and the Ocean Sea, everything to the north is called Europe. And all these lands are different, and separate from the New World; that is to say, not so much new as previously unknown to Christendom and to the ancients until the admiral showed it to the world in 1492. By the order of their Catholic majesties Fernando and Isabel, in the midst of the siege of Granada, Columbus went to the Saltés river and set sail with three caravels to look for these unknown seas and lands. The rulers made him perpetual and hereditary admiral of the Indies. After him the second admiral don Diego Colón, his son, succeeded to the title, and after him the third and present admiral don Luis Colón, son of don Diego, the second admiral.

7.2.2. The New World is indeed another thing. I do not wish to argue whether or not it was written about previously, because I discuss the matter at length and settle it in the *General History of the Indies* I am writing as their majesties' chronicler. But I must insist that by all I have seen and heard and read, never did any man or vassal do such great service to his lord or king as Christopher Columbus to the Castilian crown. As a king may grant a city or town, a dukedom or principality, even a kingdom to whomever he wishes to exalt, this famous sailor and admiral Columbus gave Castile a world full of kingdoms from which untold and priceless treasure of gold and silver, emeralds and pearls, flow to Spain.

7.2.3. This is no rumor, nor hearsay, but an eyewitness account; for I saw Columbus many times, and met his sons and grandsons, whom I know to this day. It is forty-two years since I began my travels to and in the Indies, and for the last twenty-two years I have been warden of this fortress of Santo Domingo on the island of Española as a long-term servitor of their majesties. It may well be said that I understand the Indies, and not from the vantage-point of the plaza Zocodover in Toledo or some other town far from this area, like those in Spain who write all about the Indies without having ever seen them.

TEXT

OVIEDO ON COLUMBUS

[1] From *De la Natural Historia de las Indias*

[1.1] Capítulo I: De la navegación.[1]

1.1.1. /3 verso/ La navegación desde España que comúnmente se hace para las Indias es desde Sevilla, donde V. M. tiene su Casa Real de Contratación para aquellas partes, y sus oficiales de los que les toman licencia los capitanes y maestres de las naos que aquel viaje hacen. Y se embarcan en Sanlúcar de Barrameda, donde el río de Guadalquivir entra en el mar Océano, y de allí siguen su derrota para las islas de Canaria. Y comúnmente tocan en una de dos de aquellas siete que son, y es en Gran Canaria o en la Gomera. Y allí los navíos toman refresco de agua y leña, y quesos y carnes y otras cosas, las que les parece que deben añadir sobre el principal bastimento que ya desde España llevan.

1.1.2. A estas islas desde España tardan comúnmente ocho días, poco mas o menos, y llegados allí han andado doscientas y cincuenta leguas. De las dichas islas tornando a proseguir el camino, tardan los navíos veinticinco días, poco más o menos, hasta ver la primera tierra de las islas que están antes de la que llamamos Española. La tierra que comúnmente se suele ver primero es una de las islas que llaman Todos Santos, Marigalante, la Deseada, Matitino, la Dominica, Guadalupe, San Cristóbal, etc. O alguna de las otras muchas que están con las susodichas. Pero algunas veces acaece que los navíos pasan sin ver ninguna de las dichas islas, ni de cuantas en aquel paraje hay, hasta que ven la isla de San Juan, o la Española, o la de Jamaica, o la de Cuba, que están más adelante, o por ventura ninguna de todas ellas, hasta dar en la Tierra Firme; pero esto acaece cuando el piloto no es diestro en la navegación. Pero haciéndose el viaje con marineros diestros (de los cuales hay muchos), siempre se reconoce una de las primeras islas que es dicho. Y hasta allí se navegan novecientas leguas desde las islas de Canaria, o más. Y de allí hasta llegar a la ciudad de Santo Domingo, que es en la isla Española, hay ciento cincuenta leguas. Así que desde España hasta allí hay mil y trescientas leguas, pero como se navegan, bien se andan mil y quinientas y más.

1.1.3. Tárdase en el viaje comúnmente treinta y cinco o cuarenta días. Esto lo más continuadamente, no tomando los extremos de los que tardan mucho más o llegan muy más presto, porque aquí no se ha de entender sino lo que las más veces acaece. La vuelta desde aquellas partes a éstas suele ser de algo más tiempo, así como hasta cincuenta días, pocos más o menos. No obstante lo cual, en este presente año de MD y XXV han venido cuatro naos desde Santo Domingo a Sanlúcar de España en veinticinco días. Pero como dicho es, no habemos de juzgar lo que raras veces se

[1] Oviedo 1526: fol. 3.

hace, sino lo que es más ordinario.

1.1.4. Es la navegación muy segura y muy usada /4 recto/ hasta la dicha isla, y desde allí a Tierra Firme atraviesan las naos en cinco, y seis, y siete días y más, según a la parte adonde van guiadas, porque la dicha Tierra Firme es muy grande y hay diversas navegaciones y derrotas para ella. Pero la tierra que esta más cerca de esta isla, y esta en frente Santo Domingo es esta. Todo esto es mejor remitirlo a las cartas de navegar y cosmografía nueva, la cual, ignorada por Tolomeo y los antiguos, ninguna cosa de ella hablaron. Pero porque esto no es menester para aquí, iré a las otras particularidades donde me detendré más que en esto, que es más para la *General Historia*, que de estas Indias yo escribo que no para este lugar.

[1.2] Capítulo III: De la gente natural de esta isla (de Santo Domingo) y de otras particularidades de ella.[2]

1.2.l. /5 verso/ La gente de esta isla es de estatura algo menor que la de España comúnmente, y de color loros claros. Tienen mujeres propias y ninguno de ellos toma por mujer a su hija propia, ni hermana, ni se echa con su madre; y en todos los otros grados usan con ellas, siendo o no siendo sus mujeres. Tienen las frentes anchas y los cabellos negros y muy llanos, y ninguna barba ni pelos en ninguna parte de la persona, así los hombres como las mujeres. Y cuando alguno o alguna tiene algo de esto, es entre mil uno, y rarísimo. Andan desnudos como nacieron, salvo que en las partes que menos se deben mostrar traen delante una pampanilla, que es un pedazo de lienzo, u otra tela, tamaño como una mano, pero no con tanto aviso puesto que se deje de ver cuanto tienen. Más paréceme conveniente cosa, antes que adelante se proceda, decir la manera del pan y mantenimiento que estos indios de esta isla tienen, porque menos nos quede por decir en lo de Tierra Firme; porque cuanto a esta parte los unos y los otros casi tienen un mantenimiento.

[1.3] Capítulo XI[3]

1.3.1. /19 verso/ Porque de muchos animales que ay en aquellas partes y entre ellos estos que yo aquí pondré o los más de ellos ningún escritor supo de los antiguos como quiera que están en parte y tierra que hasta nuestros tiempos era incógnita y de quien ninguna mención hacía la cosmografía del Tolomeo ni otra hasta que el Almirante don Cristóbal Colón nos la enseñó. Cosa por cierto más digna y sin comparación hazañosa y grande que no fue dar Ercoles entrada al mar Mediterráneo en el océano pues los griegos hasta él nunca lo supieron (. . .) V.M. trae por divisa con aquella su letra de *plus ultra*. Palabras en verdad dignas de tan grandísimo y universal Emperador y no convenientes a otro príncipe alguno (. . .) Por cierto señor aunque a Colón se hiciera una estatua de oro no pensaran los antiguos que le pagaban si en su tiempo fuera.

[2]Oviedo 1526: fol. 5 verso.
[3]Oviedo 1526: fols. 19 verso–20 recto.

[2] FROM *CATHÁLOGO REAL E IMPERIAL DE CASTILLA*

[2.1] Sexta Edad. En loor de España.[4]

2.1.1. /19 recto/ La sexta e última cosa o causa de la riqueza de España es la innumerable cantidad de oro, e perlas e otras joyas, e azúcar e asaz diversas mercaderías que a ella continua e ordinariamente se traen de las Islas e Indias del Mar Océano, que son de la corona de Castilla. En las cuales, desde el año que pasó de mil e quinientos e catorce hasta el presente de mil e quinientos e treinta e dos años, yo he servido a los Católicos Reyes pasados e sirvo a sus Majestades, e tengo al presente mi mujer e hijos en aquella tierra. E en este tiempo he ido e tornado tres veces e pasado seis el grande Mar Océano, e con ayuda e Dios, pienso tornar presto a aquella patria nueva a españoles e a todos los cristianos e gentes que ay en África, Asia e Europa, a usar e ejercer el oficio que allá tengo de veedor de las fundiciones del oro. E pienso ya acabar de esta vez, volviéndome Dios a mi casa, mis caminos e peregrinaciones en ella, así porque mi edad no pide ya más romerías, como porque España no me sería ni a mi propósito o salud tan conveniente por los temporales de ella y desconveniencia del verano con el invierno, de los cuales extremos las Indias carecen en eso e otras cosas. Esto he traído a consecuencia para que se crea, que pues soy oficial de Su Majestad e su veedor de las fundiciones del oro en la provincia de Castilla del Oro en Tierra Firme, e ha tanto tiempo que curso en aquella tierra, que se me puede dar crédito si dije de suso que es innumerable la cantidad de oro e perlas e otras mercaderías que se ha traído, e continua e ordinariamente se traen a España, e de mucha más cantidad e precio lo que se traerá de aquí adelante, así porque las minas cada día se descubren e hallan más rías de oro, como porque los hombres están ya más diestros y más sanos e hechos a los aires y constelación de la tierra, como porque los cristianos e las granjerías siempre crecen e se aumentan allá en todos los géneros e tractos de haciendas, e se va la tierra ennobleciendo en edificios e templos, y en todo lo demás. E la navegación está ya muy mejor entendida e por eso es de menor peligro. E caso que solamente el oro e perlas que para el tesoro real de aquella tierra ha venido sea de inenarrable cantidad y grandísima suma, quién acabará de decir e expresar el dinero o oro puro e virgen fue particulares personas han metido en España.

2.1.2. No curemos de las fábulas de Midas ni de los tesoros que tomó Perseo a las Hespérides. Hablemos historia auténtica e verdadera. No curemos de ornato de retórica para engrandecer la cosa, que aquí no solamente Gonzalo Fernández de Oviedo será pobre de palabras e estilo, por la grandeza de la materia e abundancia de oro e riqueza de las Indias, pero a los muy ornados historiales y a aquel único Tulio Cicerón les faltaran palabras para acabar de decir lo que en este paso es claro e notoriamente visto e cada día se ve, lo cual yo he tocado con las manos e visto con los ojos. E no dejo de creer que las mismas Hespérides son estas Indias, /19 verso/ conformándome con aquella autoridad de Solino, *De mirabilibus mundi*, donde dice: "Vltra Gorgades Hesperidum insule sunt (sicut Sebosus afirmat) dierum quadraginta nauigatione in intimos maris sinus reçesserunt". De manera que, cerrados los ojos, tomando por guía esta autoridad de Solino, viendo que él hablaba lo que es dicho

[4]Oviedo 1532: fol. 19.

desde Italia, e advirtiendo que las Górgades son las islas que se llaman ahora de Cabo Verde, cerrados los ojos era necesario en navegación de cuarenta días dar forzosamente en las Indias. Y no dejo de sospechar que esta autoridad levantase a don Cristóbal Colón, primero inventor o descubridor de estas Indias, enriquecedor de nuestra España, con buen ánimo e esperanza abierta a descubrir aquel Nuevo Mundo occidental de estas Indias de España. Así que tornando a nuestro propósito de la riqueza de España, qué provincia o región en el mundo se puede alegrar ni hallar tan rica ni próspera o sublimada como España

[2.2][5]
/19 verso/ De don Cristóbal Colón primero descubridor de las indias islas y tierra firme del mar océano a quien los españoles después de Santiago que primero plantó la fe en España más deben como aquel que más útil ha sido a todos por haber descubierto las dichas Indias.

[2.3][6] /427 recto/
A España pobló Túbal
Jacobo la convirtió
y Rodrigo la perdió
por sentencia divina
y Colón la enriqueció
Pero su fama inmortal
Carlos quinto se la dio

[5]Oviedo 1532: in a note on the margin of fol. 19 verso.
[6]Oviedo 1532: poem included at the end of the work, fol. 427.

[3] FROM *LA HISTORIA GENERAL Y NATURAL DE LAS YNDIAS*
PRIMERA PARTE

[3.1] Proemio[7]

3.1.1. /1 recto/ Para que más ordenadamente esta grande y natural y general Historia de las Indias se entienda, conviene hacer distinción de mis libros; y en el proemio o principio de cada uno de ellos entiendo dar particular y sumaria relación de las materias que se han de tratar y escribir en cada uno, o, a lo menos, de lo más substancial. Y así digo que en este segundo (libro) se seguirá la historia en continuación del primero y precedente libro o proemio, diciendo el motivo e intención con que yo prosigo, cumpliendo lo que por la Cesárea Majestad me está mandado. Y junto con esto, diré en qué manera sigo o, mejor diciendo, quiero o deseo imitar al Plinio, y tocaré brevemente las opiniones que hay sobre a quién él enderezó su Natural Historia. Y asimismo diré la opinión que yo tengo cerca de haberse sabido estas islas por los antiguos, y ser las Hespérides: y probarelo con historiales y autoridades de mucho crédito. Y diré quién fue don Cristóbal Colón, primero descubridor y Almirante de estas Indias, y por qué vía y forma se movió al descubrimiento de ellas; y en qué tiempo fueron halladas por él, y lo que le acaeció en el primero y segundo viajes que hizo a estas partes y lo que descubrió en ellas en cada viaje; y de la donación y título apostólico que el Sumo Pontífice hizo de estas Indias a los Reyes Católicos don Fernando y doña Isabel, y a sus sucesores en los reinos de Castilla y de León (no obstante que antiguamente fueron de España según mi opinión). Y diré quiénes fueron algunos caballeros e hidalgos que primero se hallaron en la conquista y pacificación de esta isla Española, y de los trabajos que los cristianos pasaron en ella en tanto que el Almirante fue a descubrir la isla de Jamaica.

[3.2] Libro II, cap. i: De las opiniones que hay cerca de a quién dirigió Plinio su libro de la *Natural Historia*; y también relatando en parte, sumariamente, las materias de que se trata en este libro segundo.[8]

3.21. /2 recto/ Notificaré en él (este segundo libro) la persona y ser de don Cristóbal Colón, primero inventor y descubridor y Almirante de estas Indias; y diré de su origen, y del primero, segundo, tercero y cuarto viajes que hizo a estas partes, por lo cual, habiendo respeto a sus grandes servicios, los Católicos Reyes, don Fernando y doña Isabel, que ganaron los reinos de Granada y Nápoles, etc., le hicieron merced del estado y título de Almirante perpetuo de sus Indias, y después de él a sus sucesores; y le fueron dadas las armas reales de Castilla y de León, y otras mezcladas con ellas y con las que él tenía de su linaje, en cierta forma, como adelante se dirá. Y fue hecho noble, con título de don para él y sus descendientes. Y también se dirá de qué forma se hubo en el descubrimiento que hizo en parte de la Tierra Firme, la cual creo que no es menor que todas tres juntas, Asia, África, Europa.

3.2.2. (. . .) En algunas cosas de las que en esta primera parte yo escribo, no seré largo, por ser notorias. Y también diré algunas opiniones que hoy viven acerca de este

[7]Oviedo 1535: fol. 1 recto / Oviedo 1959: 1.13.
[8]Oviedo 1535: fol. 2 recto / Oviedo 1959: 1.14–15.

descubrimiento, y de dónde hubo noticia de estas tierras este primero descubridor de ellas, estando tan incógnitas y apartadas de todo lo que Tolomeo y otros cosmógrafos escribieron. Pero no daré en este caso más crédito (ni tanto) a lo que el vulgo o algunos quisieron afirmar, porfiando que de esta tierra y mares otro fue descubridor primero, como a lo que la misma obra y el efecto del dicho Almirante consintieren. Porque, en la verdad, aunque otra cosa se pudiese presumir de los contrarios indicios o fábulas, para estorbar el loor de don Cristóbal Colón, no deben ser creídos. Suya es esta gloria, y a solo Colón, después de Dios, la deben los reyes de España pasados y católicos, y los presentes y por venir; y no solamente toda la nación de los señoríos todos de Sus Majestades, más aún los reinos extraños, por la grande utilidad que en todo el mundo ha redundado de estas Indias, con los innumerables tesoros que de ellas se han llevado y cada día se llevan, y se llevarán en tanto que haya hombres.

[3.3] Libro II, cap. ii: Del origen y persona del Almirante primero de las Indias, llamado Cristóbal Colón, y por qué vía o manera se movió al descubrimiento de ellas, según la opinión del vulgo.[9]

3.3.1. /2 verso/ Quieren algunos decir que esta tierra se supo primero grandes tiempos ha, y que estaba escrito y notado dónde es, y en qué paralelos; y que se había perdido de la memoria de los hombres la navegación y cosmografía de estas partes, y que Cristóbal Colón, como hombre leído y docto en esta ciencia, se aventuró a descubrir estas islas. Y aún yo no estoy fuera de esta sospecha, ni lo dejo de creer, por lo que se dirá adelante en el siguiente capítulo. Mas, porque es bien que a hombre que tanto se le debe, pongamos por principio y fundador de cosa tan grande como ésta, a quien él dio comienzo e industria, para todos los que viven y después de él nos vinieren, digo que Cristóbal Colón, según yo he sabido de hombres de su nación, fue natural de la provincia de Liguria, que es en Italia, en la cual cae la ciudad y señorío de Génova. Unos dicen que de Saona, y otros que de un pequeño lugar o villaje, dicho Nervi, que es a la parte del Levante y en la costa de la mar, a dos leguas de la misma ciudad de Génova; y por más cierto se tiene que fue natural de un lugar dicho Cugureo, cerca de la misma ciudad de Génova. Hombre de honestos parientes y vida, de buena estatura y aspecto, más alto que mediano y de recios miembros; los ojos vivos, y las otras partes del rostro de buena proporción; el cabello muy bermejo, y la cara algo encendida y pecoso; bien hablado, cauto y de gran ingenio, y gentil latino, y doctísimo cosmógrafo; gracioso cuando quería; iracundo cuando se enojaba.

3.3.2. El origen de sus predecesores es de la ciudad de Placencia, en la Lombardía, la cual está en la ribera del río Po, del antiguo y noble linaje de Pelestrel. Viviendo Dominico Colón, su padre, éste su hijo, siendo mancebo y bien doctrinado, y ya salido de la edad adolescente, se partió de aquella su patria y pasó en Levante, y anduvo mucha parte, o lo más, del mar Mediterráneo, donde aprendió la navegación y ejercicio de ella por experiencia; y después que algunos viajes hizo en aquellas partes, como su ánimo era para más extendidos mares y altos pensamientos, quiso ver el grandísimo mar Océano, y fuese en Portugal. Y allí vivió algún tiempo en la ciudad de

[9]Oviedo 1535: fols. 2 recto –3 recto / Oviedo 1959: 1.15–16.

Lisboa, desde la cual, y de donde quiera que estuvo siempre, como hijo grato, socorría a su padre viejo con parte del fruto de sus sudores, viviendo en una vida asaz limitada, y no con tantos bienes de fortuna que pudiese estar sin asaz necesidad

3.3.3. Quieren decir algunos que una carabela que desde España pasaba para Inglaterra cargada de mercaderías y bastimentos, así como vinos y otras cosas que para aquella isla se suelen cargar, de que ella carece y tiene falta, acaeció que le sobrevinieron tales y tan forzosos tiempos, y tan contrarios, que hubo necesidad de correr al Poniente tantos días, que reconoció una o más de las islas de estas partes e Indias; y salió en tierra, y vio gente desnuda, de la manera que acá la hay; y que cesados los vientos, que contra su voluntad acá le trajeron, tomó agua y leña para volver a su primer camino. Dicen más: que la mayor parte de la carga que este navío traía eran bastimentos y cosas de comer y vinos; y que así tuvieron con qué se sostener en tan largo viaje y trabajo; y que después le hizo tiempo a su propósito, y tornó a dar la vuelta, y tan favorable navegación le sucedió, que volvió a Europa y fue a Portugal. Pero como el viaje fuese tan largo y enojoso, y en especial a los que con tanto temor y peligro forzados le hicieron, por presta que fuese su navegación les duraría cuatro o cinco meses, o por ventura más, en venir acá y volver adonde he dicho. Y en este tiempo se murió casi toda la gente del navío, y no salieron en Portugal sino el piloto con tres o cuatro o alguno más de los marineros, y todos ellos tan dolientes que en breves días después de llegados murieron.

3.3.4. Dícese, junto con esto, que este piloto era muy íntimo amigo de Cristóbal Colón, y que entendía alguna cosa de las alturas; y marcó aquella tierra que halló de la forma que es dicho, y en mucho secreto dio parte de ello a Colón, y le rogó que le hiciese una carta y asentase en ella aquella tierra que había visto. Dícese que él le recogió en su casa, como amigo, y le hizo curar, porque también venía muy enfermo; pero que también se murió como los otros, /3 recto/ y que así quedó informado Colón de la tierra y navegación de estas partes, y en él solo se resumió este secreto. Unos dicen que este maestro o piloto era andaluz; otros le hacen portugués; otros vizcaíno; otros dicen que el Colón estaba entonces en la isla de la Madera, y otros quieren decir que en las de Cabo Verde, y que allí aportó la carabela que he dicho, y él hubo, por esta forma, noticia de esta tierra.

3.3.5. Que esto pasase así o no, ninguno con verdad lo puede afirmar; pero esta novela anda así por el mundo, entre la vulgar gente, de la manera que es dicho. Para mí, yo lo tengo por falso, y, como dice el Augustino: *Melius est dubitare de occultis. quam litigare de incertis*. Mejor es dudar en lo que no sabemos que porfiar lo que no está determinado.

[3.4] Libro II, cap. iii: En que se trata de la opinión que el autor y cronista de esta *General y Natural Historia de las Indias* tiene cerca de haberse sabido y escrito por los antiguos dónde son estas Indias, y cómo y con quién lo prueba.[10]

3.4.1. En el precedente capítulo se dijo la opinión que el vulgo tiene cerca del descubrimiento de estas Indias; ahora quiero yo decir lo que tengo creído de esto, y

[10]Oviedo 1535: fols. 3 recto–4 verso / Oviedo 1959: 1.17–20.

cómo, a mi parecer, Cristóbal Colón se movió como sabio y docto y osado varón, a emprender una cosa como ésta, de que tanta memoria dejó a los presentes y venideros; porque conoció, y es verdad, que estas tierras estaban olvidadas. Pero hallólas escritas, y para mí no dudo haberse sabido y poseído antiguamente por los reyes de España.

3.4.2. /4 verso/ (. . .) Y así como España e Italia y aquella ciudad que se dijo en Mauritania, se nombraron Hespérides y Hespéride de Hespero, rey duodécimo de España, así las islas que se dicen Hespérides, y que señalan Seboso y Solino y Plinio e Isidoro, según está dicho, se deben tener indubitadamente por estas Indias, y haber sido del señorío de España desde el tiempo de Hespero, duodécimo rey de ella, que fue, según Beroso escribe, mil seiscientos y cincuenta y ocho años antes que el Salvador del mundo naciese. Y porque al presente corren de su gloriosa Natividad mil y quinientos y treinta y cinco años, síguese que ahora tres mil ciento noventa y tres años, España y su rey Hespero señoreaban estas islas o Indias Hespérides; y así, con derecho tan antiquísimo; y por la fama que está dicha, o por la que adelante se dirá en la prosecución de los viajes del Almirante Cristóbal Colón, volvió Dios este señorío a España a cabo de tantos siglos. Y parece que como cosa que fue suya, quiere la divina justicia que lo haya tornado a ser y lo sea perpetuamente, en ventura de los bienaventurados y Católicos Reyes don Fernando y doña Isabel, que ganaron a Granada y Nápoles, etc., en cuyo tiempo y por cuyo mandado descubrió el Almirante don Cristóbal Colón este Nuevo Mundo o parte tan grandísima de él, olvidada en el universo; la cual, después, en tiempo de la Cesárea Majestad del Emperador nuestro señor, más largamente se ha sabido y descubierto, para mayor amplitud de su monarquía.

3.4.3. Así que, fundando mi intención con los autores que tengo expresados, todos ellos señalan a estas nuestras Indias. Y por tanto, yo creo que, conforme a estas autoridades, o, por ventura, a otras que con ellas Colón podría saber, se puso en cuidado de buscar lo que halló, como animoso experimentador de tan ciertos peligros y longuísimo camino. Sea ésta u otra la verdad de su motivo, que por cualquier consideración que él se moviese, emprendió lo que otro ninguno hizo antes de él en estas mares, si las autoridades ya dichas no hubiesen lugar.

[3.5] Libro II, cap. iv: Que trata cómo Cristóbal Colón fue el que mostró a navegar los españoles por las alturas del sol y norte, y de cómo fue a Portugal y otras partes a buscar quién le ayudase al descubrimiento de estas Indias y le favoreciese para ello; y cómo hubieron noticia de su persona los Católicos Reyes don Fernando y doña Isabel, por cuyo mandado hizo este descubrimiento.[11]

3.5.1. /4 verso/ Es opinión de muchos (y aun la razón lo enseña y amonesta que se crea) que Cristóbal Colón fue el primero que en España enseñó a navegar el amplísimo mar Océano por las alturas de los grados de sol y norte, y lo puso por obra; porque hasta él, aunque se leyese en las escuelas tal arte, pocos (o mejor diciendo, ninguno) se atrevían a experimentarlo en los mares, porque es ciencia que no se puede ejercitar enteramente, para saberla por experiencia y efecto, si no se usa en golfos muy

[11]Oviedo 1535: fols. 4 verso–5 verso / Oviedo 1959: 1.20–23.

grandes y muy desviados de la tierra; y los marineros y pilotos y hombres de la mar, hasta entonces arbitrariamente hacían su oficio, según el juicio del nauta o piloto; pero no puntualmente, ni con la razón que hoy se hace en estas mares, sino como en la mar Mediterránea, /5 recto/ y en las costas de España y Flandes, y en toda Europa y África, y restante del mundo donde no se apartan mucho de la tierra. Mas para navegar en demanda de provincias tan apartadas como estas Indias están de España, y servirse el piloto de la razón del cuadrante, requiérense mares de mucha longitud y latitud, como éstas que hay de aquí a Europa, o a la Especiería que tenemos al Poniente de la Tierra Firme de estas Indias.

3.5.2. Movido, pues, Colón con este deseo, como hombre que alcanzaba el secreto de tal arte de navegar (cuanto a andar el camino), como docto varón en tal ciencia, o por estar certificado de la cosa por aviso del piloto (que primero se dijo), que le dio noticia de esta oculta tierra, en Portugal o en las islas que dije (si aquello fue así), o por las autoridades que se tocaron en el capítulo antes de éste, o en cualquier manera que su deseo le llamase, trabajó, por medio de Bartolomé Colón, su hermano, con el rey Enrique VII de Inglaterra (padre de Enrique VIII que hoy allí reina), que le favoreciese y armase para descubrir estas mares occidentales, ofreciéndose a darle muchos tesoros, en acrecentamiento de su corona y estados, de muy grandes señoríos y reinos nuevos. Informado el rey de sus consejeros, y de personas a quienes él cometió la examinación de esto, burló de cuanto Colón decía, y tuvo por vanas sus palabras. El cual, no desconfiado por esto, así como vio que allí no era acogido su servicio, comenzó a mover y tratar la misma navegación con el rey don Juan, segundo de tal nombre en Portugal. Y tampoco fió de él, aunque ya era Colón casado en aquel reino, y se había hecho natural vasallo de aquella tierra por su matrimonio. Pero por eso no se le dio más crédito, ni el rey de Portugal quiso favorecer ni ayudar al dicho Colón para lo que decía. De manera que determinó de irse en Castilla, y llegado en Sevilla tuvo sus inteligencias con el ilustre y valeroso don Enrique de Guzmán, duque de Medina Sidonia; y tampoco halló en él lo que buscaba. Y movió después el negocio más largamente con el muy ilustre don Luis de la Cerda, primero duque de Medinaceli, el cual también tuvo por cosa fabulosa sus ofrecimientos, aunque quieren decir algunos que el duque de Medinaceli ya quería venir en armar al dicho Colón en su villa del Puerto de Santa María, y que no le quisieron dar licencia el Rey y Reina Católicos para ello. Y por tanto, como no era tan alto señorío, sino para cuyo es, fuese Colón a la corte de los serenísimos Católicos Reyes don Fernando y doña Isabel; y allí anduvo un tiempo con mucha necesidad y pobreza, sin ser entendido de los que le oían, procurando que le favoreciesen aquellos bienaventurados Reyes y le armasen algunas carabelas con que en su real nombre descubriese este Nuevo Mundo, o partes incógnitas de él en aquella sazón.

3.5.3. Y como esta empresa era cosa en que los que le escuchaban no tenían el concepto y gusto, o esperanza, que sólo Colón tenía del buen fin de su deseo, no solamente se le daba poco, mas ningún crédito, y aun teníase por vano cuanto decía. Y duróle casi siete años esta importunación, haciendo muchos ofrecimientos de grandes riquezas y estados para la corona de Castilla. Pero como traía la capa raída, pobre, teníanle por fabuloso y soñador de cuanto decía y hablaba, así por no ser conocido y extranjero, y no tener quien le favoreciese, como por ser tan grandes y no oídas las cosas que se profería de dar acabadas.

3.5.4. Ved si tuvo Dios cuidado de dar estas Indias, cuyas son; pues rogados Inglaterra y Portugal con ellas, y los duques que he dicho, no permitió que alguno de aquellos reyes tan poderosos ni los duques tan ricos que dije, quisiesen aventurar tan poca costa como Colón les pedía, para que, descontentos de aquellos príncipes, fuese a buscar los que halló tan ocupados, como a la sazón estaban, en la santa guerra de los moros del reino de Granada.

3.5.5. No es de maravillar si tan Católicos Rey y Reina, movidos a buscar ánimas /5 verso/ que se salvasen, más que tesoros y nuevos estados para que con mayor ocupación y cuidado reinasen, acordaron de favorecer esta empresa y descubrimiento. Ni crea ninguno que esto se podía excusar a su buena ventura; porque no vio ojo, ni oyó oreja, ni subió en corazón de hombre las cosas que aparejó Dios a los que le aman. Estas y otras muchas venturas cupieron en aquellos buenos reyes nuestros, por ser tan verdaderos siervos de Jesucristo y deseosos del acrecentamiento de la sagrada religión suya. Y por tanto, la voluntad divina les dio noticia de Cristóbal Colón; porque el mismo Dios mira todos los fines del mundo, y ve todas las cosas de debajo del cielo.

3.5.6. Y cuando llegó la hora que tan grande negociación se concluyese, fue por estos términos. En aquel tiempo que Colón, como dije, andaba en la corte, llegábase a casa de Alonso de Quintanilla, contador mayor de cuentas de los Reyes Católicos (el cual era notable varón y deseoso del acrecentamiento y servicio de sus reyes), y mandábale dar de comer necesario, por una compasibilidad de su pobreza. Y en ese caballero halló más parte y acogimiento Colón que en hombre de toda España, y por su respeto e intercesión fue conocido del reverendísimo e ilustre cardenal de España, arzobispo de Toledo, don Pedro González de Mendoza, el cual comenzó a dar audiencia a Colón, y conoció de él que era sabio y bien hablado, y que daba buena razón de lo que decía, y túvole por hombre de ingenio y de grande habilidad; y concebido esto, tomóle en buena reputación y quísole favorecer. Y como era tanta parte para ello, por medio del cardenal y de Alonso de Quintanilla, fue oído del Rey y de la Reina; y luego se principió a dar algún crédito a sus memoriales y peticiones, y vino a concluirse el negocio teniendo los Reyes Católicos cercada la grande y muy nombrada ciudad de Granada, año de mil y cuatrocientos y noventa y dos años de la Natividad de nuestro Redentor. Y desde aquel real y campo, aquellos bienaventurados príncipes le despacharon a Colón en aquella villa que en medio de sus ejército fundaron, llamada Santa Fe; y en ella, y mejor diciendo, en la misma santa fe que en aquellos corazones reales estaba, hubo principio este descubrimiento.

3.5.7. No contentándose aquellos santos príncipes con sola su empresa y conquista santísima que entre las manos tenían, con que dieron fin a la sujeción de todos los moros de las Españas (donde habían estado, en despecho y ofensa de los cristianos desde el año de setecientos y veinte que la Virgen parió al Salvador, como muchos autores en conformidad escriben); pero demás de reducir a España toda a nuestra católica religión, propusieron de enviar a buscar este otro Nuevo Mundo, a plantarla en él, por no vacar ninguna hora en el servicio de Dios. Y con este santo propósito mandaron despachar a Colón, dándole sus provisiones y cédulas reales para que en el Andalucía se le diesen tres carabelas del porte y manera que las pidió, y con la gente y bastimentos que convenía para viaje tan largo, y de que ninguna certeza se tenía mayor que el buen celo y santo fin de tan cristianísimos príncipes, en cuya ventura y por cuyo mandado tan grande cosa se comenzaba. Y porque había necesidad de dineros para su expedición, a causa de la guerra, los prestó para hacer esta primera armada de las Indias y su descubrimiento, el escribano de ración Luis de Santángel. Y esta primera capitulación y asiento que el Rey y la Reina tomaron con Colón fue en la villa de Santa Fe, en el real de Granada, a dieciocho de abril de mil y cuatrocientos y noventa y dos años, la cual pasó ante el secretario Juan de Colona. Y fuéle confirmada la dicha capitulación por un real privilegio que le fue dado desde a trece días, que se contaron treinta de abril, en la ciudad de Granada, del dicho año de noventa y dos. Y con ese despacho partió Colón donde es dicho, y fuese a la villa de Palos de Moguer, donde puso en orden su viaje.

[3.6] Libro II, cap. v: Del primero viaje y descubrimiento de las Indias, hecho por don Cristóbal Colón, primero descubridor de el las, por lo cual dignamente fue hecho Almirante perpetuo de estas mares e imperio de las Indias de estas partes.[12]

3.6.1. /6 recto/ Oído habéis cómo y de qué manera y por qué vino Cristóbal Colón a ser conocido de los Reyes Católicos don Fernando y doña Isabel, estando sobre la ciudad de Granada con sus ejércitos; y cómo le mandaron despachar y le dieron sus provisiones reales para ello, y se fue a la villa de Palos de Moguer para principiar su viaje. Debéis saber que desde allí principió su camino con tres carabelas: la una y mayor de ellas llamada la *Gallega*, y las otras dos eran de aquella villa de Palos, y fueron abastecidas y armadas de todo lo necesario. Y según la capitulación que con Colón se tomó, había de haber después una décima parte en las rentas y derechos que el rey hubiese en lo que fuese por Colón descubierto; y así se le pagó todo el tiempo que él vivió después que descubrió esta tierra; y así lo gozó el segundo Almirante, don Diego Colón, su hijo; y así lo goza don Luis Colón, su nieto, tercero Almirante, que al presente tiene su casa y estado.

3.6.2. Antes que Colón entrase en la mar algunos días, tuvo muy largas consultaciones con un religioso llamado fray Juan Pérez, de la Orden de San Francisco, su confesor, el cual estaba en el monasterio de La Rábida que es media legua de Palos, hacia la mar. Y este fraile fue la persona sola de esta vida a quien Colón más comunicó de sus secretos; y aun del cual y de su ciencia se dice, hasta hoy, que él recibió mucha ayuda y buena obra, porque este religioso era grande cosmógrafo. Con el cual estuvo en el monasterio que es dicho, de La Rábida, algún tiempo, y él lo hizo ir al real de Granada cuando se concluyó su despacho y entendió en ello. Y después se fue Colón al mismo monasterio y estuvo con el fraile comunicando su viaje y ordenando su alma y vida, y apercibiéndose primeramente con Dios, y poniendo, como católico, en sus manos y misericordia su empresa, como fiel cristiano, y como negocio en que Dios esperaba ser tan servido por el

[12]Oviedo 1535: fols. 5 verso–7 verso / Oviedo 1959: 1.23–26.

acrecentamiento de su república cristiana. Y después de haberse confesado, recibió el santísimo sacramento de la Eucaristía, el día mismo que entró en la mar; y en el nombre de Jesús mandó desplegar las velas y salió del puerto de Palos por el río de Saltes a la mar Océana con tres carabelas armadas, dando principio al primer viaje y descubrimiento de estas Indias, viernes tres días de agosto año del nacimiento de nuestro Salvador de mil y cuatrocientos y noventa y dos años con la buena ventura, efectuando este memorable hecho movido por Dios, el cual quiso hacer a este hombre arbitrario y ministro para tan grande y señalada cosa.

3.6.3. De estas tres carabelas era capitana la *Gallega*, en la qual iba la persona de Colón; de las otras dos, la una se llamaba la *Pinta*, de que iba por capitán Martín Alonso Pinzón; y la otra se decía la Niña, e iba por capitán de ella Francisco Martín Pinzón, con el cual iba Vicente Yáñez Pinzón. Todos estos tres capitanes eran hermanos y pilotos, y naturales de Palos. Y serían por todos, hasta ciento y veinte hombres; con las cuales, después que estas tres carabelas se dieron a la mar, tomaron su derrota para las islas de Canarias, que los antiguos llamaron Afortunas.

3.6.4. Las cuales estuvieron mucho tiempo que no se navegaban ni se sabían navegar, hasta que después, en tiempo del rey don Juan, segundo de tal nombre en Castilla, siendo niño y debajo de la tutela de la serenísima reina doña Catalina, su madre, fueron halladas y tornadas a navegar y conquistarse estas islas por su mandado y licencia, como más largamente se escribe en la *Crónica* del mismo rey don Juan segundo. Después de lo cual muchos años Pedro de Vera, noble caballero de Jerez de la Frontera, y Miguel de Móxica, conquistaron la Gran Canaria en nombre de los Católicos Reyes don Fernando y doña Isabel, y las otras, excepto la Palma y Tenerife, que por mandado de los mismos reyes las conquistó Alonso de Lugo, al cual hicieron Adelantado de Tenerife.

3.6.5. Esta gente de los canarios era de mucho esfuerzo, aunque casi desnuda y tan silvestre que se dice y afirman algunos que no tenían lumbre ni la tuvieron hasta que los cristianos ganaron aquellas islas. Sus armas eran piedras y varas, con las cuales mataron muchos cristianos, hasta /6 verso/ ser sojuzgados y puestos, como están, debajo de la obediencia de Castilla, del cual señorío son las dichas islas. Y están doscientas leguas de España las primeras, y la isla de Lanzarote y la de Hierro, a doscientas y cuarenta; por manera que todas ellas se incluyen en espacio de cincuenta o sesenta leguas, pocas más o menos. Y están asentadas desde veintisiete hasta veintinueve grados de la línea equinoccial, a la parte de nuestro polo ártico; la última isla de ellas, o más occidental, está del oeste al este con el cabo de Bojador en África, y a sesenta y cinco leguas de él. Son todas estas islas fértiles y abundantes de las cosas necesarias a la vida del hombre, y de muy templados aires. Pero ya, de la gente natural que había cuando fueron conquistadas, hay pocas; mas todas están muy pobladas de cristianos.

3.6.6. Y allí, como en lugar apropiado y para la navegación al propósito, llegó Colón, continuando su primero descubrimiento de estas Indias, con las tres carabelas que tengo dicho, y tomó allí agua y leña, y carne, y pescado, y otros refrescos, los que le convino para proseguir su viaje. El cual efectuando con su armada, partió de la isla de la Gomera a seis días de septiembre de aquel año de mil y cuatrocientos y noventa y dos años; y anduvo muchos días por el grande mar Océano, hasta tanto que ya los que con él iban comenzaron a desmayar y quisieron dar la vuelta, y temiendo de su camino murmuraban de la ciencia de Colón y de su atrevimiento; y amotinábasele la gente y los capitanes, porque cada hora crecía el temor en ellos, y menguaba la esperanza de ver la tierra que buscaban. De forma que desvergonzadamente y público le dijeron que los había engañado y los llevaba perdidos; y que el Rey y la Reina habían hecho mal y usado con ellos de mucha crueldad en fiar a un hombre semejante, y dar crédito a un extranjero que no sabía lo que se decía. Y llegó la cosa a tanto, que le certificaron que si no se tornaba le harían volver a mal de su grado, o le echarían en la mar; porque les parecía que él estaba desesperado, y decían que ellos no lo querían ser, ni creían que pudiese salir con lo que había comenzado, y por tanto, a una voz acordaban de no seguirle.

3.6.7. En esta sazón y contienda hallaron en la mar grandes praderías, al parecer, de hierbas sobre el agua; y pensando que era tierra anegada, y que eran perdidos, doblábanse los clamores. Y para quien nunca había visto aquello sin duda era cosa para mucho temer. Mas luego se paso aquella turbación, conociendo que no había peligro en ella, porque son unas hierbas que llaman sargazos, y se andan sobreaguadas en la superficie de la mar. Las cuales, según los tiempos y los aguajes suceden, así corren y se desvían o allegan a Oriente o Poniente, o al Sur, o a la Tramontana; y a veces se hallan a medio golfo, y otras veces, más tarde y lejos, o más cerca de España. Y algunos viajes acaece que los navíos topan muy pocas o ninguna de ellas; y también a veces hallan tantas que, como he dicho, parecen grandes prados verdes y amarillos o de color jalde; porque en estas dos colores penden en todo tiempo.

3.6.8. Salidos, pues, de este cuidado y temor de las hierbas, determinados todos tres capitanes y cuantos marineros allí iban, de dar la vuelta, y aun consultando entre sí de echar a Colón en la mar, creyendo que los había burlado, como él era sabio y sintió la murmuración que de él se hacía, como prudente comenzó a confortarlos con muchas y dulces palabras, rogándoles que no quisiesen perder su trabajo y tiempo. Recordábales cuánta gloria y provecho de la constancia se les seguiría, perseverando en su camino; prometíales que en breves días darían fin a sus fatigas y viaje, con mucha e indubitada prosperidad, y en conclusión les dijo que dentro de tres días hallarían la tierra que buscaban; por tanto, que estuviesen de buen ánimo y prosiguiesen su viaje, que para cuando decía él les enseñaría un Nuevo Mundo y tierra, y habrían concluido sus trabajos, y verían que él había dicho verdad siempre, así al Rey y Reina Católicos como a ellos; y que si no fuese así, hiciesen su voluntad y lo que les pareciese, que él ninguna duda tenía en lo que les decía.

3.6.9. Con estas palabras movió los corazones de los enflaquecidos ánimos de los que allí iban a alguna vergüenza, /7 recto/ en especial a los tres hermanos capitanes pilotos que he dicho; y acordaron de hacer lo que les mandaba, y de navegar aquellos tres días, y no más, con determinación y acuerdo que en fin de ellos darían la vuelta a España, si tierra no viesen. Y esto era lo que ellos tenían por más cierto; porque ninguno había entre ellos que pensase que en aquel paralelo y camino que hacían se había de hallar tierra alguna. Y dijeron a Colón que aquellos tres días que él tomaba de término y les asignaba, le seguirían; pero no una hora más, porque creían que ninguna cosa de cuantas les decía había de ser cierta; y en una conformidad todos, rehusaban pasar adelante, diciendo que no querían morir a sabiendas, y que el bastimento y agua que tenían no podía bastar para tornarlos a España sin mucho peligro, por bien que se reglasen en el comer y beber.

3.6.10. Y como los corazones que temen, ninguna cosa sospechan que pueda aflojar sus fatigas, en especial en ejercicio de navegación y semejante, ningún momento cesaban en su murmurar, amenazando a su principal capitán y guía. Ni él tampoco reposaba ni cesaba un punto de confortar y animar a todos a la prosecución de su camino; y cuanto más turbados los veía, más alegre semblante él mostraba, esforzándolos y ayudándolos a desechar su temerosa turbación. Y aquel mismo día que el Almirante Colón estas palabras dijo, conoció realmente que estaba cerca de tierra, en semblante de los celajes de los cielos; y amonestó a los pilotos que, si por caso las carabelas se apartasen, por algún caso fortuito, la una de la otra, que pasado aquel trance corriesen hacia la parte o viento que les ordenó, para tornar a reducirse en su conserva. Y como sobrevino la noche, mandó apocar las velas y que corriesen con solos los trinquetes bajos; y andando así, un marinero de los que iban en la capitana, natural de Lepe, dijo: "¡Lumbre! . . . ¡Tierra! . . ." Y luego un criado de Colón, llamado Salcedo, replicó diciendo: "Eso ya lo ha dicho el Almirante, mi señor"; e incontinente Colón dijo: "Rato ha que yo lo he dicho y he visto aquella lumbre que está en tierra". Y así fue, que un jueves, a las dos horas después de medianoche, llamó el Almirante a un hidalgo dicho Escobedo, repostero de estrados del Rey Católico, y le dijo que veía lumbre. Y otro día de mañana en esclareciendo, y a la hora que el día antes había dicho Colón, desde la nao capitana se vio la isla que los indios llaman Guanahani, de la parte de la Tramontana o Norte. Y el que vio primero la tierra, cuando ya fue de día, se llamaba Rodrigo de Triana, a once días de octubre del año ya dicho de mil y cuatrocientos y noventa y dos.

3.6.11. Y de haber salido tan verdadero el Almirante en ver la tierra en el tiempo que había dicho, se tuvo más sospecha que él estaba certificado del piloto que se dijo que murió en su casa, según se tocó más arriba. Y también podría ser que, viendo determinados a cuantos con él iban para tornarse, dijese que si en tres días no viesen la tierra se volviesen, confiando en que Dios se la enseñaría en aquel término que les daba para no perder trabajo y tiempo.

3.6.12. Tornando a la historia: aquella isla que se vio primero, según he dicho, es una de las islas que dicen de los Lucayos. Y aquel marinero que dijo primero que veía lumbre en tierra, tornado después en España, porque no se le dieron las albricias, despechado de esto, se pasó en África y renegó de la fe. Este hombre, según yo oí decir a Vicente Yáñez Pinzón y a Hernán Pérez Mateos, que se hallaron en este primero descubrimiento, era de Lepe, como he dicho.

3.6.13. Así como el Almirante vio la tierra, hincado de rodillas y saltándosele las lágrimas de los ojos del extremado placer que sentía, comenzó a decir con Ambrosio y Augustino: *Te Deum laudamus. Te Dominum confitemur* etc. Y así, dando gracias a Nuestro Señor con todos los que con él iban, fue inestimable el gozo que los unos y los otros hacían. Tomabanle unos en brazos, otros le besaban las manos, y otros le demandaban perdón de la poca constancia que habían mostrado. Algunos le pedían mercedes y se ofrecían por suyos; En fin, tamaña era la leticia /7 verso/ y regocijo que, abrazándose unos con otros, no se conocían en el placer de su buena andanza. Lo cual yo creo bien, porque, sabiendo como sabemos los que ahora vienen de España, y los que de acá vuelven de allá, que el viaje y camino es seguro y cierto, no tiene comparación otro placer con el que reciben los que ha días que navegan, cuando ven la tierra. Ved qué tal sería el de los que en tan dudosa jornada se hallaron, viéndose certificados y seguros de su descanso.

3.6.14. Pero habéis de saber que, por el contrario dicen algunos lo que aquí se ha dicho de la constancia de Colón: que aún afirman que él se tornara de su voluntad del camino y no lo concluyese, si estos hermanos Pinzones no le hicieran ir adelante. Y diré más, que por causa de ellos se hizo el descubrimiento, y que Colón ya ciaba y quería dar la vuelta. Esto será mejor remitirlo a un largo proceso que hay entre el Almirante y el fiscal real, donde a pro y contra hay muchas cosas alegadas, en lo cual yo no me entremeto; porque como sean cosas de justicia, y por ella se han de decidir, quédense para el fin que tuvieren. Pero yo he dicho en lo uno y en lo otro ambas las opiniones: el lector tome la que más le dictare su buen juicio.

3.6.15. Tardóse el Almirante en llegar desde las islas de Canaria hasta ver la primera tierra que he dicho, treinta y tres días; pero él llegó a estas islas, primeras que vio, en el mes de octubre del año de mil y cuatrocientos y noventa y dos años.

[3.7] Libro II, cap. vi: Cómo el Almirante descubrió esta isla Española y dejó en ella treinta y ocho cristianos en tierra del rey o cacique Goacanagari, en tanto que llevaba las nuevas del descubrimiento primero de estas partes; y cómo volvió a España en salvamento.[13]

3.7.1. En aquella isla que he dicho de Guanahani hubo el Almirante y los que con él iban, vista de indios y gente desnuda, y allí le dieron noticia de la isla de Cuba. Y como parecieron luego muchas isletas que están juntas y en torno de Guanahani, comenzaron los cristianos a llamarlas islas Blancas (porque así lo son por la mucha arena), y el Almirante les puso nombre las Princesas, porque fueron el principio de la vista de estas Indias. Y arribó a ellas, en especial a la de Guanahani, y estuvo entre ella y otra que se dice Caicos; pero no tomó tierra en ninguna de ellas, según afirma Hernán Pérez Mateos, piloto que hoy día está en esta ciudad de Santo Domingo, que dice que se halló allí. Pero a otros muchos he oído decir que el Almirante bajó en tierra en la isla de Guanahani y la llamó San Salvador, y tomó allí la posesión; y esto es lo más cierto y lo que se debe creer de ello. Y de allí vino a Baracoa, puerto de la isla de Cuba de la banda del Norte; el cual puerto es doce leguas más al Poniente de la punta que llaman Maicí. Y allí halló gente, así de la propia isla de Cuba como de las otras que están el Norte opuestas, que son la isla Guanahani, que tengo dicho, y otras muchas que hay allí, que se llaman islas de los Lucayos generalmente todas ellas, no obstante que cada una tiene su propio nombre y son muchas: así como Guanahani, Caicos, Jumeto, Yabaque, Mayaguana, Samana, Guanima, Yuma, Curateo, Ciguateo, Bahama (que es la mayor de todas), el Yucayo y Necua, Habacoa y otras muchas

[13]Oviedo 1535: fols. 7 verso–9 recto / Oviedo 1959: 1.26–29.

isletas que por allí hay.

3.7.2. Tornando a la historia: llegado, pues, el Almirante a la isla de Cuba, donde he dicho, saltó en tierra con algunos cristianos, y preguntaba a los indios por Cipango y ellos por señas le respondían y señalaban que era esta isla de Haití, que ahora llamamos Española. Y creyendo los indios que el Almirante no acertaba el nombre, decían ellos: "¡Cibao! ¡Cibao!", pensando que por decir Cibao decían Cipango; porque Cibao es donde en esta isla Española están las minas más ricas y de más fino oro. Y así el Almirante con las tres carabelas, guiados por los indios, de los cuales algunos, de su grado, se entraron en los navíos, se embarcó en aquel puerto de Baracoa de Cuba y vino a esta isla de Haití, que ahora llamamos Española, y de la parte o banda del Norte surgió en un muy buen puerto y llamóle Puerto Real. Y a la entrada de él tocó en tierra la nao capitana, llamada *Gallega*, y abrióse. Pero no peligró ningún hombre; antes muchos pensaron que mañosamente la habían hecho tocar para dejar en la tierra parte de la gente, como quedó. Y allí salió el Almirante con toda su gente; y luego vinieron /8 recto/ a habla y conversación con los cristianos muchos indios de paz de aquella tierra, la cual era del señorío del rey Guacanagari (que los indios llaman *cacique*, así como los cristianos decimos rey), con el cual se trató luego la paz y amistad. Y él vino a ella muy de grado, y se vio con el Almirante y los cristianos muy domésticamente y muy continuo, y se le dieron algunas cosas de poco valor entre los cristianos, pero de los indios muy estimadas, así como cascabeles, alfileres, agujas y algunas cuentas de vidrio de diversas colores; lo cual el cacique y sus indios, con mucha admiración contemplando, mostraban apreciarlo y estimar, y holgaban mucho de que algo así se les daba, y ellos traían a los cristianos de sus manjares y cosas que tenían.

3.7.3.Viendo el Almirante que esta gente era tan doméstica, parecióle que seguramente podría dejar allí algunos cristianos para que en tanto que él volvía a España, aprendiesen la lengua y costumbres de esta tierra. E hizo hacer un castillo cuadrado, a manera de palenque, con la madera de la carabela capitana o *Gallega* (que es dicho que tocó al entrar del puerto), y con fajina y tierra, lo mejor que se pudo fabricar, en la costa, a par del puerto y arrecifes de él, en un arenal. Y dio orden el Almirante a treinta y ocho hombres que allí mandó quedar, de lo que habían de hacer en tanto que él llevaba tan prósperas nuevas de su descubrimiento a los Reyes Católicos, y tornaba con muchas mercedes para todos, ofreciéndoles cumplidos galardones a los que así quedaban. Y nombró entre aquéllos por capitán a un hidalgo llamado Rodrigo de Arana, natural de Córdoba, y mandóles que le obedeciesen como a su persona. Y para si aquel muriese en tanto que él volvía, señaló otro, y para después del segundo nombró otro tercero; de forma que nombró dos para después de los días del primero. Y dejó con ellos a un maestro Juan, cirujano, buena persona. Y amonestó a todos que no entrasen en la tierra adentro, ni se desacaudillasen, ni dividiesen, ni tomasen mujeres, ni diesen pesadumbre ni enojo alguno a los indios por ningún caso, en cuanto posible les fuese.

3.7.4. Y como se perdió la nao capitana, pasóse el Almirante a la carabela la *Niña*, en que iban Francisco Martín y Vicente Yáñez Pinzón. Mas como de la quedada de esta gente no le plugo al capitán de la otra carabela, *Pinta*, llamado Martín Alonso

Pinzón, hermano de estos otros, contradíjolo todo cuanto él pudo. Y decía que era mal hecho que aquellos cristianos quedasen tan lejos de España, siendo tan pocos, y porque no se podrían proveer ni sostener y se perderían. Y a este propósito dijo otras palabras, de que el Almirante se resabió, y sospechóse que le quisiera prender; y el Martín Alonso, con temor que hubo de esta sospecha, se salió a la mar con su carabela *Pinta*, y fuese al puerto de Gracia, veinte leguas al Este u Oriente apartado del dicho Puerto Real.

3.7.5. Y en tanto que el Almirante tardó en la obra que dije de aquel castillo, súpose de los indios de la tierra, dónde estaba el Alonso Martín y la otra carabela. Y luego los otros dos hermanos Pinzones, que estaban con el Almirante, procuraron de reconciliarle y volverle a la gracia del Almirante, y acabaron con él que le perdonase. Y él lo hizo así por muchos respectos, y en especial porque la mayor parte de cuantos hombres de la mar tenía, eran parientes y amigos de estos Pinzones hermanos, y de una tierra, y estos tres eran los más principales. Y así como le perdonó, le escribió una carta muy generosa, como en el caso convenía, y mandó que aquel puerto se llamase Puerto de Gracia, y así se nombra hasta ahora. Y los indios que llevaron la carta, volvieron otra, respondiendo Martín Alonso al Almirante y teniéndole en merced el perdón. Y así se concertaron para que en cierto día el Martín Alonso, desde donde estaba con aquella carabela, y el Almirante con la otra, se fuesen a juntar en la Isabela, y allí saltaron todos en tierra muy conformes. Aquel asiento de la Isabela es en la misma costa, dieciocho leguas, o poco más, al Este de Puerto Real.

3.7.6. No fue poca maravilla para los indios ver cómo por las cartas los cristianos se entendían; y llevábanlas puestas los mensajeros en un palillo, porque con temor y acatamiento las miraban, y creían que cierto tenían un algún espíritu y hablaban, como otro hombre, por alguna deidad o no arte humana.

3.7.7. Juntos el Almirante y su gente, y quedando los treinta y ocho hombres donde se dijo, tomaron agua y leña, y lo que más pudieron de los bastimentos de esta tierra, para que más /8 verso/ les durasen los que les quedaban de los que trajeron de Castilla; y salieron de la Isabela, el cual nombre el Almirante puso a aquella provincia y puerto en memoria de la Católica Reina doña Isabel. Y desde allí ambas carabelas fueron a Puerto de Plata, el cual nombre le puso el Almirante; y después fueron a puerto de Samaná, así llamado por los indios. Y desde Samaná (que esa en esta isla Española, de la banda del Norte) tomaron estas dos carabelas su derrota para Castilla, con mucho placer, encomendándose todos a Dios y la buena ventura de los Católicos Reyes de España, que tan grandes nuevas esperaban, aunque no confiados de la ciencia de Colón, sino de la misericordia de Dios.

3.7.8. Y llevó de este camino el Almirante nueve o diez indios consigo, para que, como testigos de su buena ventura, besasen las manos al Rey y a la Reina, y viesen la tierra de los cristianos y aprendiesen la lengua, para que cuando estos acá tornasen, ellos y los cristianos que quedaban encomendados a Goacanagari, y en el castillo que es dicho de Puerto Real fuesen lenguas e intérpretes para la conquista y pacificación y conversión de estas gentes.

3.7.9. Y así como Dios Nuestro Señor fue servido que estas tierras se descubriesen, y que para hallarlas hubiese sido próspera y acertada la navegación de este primer viaje, y en breve tiempo, así tuvo por bien y permitió que fuese favorable la vuelta, y llevó en salvamento este primero descubridor de estas Indias a España. Y fue a reconocer las islas de los Azores, y a cuatro días de marzo de mil y cuatrocientos y noventa y tres entró en Lisboa, desde donde se fue al puerto de Palos, adonde se había embarcado cuando comenzó esta jornada.

3.7.10. Y no estuvo desde que partió de esta isla hasta que en Castilla tomó tierra, sino cincuenta días. Pero estando ya cerca de Europa, por tormenta, se apartó la una carabela de la otra, y corrió el Almirante a Lisboa, y el Martín Alonso a Bayona de Galicia. Y después cada navío de estos tomó su camino para el río de Saltes, y de caso entraron en un mismo día; y entró el Almirante por la mañana, y la otra carabela llegó en la tarde. Y porque se tuvo sospecha que por las cosas pasadas el Almirante haría prender al Martín Alonso Pinzón, salióse en una barca del navío, así como entraba a la vela, y fuese donde le pareció, secretamente, y el Almirante luego se partió para la corte con la grande nueva de su descubrimiento. Y como el Martín Alonso supo que era ido, fuese a Palos, a su casa, y murió desde a pocos días, porque iba muy doliente.

3.7.11. Tardó el Almirante en reconocer la primera tierra de estas Indias en las islas de los Lucayos, según he dicho, desde que de España partió, casi tres meses, y en volver a España, y en lo que acá se detuvo, otros tres; y en todo estuvo en la venida y vuelta seis meses, diez días más o menos.

3.7.12. Tornando a la historia: digo que después que Colón salió en Palos con los indios que llevaba de estas islas (de los cuales uno se le habla muerto en la mar) tomó los seis que iban sanos, y dejó allí dos o tres que estaban dolientes, y fuese a la corte de los Católicos Reyes a darles cuenta de su prosperidad y de lo que Dios acrecentaba en los reinos y señoríos de Castilla. La cual nueva no se esperaba en tan breve tiempo, porque, en la verdad, fue cosa de admiración, según lo que después tardaban otras naos y carabelas en venir y volver desde acá, hasta que esta navegación se fue mejor entendiendo. Y aun hoy que se sabe mejor, sería asaz dos navíos andar lo que aquéllos anduvieron en tan breve tiempo; puesto que, como digo, ahora está la navegación entendida, y entonces la anduvieron a tiento y con la sonda siempre en la mano, y apocando las velas de noche, y en recelo, como lo suelen hacer los que son prudentes y sabios pilotos, cuando descubren y van por mares que no se saben ni han navegado.

[3.8] Libro II, cap. vii: De cuatro cosas notables en el año de mil y cuatrocientos y noventa y dos años; y de cuando el Almirante don Cristóbal llegó a la corte de los Reyes Católicos don Fernando y doña Isabel, y de las mercedes que le hicieron después que volvió a España del primero descubrimiento de las Indias; y la razón porque se debe creer que en estas partes fue predicado el Evangelio por los apóstoles o por alguno de ellos.[14]

3.8.1. /9 recto/ Con menor autoridad enseña el que habla las cosas que oyó, que el que dice las que vio. Esto San Gregorio lo dice sobre los capítulos catorce y quince de Job; mas yo no lo traigo aquí a consecuencia solamente por los que estas cosas de Indias las han escrito desde España por oídas, sino dígolo porque hablaré aquí de las

[14]Oviedo 1535: fols. 9 recto–10 verso / Oviedo 1959: 1.29–32.

de España desde las Indias. Mas hay en ello lo uno y lo otro, aunque vivo acá, vi lo que acaeció acullá.

3.8.2. Y porque no es fuera de mi propósito, digo que fue muy notable en España el año de mil y cuatrocientos y noventa y dos años, en el cual a los dos días del mes de enero tomaron los Católicos Reyes don Fernando y doña Isabel, la muy nombrada y gran ciudad de Granada. El mismo año, en fin de julio, echaron los judíos de sus reinos. El mismo año, viernes siete días del mes de diciembre, un villano, natural del lugar de Remensa, del principado de Cataluña, llamado Juan de Cañamares, dio en Barcelona una cuchillada al rey Católico en el pescuezo, tan peligrosa que llegó a punto de muerte; del cual traidor fue hecha muy señalada justicia, no obstante que, según pareció, él estaba loco, y siempre dijo que si le matara, él fuera rey. Y en aquel mismo año descubrió Colón estas Indias, y llegó a Barcelona en el siguiente de mil y cuatrocientos y noventa y tres años, en el mes de abril, y halló al Rey asaz flaco, pero sin peligro de su herida.

3.8.3. Estos notables se han traído a la memoria para señalar el tiempo en que Colón llegó a la corte, en lo cual yo hablo como testigo de vista, porque me hallé paje, muchacho, en el cerco de Granada, y vi fundar la villa de Santa Fe en aquel ejército, y después vi entrar en Granada al Rey y Reina Católicos, cuando se les entregó; y vi echar los judíos de Castilla; y estuve en Barcelona cuando fue herido el Rey como he dicho; y vi allí venir al Almirante don Cristóbal Colón, con los primeros indios que de estas partes fueron en el primer viaje y descubrimiento. Así que no hablo de oídas en ninguna de estas cuatro cosas, sino de vista, aunque las escriba desde aquí, o, mejor diciendo, ocurriendo a mis memoriales, desde el mismo tiempo escritas en ellos. Volvamos a nuestra historia.

3.8.4. Después que fue llegado Colón a Barcelona, con los primeros indios que de estas partes a España fueron, o él llevó, y con algunas muestras de oro y muchos papagayos y otras cosas de las que acá estas gentes usaban, fue muy benigna y graciosamente recibido del Rey y de la Reina. Y después que hubo dado muy larga y particular relación de todo lo que en su viaje de descubrimiento había pasado, le hicieron muchas mercedes aquellos agradecidos príncipes, y le comenzaron a tratar como a hombre generoso y de estado, y que por el gran ser de su persona propia tan bien lo merecía.

3.8.5. Mas a mi parecer (so la protestación por mí hecha en el proemio o libro I), digo que en estas nuestras Indias justo es que se tenga y afirme que fue predicada en ellas la verdad evangélica; y primero en nuestra España por el apóstol Santiago, y después la predicó en ella el apóstol San Pablo, como lo escribe San Gregorio. Y si desde nuestra Castilla se cultivó acá y transfirió la noticia del Santo Evangelio en nuestros tiempos, no cesa por eso que, desde el tiempo de los apóstoles, no supiesen estas gentes salvajes de la redención cristiana y sangre de nuestro Redentor Jesucristo vertió por el humano linaje. Antes es de creer que ya estas generaciones e indios de estas partes lo tenían olvidado, /9 verso/ pues que *in omnem terram exivit sonus eorum, et in fines orbis terrae verba eorum*. Conforme a lo que es dicho del salmista David, dice San Gregorio, sobre el capítulo dieciseis de Job, estas palabras: La Santa Iglesia ha ya predicado en todas las partes del mundo el misterio de nuestra

Redención. Así que estos indios ya tuvieron noticia de la verdad evangélica y no pueden pretender ignorancia en este caso; quédese esto a los teólogos, cuya es esta materia. Pero decir que, puesto que de nuestra santa fe católica acá hubiesen habido noticia los antecesores de estos indios, ya estaba fuera de la memoria de estas gentes. Y así fue grandísimo servicio el que a Dios hicieron los Reyes Católicos en el descubrimiento de estas Indias. Y grande fue el mérito que adquirió nuestra nación en ser por españoles buscadas estas provincias, y tantos reinos de gentes perdidas e idólatras, por la industria y en compañía y debajo de la guía del primer Almirante don Cristóbal Colón, reedificando y tornando a cultivar en estas tierras, tan apartadas de Europa, la sagrada pasión y mandamientos de Dios y de su Iglesia Católica, donde tantos millones de ánimas gozaba, o mejor diciendo, tragaba el infierno; y donde tantas idolatrías y diabólicos sacrificios y ritos que en reverencia de Satanás se hacían muchos siglos había, cesasen; y donde tan nefandos crímenes y pecados se ejercitaban, se olvidasen.

3.8.6. En esto se podría decir tanto que en muchas historias no se pudiese acabar de relatar los méritos de los Reyes Católicos don Fernando y doña Isabel, y de sus sucesores, por la continuación del santo celo y obra para la conversión de estas gentes. Porque, en la verdad, por su real voluntad y expresos mandamientos y muy continuado cuidado, siempre han proveído en el remedio de las ánimas de estos indios, y en el buen tratamiento de ellos. Y si en este caso algo ha faltado, es a causa de los ministros; y no tiene la culpa otro sino el que acá viene por gobernador o prelado y en esto se descuida; pero no dura más su negligencia de cuanto tarda de llegar a noticia de César o de su Real Consejo de Indias, donde luego se provee con grande atención en el reparo y enmienda, como conviene.

3.8.7. Yo, en la verdad, la principal causa de lo que en este caso puede haber mal sucedido, o no tan bien efectuándose como fuera razón, tampoco la quiero dar a los oficiales o ministros de tan santa y pía obra como es doctrinar esta generación de indios, sino a ellos mismos, especialmente por su incapacidad y malas inclinaciones; porque es cierto que son muy raros, y aun rarísimos, aquellos que en tanta multitud de ellos perseveran en la fe; antes deslizan de ella como el granizo de las puntas de las lanzas. Es menester que Dios ponga en esto su mano para que así los que enseñan como los enseñados, aprovechen más que hasta aquí. Vuelvo a la historia.

3.8.8. Seis indios llegaron con el primer Almirante a la corte, a Barcelona, cuando he dicho; y ellos, de su propia voluntad, y aconsejados, pidieron el bautismo, y los Reyes Católicos, por su clemencia, se lo mandaron dar; y juntamente con sus Altezas, el serenísimo príncipe don Juan, su primogénito y heredero, fueron los padrinos. Y a un indio, que era el más principal de ellos, llamaron don Fernando de Aragón, el cual era natural de esta isla Española, y pariente del rey o cacique Goacanagari; y a otro llamaron don Juan de Castilla. Y a los demás se les dieron otros nombres, como ellos los pidieron o sus padrinos acordaron que se les diese, conforme a la Iglesia Católica. Mas a aquel segundo, que se llamó don Juan de Castilla, quiso el príncipe para sí, y que quedase en su real casa, y que fuese muy bien tratado y mirado, como si fuera hijo de un caballero principal a quien tuviera mucho amor. Y le mandó doctrinar y enseñar en las cosas de nuestra santa fe, y dio cargo de él a su mayordomo Patiño, al cual indio yo vi en estado que hablaba ya bien la lengua castellana, y después, de allí a dos años, murió.

3.8.9. Todos los otros indios volvieron a esta isla en el segundo viaje que a ella hizo el Almirante; al cual aquellos gratísimos Príncipes Católicos /10 recto/ hicieron señaladas mercedes, y en especial le confirmaron su privilegio, en la dicha Barcelona, a veintiocho de mayo de mil y cuatrocientos y noventa y tres. Y entre otras, demás de le hacer noble y dar título de Almirante perpetuo de estas Indias a él y a sus sucesores, por vía de mayorazgo, y que todos los que de él dependiesen,y aun sus hermanos, se llamasen *don*, le dieron las mismas armas reales de Castilla y de León, mezcladas y repartidas con otras que asimismo le concedieron de nuevo, aprobando y confirmando de su autoridad real las otras armas antiguas de su linaje. Y de las unas y las otras formaron un nuevo y hermoso escudo de armas con su timbre y divisa, en la manera y forma que aquí se contiene y se ve patente:

3.8.10. Un escudo con un castillo de oro en campo de gules o sanguino, con las puertas y ventanas azules, y un león de púrpura o morado en campo de plata, con una corona de oro, la lengua sacada, y rampante, así como los reyes de Castilla y León los traen. Y este castillo y león han de estar en el chief o cabeza del escudo, en la parte derecha, y el león en la siniestra. Y de allí abajo, las dos partes restantes del escudo todo han de estar partidas en mantel; y en la parte derecha una mar en memoria del grande mar Océano: las aguas al natural, azules y blancas, y puesta la Tierra Firme de las Indias que tome casi la circunferencia de este cuarto, dejando la parte superior y alta de él abierta, de manera que las puntas de esta tierra grande muestran ocupar las partes del Mediodía y Tramontana; y la parte inferior, que significa /10 verso/ el Occidente, sea de tierra continuada que vaya desde la una punta a la otra de esta tierra; y entre estas puntas lleno el mar de muchas islas grandes y pequeñas, de diversas formas; porque esta figura, según está blasonada en este cuarto, es de la manera que se pueden significar estas Indias. La cual tierra e islas han de estar muy verdes, y con muchas palmas y árboles, porque nunca en ella pierden la hoja sino muy pocos; y ha de haber en esta Tierra Firme muchos matices y granos de oro, en memoria de las innumerables y riquísimas minas de oro que en estas partes e islas hay. Y por esta pintura, si el lector no quedó bien informado de lo que se tocó en el primer capítulo, libro II, de la grandeza y forma del asiento de la Tierra Firme, lo podrá algo más claramente entender. Y yo tornaré a definir estas armas de que ahora se trata. Y digo que en el otro cuarto siniestro del escudo hay cinco áncoras de oro en campo azul, como insignia apropiada al mismo oficio y título de Almirante perpetuo de estas Indias; y en la parte inferior del escudo, las armas de la prosapia del linaje de Colón, conviene saber: un chief o cabeza, o parte alta de gules, vel sanguina; y de allí abajo una banda azul en campo de oro; y sobre el escudo un baúl de estado, al natural, de ocho lumbres o vistas, con un rollo y dependencias azules y de oro, y sobre el baúl, por timbre y cimera, un mundo redondo con una cruz encima de gules; y en el mundo pintada la Tierra Firme e islas, de la manera que están arriba blasonadas; y por de fuera del escudo, una letra en un rótulo blanco, con unas letras de sable que dicen: *Por Castilla y por León nuevo mundo halló Colón.*

3.8.11. Asimismo, por respeto del Almirante, hicieron los Reyes Católicos

Adelantado de esta isla Española a don Bartolomé Colón, su hermano; y le hicieron otras mercedes que, por evitar prolijidad aquí no se dicen, como más largamente parece por su privilegio real que le concedieron; y yo he visto algunas veces.

[3.9] Libro II, cap. viii: Del segundo viaje que el Almirante primero, don Cristóbal Colón, hizo desde España a esta isla de Haití o Española; y de cómo halló muertos los cristianos que había dejado en tierra del rey Guacanagari; y de la concesión que el Papa Alejandro VI hizo de estas Indias a los Reyes Católicos don Fernando y doña Isabel, y sus sucesores en los reinos de Castilla y de León. Y del descubrimiento de las islas de los indios flecheros, llamados caribes, y otras cosas notables.[15]

3.9.1. ¿Quién hay que no sepa que dio el Señor las cosas terrenas para nuestros usos, y que crió las ánimas de los hombres para los suyos, como nos lo recuerda San Gregorio? Así, pues, conforme a esto, los bienaventurados reyes don Fernando y doña Isabel, deseando que las ánimas de estos indios fuesen para Dios, mandaron que el Almirante don Cristóbal Colón volviese a esta isla de Haití o Española con muy buena armada, en que vinieron algunos caballeros e hidalgos de su casa real y otros nobles varones y hombres de claros linajes, deseosos de ver esta nueva tierra y las cosas de ella.

3.9.2. Y hubieron primero aquellos santos príncipes la merced y concesión de estas Indias por el Sumo Pontífice, así porque con más justo titulo su santo propósito se efectuase (que era ampliar la religión cristiana como siervos de Dios, y aunque para esto no tuviesen necesidad, tomaron licencia y título del vicario de Cristo, a quien ellos siempre con fiel corazón tuvieron obediencia) como por ser estas mares e imperio de la corona y conquista de Castilla y haberse solamente los Católicos Reyes don Fernando y doña Isabel, ocupado en este memorable y santo ejercicio; cuanto más que, por lo que tengo dicho, ya muchos siglos antes fue este señorío de los reyes de España.

3.9.3. Y así el Papa dio al rey y reina y sus sucesores en los reinos de Castilla y de León estas Indias, y todo lo demás, fabricando una línea de polo a polo, por diámetro, desde cien leguas adelante de las islas /11 recto/ de los Azores y de las de Cabo Verde, y desde allí, discurriendo al Poniente, todo lo que en el mundo se hallase, de que no tuviese actual posesión algún príncipe cristiano.

3.9.4. Después de lo cual fue convenido y sentado entre España y Portugal que desde las dichas islas que dije más arriba, trescientas y setenta leguas de ellas al Occidente, se hiciese una línea de polo a polo, y lo que quedase entre esta línea y la que se dijo primero, fuese de Portugal. Y de aquí los portugueses interpretan que les queda todo lo del Oriente, en lo cual se engañan. De manera que conforme a la bula o donación apostólica hecha a Castilla y a los reyes de ella, se comprenden todas las islas de la Especiería y de Maluco y Bruney (donde se coge la canela), con toda la Especiería y lo demás del mundo, hasta tornar por el Oriente a la línea primera que se dijo del diámetro, significada a las cien leguas de las islas de los Azores y de Cabo Verde. Y esto, como he dicho, cae en la parte así concedida a los Reyes Católicos, de

[15]Oviedo 1535: fols. 10 verso–12 recto / Oviedo 1959: 1.33–36.

gloriosa memoria, y pertenece a la corona de Castilla.

3.9.5. Pero, porque estas cosas están aprobadas por el vicario de Dios y de la sagrada Iglesia, no es necesario decir otra cosa sino que yo he visto un traslado autorizado y signado de la Bula apostólica, la data de la cual dice: *Datis Romae apud Sanctus Petrum, anno Icarnationis Domini millesimo quadrigentessimo nonagessimo tertio, quarto nonas maii, pontificatus nostri anno primo.*

3.9.6. Pues conforme a lo amonestado por el Santo Padre en su bula y donación apostólica, cerca del cuidado que se debe tener en la conversión de los indios, vinieron religiosos, personas de aprobada y santa vida y letras. En especial fue escogido para esto fray Buyl, de la orden de San Benito, natural de Cataluña; al cual el mismo Santo Padre dio plenísimo poder para la administración de la Iglesia en estas partes, como prelado y cabeza de los clérigos y religiosos que en esta sazón acá pasaron para el servicio del culto divino y conversión de estos indios. Y trajeron los ornamentos y cruces y cálices e imágenes, y todo lo que era necesario para las iglesias y templos que se hiciesen. Y en la bula susodicha apostólica amonestó y mandó el Papa, en virtud de santa obediencia, al Rey y a la Reina que enviasen para lo que es dicho, a estas Indias, buenos varones y temerosos de Dios, doctos y expertos, para instruir y enseñar los habitadores de estas nuevas tierras en la fe católica y en buenas costumbres, con la debida diligencia que para tan santa y ardua cosa convenía.

3.9.7. Y así, conforme a esta amonestación del Sumo Pontífice y al santo celo que los Católicos Reyes tuvieron para cumplir por su parte lo que en ellos era, en cumplimiento de lo que es dicho, buscaron en todos sus reinos tales personas como eran necesarias, así de eclesiásticos como de seglares. Y con una muy hermosa armada, y lucida y noble compañía de gente, cual he dicho, se partió el mismo año el Almirante de la corte, desde la ciudad de Barcelona para la provincia de Andalucía; y llegado a la ciudad de Sevilla, comenzóse allí a juntar la gente, y las naos y carabelas, en la bahía de Cádiz, para esta flota.

3.9.8. Desde allí, hecho su alarde, y dada la orden y derrota a cada capitán y a los maestros y pilotos para su viaje, con la buena ventura salió con su armada a la vela, miércoles veinticinco días del mes de septiembre de mil y cuatrocientos y noventa y tres años. Y al cuarto del alba soltó las velas la nao capitana, y lo mismo hicieron todas las otras naos y carabelas, que eran, por todas, diecisiete velas, en que había mil y quinientos hombres de hecho, muy bien aderezados y proveídos de armas y municiones y bastimentos y de todo lo necesario, la cual gente vino al sueldo real. Y en esta armada vinieron personas religiosas, y caballeros e hidalgos y hombres de honra, y tales cuales convenía para poblar tierras nuevas y cultivarlas santa y rectamente en lo espiritual y temporal. Y como por tan cristianísimos príncipes proveído, muchos criados de su casa real, y a todos los más de los principales de ellos los vi y conocí. Y algunos al presente hay /11 verso/ vivos en estas Indias y en España, aunque son ya muy pocos los que quedan de ellos.

3.9.9. Tornando la historia al camino, digo que el Almirante, como más diestro en la navegación, por la experiencia del primer viaje, trajo más derecha y justa su derrota en este segundo. Y la primera tierra que halló y reconoció fue una isla que él nombró, así como la vio, la Deseada, conforme al deseo que él y todos los de su flota traían de ver la tierra. Y asimismo se vio luego otra isla, y llamóla Marigalante, porque la nao capitana en que el mismo Almirante venía se llamaba así. Y puso nombre a todas las otras islas que están en aquel paraje de Norte a Sur, o de polo a polo, conviene a saber: a la parte de la Tramontana, primera y más cercana isla, Guadalupe, la Barbada, el Aguja, el Sombrero, y otras. Y más cercanas a ella, el Anegada, desde la cual, al Poniente, están muchas isletas que llaman las Vírgenes, y más adelante está la isla Boriquén que ahora se llama San Juan, la cual isla es muy rica y de las más notables, como se dirá adelante en su lugar. A la parte austral de la dicha isla Deseada, la más próxima a ella es la isla Dominica, a la cual el Almirante nombró así porque en domingo fue vista. Y los Todos Santos es otra isla; y más al Mediodía está Matinino, la cual han querido algunos cronistas decir que era poblada de amazonas, y otras fábulas muy desviadas de la verdad, como parece por sus tratados, y se ha después averiguado por los que habemos visto la isla y las otras de su paraje. Y es todo falso lo que de ésta se ha dicho cuanto a ser poblada de mujeres solamente, porque no lo es, ni se sabe que jamás lo fuese.

3.9.10. Hay otras islas por allí, así como Santa Lucía, San Cristóbal, los Barbados, y otras que no hacen mucho al caso, porque son muchas y pequeñas. Pero cuando se diga del descubrimiento de la Tierra Firme, se dirán otras que hay entre éstas que he nombrado y la costa de Tierra Firme, de éstas que he dicho y otras que están con ellas, así como Libuqueira, a la cual los cristianos llamamos Santa Cruz y el cronista Pedro Mártir la llama Ayay.

3.9.11. Y las de al par de ella todas, o las más, estaban pobladas de indios flecheros llamados caribes, que en lengua de los indios quiere decir bravos y osados. Estos tiran con hierba tan pestífera y enconada que es irremediable; y los hombres que son heridos con ella mueren rabiando y haciendo muchas bascas y mordiéndose sus propias manos y carnes, desatinados del dolor grandísimo que sienten. Y cuando alguno escapa es por sobrada dieta y diligencia de algunas medicinas apropiadas contra ponzoña, de las cuales, hasta ahora, acá se ven pocas que aprovechen. Pero lo más cierto, cuando alguno sana, es por ser hecha la hierba de mucho tiempo, o por faltarle alguno de los materiales ponzoñosos de que es compuesta, como adelante se dirá; porque en diversas partes, diversa manera de hacer esta hierba tienen los indios. Estos flecheros de estas islas que tiran con hierba comen carne humana, excepto los de la isla de Boriquén. Pero, demás de estos de las islas, también la comen en muchas partes de la Tierra Firme, como se dirá en su lugar. Y esto mismo dice Plinio que hacen los antropófagos en Escitia; el cual autor dice, asimismo, que demás de comer carne humana, beben con las cabezas o calaveras de los hombres muertos, y que los dientes, con los cabellos de ellos, traen por collares; y de estos tales collares he yo visto algunos en la Tierra Firme.

3.9.12. Tornemos a nuestra historia y camino: que para lo que se toca más arriba, y de otras criminales costumbres de los indios, en su lugar se dirá más largamente. Digo, pues, así: que reconocidas estas primeras islas Deseada y las que están más cercanas a ella, pasó el Almirante y su armada, prosiguiendo su viaje, entre las unas y las otras, después que hubieron tomado agua en una de ellas; e idos adelante reconocieron la isla de Boriquén, que, como se dijo más arriba, es ahora llamada San

Juan. Y ésta es la mayor isla de las que hay en aquel paraje y más principal, de cuyo sitio y medida, y asiento y gente, y de lo que hay desde España hasta ella y a las que tengo dicho, se hará especial mención en su lugar, cuando convenga. Y no entienda el /12 recto/ lector, como han querido afirmar algunos que han escrito estas cosas de Indias, que todas estas islas que he nombrado las descubrió el Almirante en este segundo viaje; porque, aunque halló la Deseada y las que, viendo aquélla, era forzado que asimismo se viesen, por ser tan propincuas unas con otras, después andando el tiempo, se hallaron y se conquistaron por diversos capitanes, y se descubrieron las más de ellas por la continuación de la navegación de estas mares.

3.9.13. Tornando a nuestro propósito y camino, digo que después que pasó esta armada de la isla de Boriquén o San Juan, vino a esta de Haití, que llamamos Española, y tomó puerto en ella el mes de diciembre del mismo año de mil y cuatrocientos y noventa y tres, en Puerto de Plata, que es de la banda del Norte. Y desde allí fue por la costa abajo al Occidente, a la Isabela. Y de allí pasó a Monte Cristo, donde señoreaba el rey Goacanagari, que es adonde ahora se llama Puerto Real. La cual tierra poseía un hermano suyo, a quien él había dado aquella provincia; y allí habían quedado los treinta y ocho hombres que dejó el Almirante en el primer viaje, cuando descubrió esta tierra e isla; a los cuales todos habían muerto los indios, no pudiendo sufrir sus excesos, porque les tomaban las mujeres y usaban de ellas a su voluntad, y les hacían otras fuerzas y enojos, como gentes sin caudillo y desordenada. Y habíanse apartado unos de otros, uno a uno, y dos a dos, y cuando más, tres o cuatro juntos, por diversas partes la tierra adentro, por donde querían, continuando su desorden. Y como los indios los vieron así divisos y separados, acordaron de matarlos, desconfiando de la vuelta del Almirante y creyendo que no habían de volver jamás otros cristianos; y así acabaron aquellos pocos que entre ellos estaban esparcidos dándoles enojo. También fue la causa ser naturalmente la gente de esta tierra de poca o ninguna prudencia, porque nunca tienen respeto a lo porvenir.

3.9.14. Murieron aquellos treinta y ocho cristianos (según después se supo de los mismos indios) por lo que es dicho y porque no quisieron estar quedos en el asiento que el Almirante los había dejado. El cual, como fue certificado de la verdad, se volvió a poblar en la Isabela; e hizo allí un pueblo de la gente que trajo (que, como se dijo más arriba serían mil y quinientos hombres), y puso nombre a aquella ciudad Isabela en memoria de la serenísima y Católica Reina doña Isabel.

3.9.15. Esta fue la segunda población de cristianos que hubo en las Indias y se fundó en esta isla de Haití, que ahora llaman Española. Y hasta el año de mil y cuatrocientos y noventa y ocho duró aquella república; porque el primer pueblo que hubo fue aquel de los treinta y ocho cristianos que quedaron del primer viaje. Y desde la Isabela se pasó después toda aquella vecindad a esta ciudad de Santo Domingo, como adelante diré. (. . .)

[3.10] Libro II, cap. ix: Del viaje que desde España se hace para estas Indias, y de la manera y forma que se tiene en la navegación; y del árbol maravilloso de la isla de

Hierro, que es una de las islas Afortunas, que ahora llaman las Canarias.[16]

3.10.1. /13 verso/ (. . .) Solamente digo en este caso que quien desde la isla del Hierro, de quien queda hecha mención (que es una de las siete Afortunas, o de Canaria, y tan notable por su agua) fuere en demanda de costa o Tierra Firme, y a buscar aquel gran río llamado Marañón que está en ella, hallará a la Tierra Firme y aquella costa, navegando seiscientas leguas o menos, como mejor lo podrá entender, quien fuere curioso, por la moderna y experimentada cosmografía de estas Indias. Pues Tolomeo, antiguo y cierto cosmógrafo, no habló cosa alguna de la Tierra Firme, y lo que se dijo de Aristóteles y Solino y Plinio e Isidoro, en el capítulo ii de este libro, aquellas autoridades islas Hespérides dicen, y en islas hablan y no en Tierra Firme. A lo que yo alcanzo (so enmienda de los que otra cosa hubieren leído), para mí bien creo que el Almirante primero don Cristóbal Colón no comenzó este descubrimiento a lumbre de pajas, sino con muy encendidas y claras autoridades y verdadera noticia de estas Indias (. . .).

[3.11] Libro II, cap. xii: /16 verso/ De lo que hizo el Almirante don Cristóbal Colón, después que supo que los indios habían muerto los cristianos que dejó en esta isla Española el primer viaje; y cómo fundó la ciudad de la Isabela y la fortaleza de Santo Tomás; y cómo descubrió la isla de Jamaica, y vio particularmente la isla y costa de Cuba; y de las primeras muestras de oro de minas que se llevaron a España.[17]

3.11.1. /17 recto/ Dicho se han el primero y segundo viajes que el Almirante don Cristóbal Colón hizo a estas islas e Indias, y cómo en el primero camino dejó treinta y ocho hombres en tierra del rey o cacique Goacanagari. Aquellos cristianos escogió que le parecieron de mejor tiento y esfuerzo. Pero como conocía la fragilidad de esa humana vida dejó tantos porque si algunos muriesen, otros quedasen que él pudiese hallar cuando volviese; y también para que fuesen parte para corregir y enmendar los unos a los otros, si entre ellos algún exceso se cometiese. Y no dejó más de aquéllos porque tenía necesidad de los que le quedaban en los navíos para volver a España, y porque esta gente le pareció muy doméstica y mansa. Así que para fronteros o hacer guerra no quedaban, ni el pensamiento del Almirante fue que los indios tal tentarían, según su mansedumbre, porque si él esto sospechara, no los dejara. Pero para lenguas y sostenerse en paz eran muchos; y cierto, para aquel lo bastaran diez o doce, y no había de dejar más; o habían de quedar doscientos, y él no los tenía. Finalmente, su intención erró menos en mandarlos quedar, que ellos mismos en no saberse conservar y estar bien ordenados. Con todo eso, el Almirante les hizo muchas amonestaciones, y dioles la orden que debían tener para conservarse entre estas gentes salvajes. Prometiéndoles muchas mercedes, partió con ellos así de los bastimentos, como de todo lo demás que él pudo darles para su vestuario. Dejóles armas, de las cuales les exhortó que no usasen de ninguna manera, sino siendo muy forzados y no siendo jamás los agresores y encomendólos, cuanto más aficionadamente lo supo mostrar, al señor de la tierra, Goacanagari, al cual dio asimismo muchas cosas, porque mejor los

[16]Oviedo 1535: fol. 13 verso / Oviedo 1959: 1.38–39.
[17]Oviedo 1535: fols. 16 verso–17 verso / Oviedo 1959: 1.45–47.

tratase y favoreciese. Y quedó por capitán con esta gente, como tengo dicho, un buen hidalgo, natural de Córdoba, llamado Rodrigo de Arana, y asimismo quedó con ellos otro hombre de bien, llamado maestre Juan, gentil cirujano. Pero como los más de aquellos hombres que sí quedaron eran marineros, y estos tales es gente sobre sí y tan diferentes de los de la tierra como lo es su oficio, muy pocos de ellos o ninguno hubo capaz para lo que el Almirante los quería, que era saberse comportar y regirse entre los indios, y aprender la lengua y sus costumbres, y comportar los defectos y bestialidades que en los indios viesen. Mas, en la verdad, hablando sin perjuicio de algunos marineros que hay, hombres de bien, soy de opinión que por la mayor parte, en los hombres que ejercitan el arte de la mar, hay mucha falta en sus personas y entendimiento para las cosas de la tierra; porque, demás de ser, por la mayor parte, gente baja y mal doctrinada, son codiciosos e inclinados a otros vicios, así como gula, y lujuria, y rapiña, y mal sufridos, como no cupo en los que Colón dejó en esta isla, alguna parte de prudencia ni vergüenza para sostenerse, obedeciendo a los precepto de tan prudente varón, ni quisieron estar quedos donde él los había dejado, dieron mala cuenta de sus personas, o no dieron ninguna, pues no les quedó vida para ello.

3.11.2. Luego se supo de los indios cómo aquellos cristianos les hacían muchos males, y les tomaban las mujeres y las hijas y todo lo que tenían, según lo querían hacer. Y con todo esto, vivieron en tanto que estuvieron quedos y acaudillados; mas así como se descomidieron con el capitán que les quedó y se entraron la tierra adentro, pocos a pocos y desviados los unos de los otros, todos los mataron sin que alguno quedase. Súpose asimismo que la elección de los dos capitanes que el Almirante mandó que quedasen para después del primero, fue mucha causa de su separación, porque, según los indios decían, cada uno de los otros quiso ser capitán; y así como el Almirante se partió para España, comenzaron a estar diferentes y dividirse, y cada uno de ellos quiso ser la cabeza y el principal. Y la señoría de muchos no es útil en los hechos de guerra, según dice Livio. Y así hubo lugar su perdición por sus diferencias; y no teniendo en nada a los indios, de dos en dos, y tres en tres, y pocos juntos, se esparcieron en diversas partes, usando de sus ultrajes en tal manera que los indios, no pudiéndolo ya comportar, y durmiendo unos y otros descuidados dejando las /17 verso/ armas, o cuando mejor aparejo se hallaba, a todos les dieron la muerte, sin que ninguno de ellos quedase.

3.11.3. Y como el Almirante volvía consigo algunos de los indios que había llevado a España, entre ellos uno que se llamaba Diego Colón y había mejor que los otros aprendido, y hablaba ya medianamente la lengua nuestra, por su interpretación el Almirante fue muy enteramente informado de muchos indios y del propio rey Goacanagari de cómo había pasado lo que es dicho, mostrando este cacique mucho pesar de ello. Pero muy mayor le sintió el Almirante, el cual, después de haberse certificado de esto, desde a pocos días que estuvo en Puerto Real se vino a una provincia de esta isla e hizo allí una ciudad que nombró la Isabela.

3.11.4. Desde aquélla partió con dos carabelas el Almirante a descubrir, y dejó en esta isla Española por su teniente y gobernador a don Diego Colón, su hermano, entre tanto que llegaba don Bartolomé Colón, Adelantado y hermano suyo asimismo, que había quedado en España y venía de Inglaterra a buscar al Almirante. Y dejó al comendador mosén Pedro Margarite por alcalde de una fortaleza que el Almirante había mandado hacer en las minas que llaman de Cibao (que son las más ricas de esta isla, a par de un río que llaman Janico), así como se tuvo noticia de ellas; en las cuales se cogieron algunos granos de oro por los españoles, porque los indios no lo sabían coger si no se lo hallaban encima de la tierra. Y también los españoles no tenían aquella experiencia que los antiguos asturianos, y lusitanos, y gallegos tuvieron antiguamente en este ejercicio de las minas en las provincias que he dicho en España, de donde los romanos tan grandes tesoros hubieron.

3.11.5. Esta fortaleza fue la segunda que hubo en esta isla, y allí que fue el comendador mosén Pedro Margarite primero alcalde de ella Y llamáronla Santo Tomás, porque como estaban en duda del oro, y quisieron ver y creer, como de esto fueron certificados los cristianos, quiso el Almirante que la fortaleza se llamase como he dicho. Pero en aquel principio no se sacó sino poco oro, con el cual envió el Almirante, en ciertos navíos, al capitán Corvalán. Y este hidalgo llevólas nuevas del oro y minas ricas de Cibao a los Católicos Reyes don Fernando y doña Isabel; por lo cual le hicieron mercedes, aunque otros quieren decir que el que primero trajo las muestras del oro a España, por mandado del Almirante, fue el capitán Antonio de Torres, hermano del ama del príncipe don Juan, de gloriosa memoria.

3.11.6. Así que hallado el oro, el Almirante puso en efecto su camino y salió de la Isabela, y con él otros caballeros, y los que le pareció que convenía llevar en dos carabelas muy bien armadas y proveídas. En tanto que él iba a descubrir, se siguieron muchos trabajos a los cristianos que aquí quedaban, como se dirá adelante. Y aquel mismo año de noventa y cuatro se perdieron en la Isabela cuatro navíos, uno de los cuales fue la nao capitana llamada *Marigalante*.

3.11.7. De este viaje descubrió el Almirante la isla de Jamaica, que ahora se llama Santiago, hasta la cual hay, desde la parte más occidental de esta isla (que es la punta del Tiburón), veinticinco leguas. Pero la verdad es que el Almirante llamó el principio o parte más oriental de esta isla cabo de San Rafael, y al cabo último y más occidental de la isla llamó cabo de San Miguel; al cual, ahora, algunos ignorantes de la verdad le llaman el cabo del Tiburón.

3.11.8. Tornando a Jamaica, digo que está aquella isla en diecisiete grados de la línea equinoccial; tiene de longitud cincuenta leguas o más, de latitud, veinticinco. Pero, primero que el Almirante la descubriese, fue a la isla de Cuba, y vio sus costas más particularmente que cuando la había descubierto en el primer viaje; la cual ahora se llama isla Fernandina, en memoria del serenísimo y Católico Rey don Fernando, de gloriosa memoria. Esta isla es la que creo yo que es la que el cronista Pedro Mártir quiso intitular Alfa, y otras veces la llama Juana; pero de tales nombres no hay en estas partes e Indias isla alguna. Y no sé qué le pudo mover a nombrarla así; pero, pues de estas islas adelante: se ha de tratar más especificadamente, basta lo que en esto está ya dicho.

[3.12] Libro II, cap. xiii: Que trata de los trabajos y guerras que pasaron los cristianos que quedaron con don Diego Colón y con el Adelantado don Bartolomé Colón en la villa de la Isabela, en tanto que el Almirante fue a descubrir desde allí; y de lo que acaeció con ciertas tórtolas al alcalde mosén Pedro Margarite en la fortaleza de Santo Tomás; y de la población y fundamento de esta ciudad de Santo Domingo, adonde el Almirante tornó después de haber descubierto a Jamaica y otras cosas, etc.[18]

3.12.1. /18 recto/ Cuando el Almirante primero partió de la ciudad de la Isabela, dejó por su teniente y gobernador de esta isla, y con toda la más gente de los cristianos, a don Diego Colón, su hermano, entretanto que venía, como después vino el Adelantado don Bartolomé Colón, su hermano.

3.12.2. Habéis de saber que como luego que se pobló aquella ciudad y el Almirante repartió los solares para que los españoles hiciesen, como hicieron, sus casas, y les señaló las caballerías y tierras para sus heredamientos, viendo los indios que esta vecindad les había de durar, pesóles de ver el propósito de los cristianos. Y para excusar esto y darles ocasión que se fuesen de esta tierra, pensaron un mal ardid con que murieron más de las dos partes o la mitad de los españoles, y de los propios indios murieron tantos que no se pudieran contar. Y esto se hizo de forma que no se pudo entender ni remediar, porque como eran tan nuevos en la tierra los cristianos, no caían en el trabajo en que estaban, ni lo entendieron, y fue esto: acordaron todos los indios de aquella provincia de no sembrar en el tiempo que lo debían hacer, y como no tuvieron maíz, comieronse la yuca, que son dos maneras de pan, y el principal mantenimiento que acá hay. Los cristianos comieronse sus bastimentos; y aquéllos acabados, queriéndose ayudar de los de la tierra, que los indios acostumbran, no lo tenían para sí ni para ellos. Y de esta manera se caían los hombres muertos de hambre, en aquella ciudad, los cristianos. Y en la fortaleza que es dicha de Santo Tomás, donde estaba el comendador mosén Pedro Margarite, también por la misma necesidad se le murió la mitad de la gente, y por toda la tierra estaban los indios muertos a cada parte. El hedor era muy grande y pestífero; las dolencias que acudieron sobre los cristianos fueron muchas, además del hambre. Y de esta manera los indios efectuaban su mal deseo, que era, o que los cristianos se fuesen huyendo por falta de bastimento, o que se muriesen, si quedasen, no lo teniendo. Los indios que escapaban metíanse la tierra adentro y desamparaban la conversación de los nuestros, por les hacer más daño e ir a buscar de comer por otras provincias.

3.12.3. En este tiempo de tanta necesidad se comieron los cristianos cuantos perros gozques había en estas islas, los cuales eran mudos, que no ladraban. Y comieron también los que de España habían traído, y comieronse todas las hutías que pudieron haber, y todos los quemis y otros animales que llaman mohuy, y todos los otros que llaman corís, que son como gazapos o conejos pequeños. Estas cuatro maneras de animales se cazaban con los perros que se habían traído de España; y después que hubieron acabado los de la tierra, comieronse a ellos también, en pago de su servicio. Y no solamente dieron fin a estos cinco géneros de animales de cuatro pies, que solamente había en esta isla. Pero acabados aquéllos se dieron a comer unas sierpes que se llaman iguanas, que es de cuatro pies, de tal vista que, para quien no la conoce, es muy espantoso animal. Ni perdonaron lagartos, ni lagartijas, ni culebras, de las cuales hay muchas y de muchas maneras de pinturas, pero no ponzoñosas. Así que,

[18]Oviedo 1535: fols. 17 verso–20 recto / Oviedo 1959: 1.48–53.

por vivir, a ninguna bestia o animal de cuantos he dicho perdonaban; porque cuantos podían haber iban al fuego, y, cocidos o asados, no faltaba a su necesidad apetito para comer esas cosas tan temerosas a la vista. De lo cual y de la humedad grandísima de esta tierra, muchas dolencias graves e incurables, a los que quedaron con la vida, se les siguieron. Y de esta causa, aquellos primeros españoles que por acá vinieron, cuando tornaban a España algunos de los que venían en esta demanda del oro, si allá volvían, era con la misma color de él; pero no con aquel lustre, sino hechos azamboas y de color de azafrán o ictericia; y tan enfermos que luego, o desde /18 verso/ a poco que allá tornaban, se morían, a causa de lo que acá habían padecido, y porque los bastimentos y el pan de España son de más recia digestión que estas hierbas y malas viandas que acá gustaban, y los aires más delgados y fríos que los de esta tierra. De manera que, aunque volvían a Castilla, presto daban fin a sus vidas, llegados a ella.

3.12.4. Padecieron más estos cristianos, primeros pobladores de esta isla, muchos trabajos con las niguas, y muy crueles dolores y pasión del mal de las búas, porque el origen de ellas son las Indias. Y digo bien las Indias, así por la tierra donde tan natural es esta dolencia, como por las indias mujeres de estas partes, por cuya comunicación pasó esta plaga a algunos de los primeros españoles que con el Almirante vinieron a descubrir estas tierras, porque, como es mal contagioso, pudo ser muy posible. Y de éstos, después de tornados en España y haber sembrado en ella tal enfermedad, de ahí pasó a Italia y a otras partes, como adelante diré, sin desacordarme de hacer relación particularmente donde convenga, de once cosas notables que en ese capítulo se han tocado, que son cinco animales de cuatro pies, conviene a saber: perro, hutia, quemi, mohuy, cori; y asimismo se dirá de la iguana, que es una serpiente, también de cuatro pies. Y no olvidaré las lagartijas, culebras, lagartos, que hay en esta tierra; y diré de la pasión de la nigua, y de la dolencia aborrecible de las búas, con que se dará cuenta de las once cosas arriba tocadas.

3.12.5. Así que, continuando lo que prometí en el título de este capítulo xiii, digo que al tiempo que en la Isabela los cristianos padecían estos males que he dicho, y otras muchas necesidades (que por evitar prolijidad se dejan de decir), estaba el comendador mosén Pedro Margarite con hasta treinta hombres en la fortaleza de Santo Tomás, en las minas de Cibao, sufriendo las mismas angustias que los de la Isabela; porque también les faltaba de comer, y tenían muchas enfermedades, y padecían aquellos trabajos a que están obligados los primeros pobladores de tierras tan apartadas, y tan salvajes y dificultosas para los que tan lejos de ellas se criaron; y por estas causas, los que en esta fortaleza estaban se morían y de cada día eran menos. Porque para salir de la fortaleza eran pocos; dejarla sola era mal caso; la lealtad de aquel caballero era la que debía; el Almirante estaba fuera de la isla, en el descubrimiento que he dicho; los que en la Isabela estaban con el Adelantado don Bartolomé, tenían tanto trabajo que no se podían valer; los indios habíanse ido la tierra adentro los que querían o podían escapar de la hambre; de manera que, estando este alcalde y su gente a tan fuerte partido, vino un día un indio al castillo (porque, según él decía, el alcalde mosén Pedro Margarite le parecía bien y era hombre que no hacía ni consentía que fuese hecha violencia ni enojo a los indios y naturales de la tierra), y trajo este indio al alcaide un par de tórtolas vivas presentadas. Y siéndole dicho al alcalde, mandó que lo dejasen subir a la torre donde él estaba. Y subido el indio le dio las tórtolas, y el alcalde le dio las gracias de la recompensa en ciertas cuentas de vidrio (que los indios en esa sazón preciaban mucho), para se poner al cuello. Y el indio ido muy gozoso con su sartal, dijo el alcalde a los cristianos que con él estaban en el castillo, que le parecía que aquellas tórtolas eran pocas para comer todos de ellas, y que para él solo tendría que comer aquel día en ellas. Todos dijeron que él decía bien, y que para todos no había nada en aquel presente, y él podría pasar aquel día con las tórtolas y las había más menester porque estaba más enfermo que ninguno. Entonces dijo el alcaide: "Nunca plega a Dios que ello se haga como lo decís; que pues me habéis acompañado en la hambre y trabajos de hasta aquí, en ella y en ellos quiero vuestra compañía, y pareceros, viviendo o muriendo, hasta que Dios sea servido que todos muramos de hambre o que todos seamos de su misericordia socorridos. Y diciendo esto, soltó las tórtolas, que estaban vivas, desde una ventana de la torre, y fuéronse volando.

3.12.6. Con esto quedaron todos tan contentos y hartos, y como si a cada uno de los que allí estaban se las diera; y tan obligados se hallaron por esta gentileza del alcaide, para sufrir con él lo que les viniese, que ninguno quiso dejar la fortaleza ni su compañía, por trabajo que tuviese. Estando, pues, en tanta necesidad los cristianos, por la continuación de estas fatigas y dolencias /19 recto/ que he dicho, y porque para ser cumplidos sus males no les faltasen ningún afán, sobrevinieron muchos vientos del Norte (que en Castilla se llama cierzo), y en esta isla es enfermo; y moríanse, no solamente los cristianos, pero, como es dicho, los naturales indios.

3.12.7. No teniendo ya otro socorro sino el de Dios, El permitió su remedio; y éste fue la mudanza de la ciudad de la Isabela, donde estaban los españoles avecindados. Y para esta transmigración ocurrió que un mancebo aragonés, llamado Miguel Díaz, hubo palabras con otro español, y con un cuchillo diole ciertas heridas; y aunque no murió de ellas, no osó atender, puesto que era criado del Adelantado don Bartolomé Colón, y ausentóse del temor del castigo, y con él, siguiéndole y haciéndole amigable compañía, cinco o seis cristianos; algunos de ellos porque habían sido participantes en la culpa del delito del Miguel Díaz, y otros porque eran sus amigos. Y huyendo de la Isabela, fuéronse por la costa arriba hacia el Este o Levante, y bojáronla hasta venir a la parte del Sur, adonde ahora está esta ciudad de Santo Domingo, y en este asiento pararon, porque allí hallaron un pueblo de indios. Y aquí tomó este Miguel Díaz amistad con una cacica, que se llamó después Catalina, y hubo en ella dos hijos, andando el tiempo. Pero desde a poco que aquí se detuvo, como aquella india principal le quiso bien, tratóle como amigo que tenía parte en ella, y por su respeto a los de demás. Y diole noticia de las minas que están siete leguas de esta ciudad, y rogóle que hiciese que los cristianos que estaban en la Isabela que él mucho quisiese, los llamase y se viniesen a esta tierra que tan fértil y hermosa es y de tan excelente río y puerto; y que ella los sostendría; y daría lo que hubiesen menester. Entonces este hombre, por complacer a la cacica, y más porque le pareció que llevando nueva de tan buena tierra y abundante, el Adelantado, por estar en parte tan estéril y enferma, le perdonaría, y principalmente porque Dios quería que así fuese y no se acabasen aquellos cristianos que quedaban, acordó de ir al Adelantado, y atravesó con sus compañeros por la tierra, guiándole ciertos indios que aquella su amiga mandó ir con él hasta que llegaron a la Isabela, que está cincuenta leguas de esta ciudad, poco más o menos. Y secretamente tuvo manera de hablar con algunos amigos suyos, y supo que aquel hombre que había herido estaba sano; y así osó ver al Adelantado, su señor, y pedirle perdón en pago de sus servicios y de la buena nueva que le llevaba de esta tierra y de las minas de oro. Y el Adelantado le recibió muy bien y le perdonó, e hizo las amistades entre él y su contendiente. Y después que le hubo oído muy particularmente las cosas de esta provincia y de esta ribera, determinó de venir en persona a verla, y con la compañía que le pareció vino aquí, y halló ser verdad todo lo que Miguel Díaz había dicho; y entró en una canoa o barca de las que tienen los indios, y tentó este río llamado Ozama, que por esta ciudad pasa, e hízolo sondar, tentó la hondura de la entrada del puerto, y quedó muy satisfecho y tan alegre como era razón. Y fue a las minas y estuvo en ellas dos días, y cogióse algún oro. Y desde allí se volvió a la Isabela y dio muy grande placer a los españoles todos, después que les hubo dicho lo que había visto por acá. Y dio luego orden cómo la gente toda viniese con él por tierra a este asiento, y mandó traer por la mar lo que allá tenían los cristianos, en dos carabelas que tenían. Y llegó a este puerto, según algunos dicen, domingo día del glorioso Santo Domingo, a cinco días de agosto del mil y cuatrocientos y noventa y cuatro años. Y fundó el dicho Adelantado don Bartolomé esta ciudad, no donde ahora está, por no quitar de aquí a la cacica Catalina y a los indios que aquí vivían, sino de la otra parte de este río de la Ozama, junto a la costa y enfrente de esta población nuestra. Pero inquiriendo yo y deseando saber la verdad por qué esta ciudad se llamó Santo Domingo, dicen que, demás de haber allí venido a poblar en domingo y día de Santo Domingo, se le dio tal nombre porque el padre del primero Almirante y del Adelantado, su hermano, se llamó Dominico, y que en su memoria el hijo llamó Santo Domingo a esta ciudad.

3.12.8. Desde a dos meses y medio, pocos más o menos días, vino el Almirante y los que con él habían ido a descubrir; y llegado a esta ciudad envió luego a saber si era vivo mosén Pedro Margarite, y mandó por su carta que él y todos los que con él hubiese, se /19 verso/ viniesen para él y dejasen la fortaleza en poder del capitán Alonso de Hojeda, que fue el segundo alcalde de ella, y así lo hicieron. Y llegados aquí, se repararon todos por la abundancia y fertilidad de la tierra, y cobraron salud

3.12.9. Después que todos fueron juntos, como nuestro común adversario nunca se cansa ni cesa de ofender y tentar a los fieles, sembrando discordias entre ellos, anduvieron muchas diferencias entre el Almirante y aquel padre reverendo fray Buyl. Y esto hubo principio porque el Almirante ahorcó a algunos, y en especial a un Gaspar Ferriz, aragonés, y a otros azotó, comenzó a mostrarse severo y con más rigurosidad de la que solía, puesto que, aunque fuese razón de ser acatado, y se le acordase de aquella grave sentencia del emperador Otto: *Pereunte obsequio imperium quoque intercidit*, que dice: Si no hay obediencia, no hay señoría. También dice Salomón: *Universa delicta operit charitas*. Pues si todos los delitos encubre la caridad, como el sabio dice en el proverbio alegado, mal hace quien no se abraza con la misericordia, en especial en estas tierras nuevas, donde, por conservar la compañía de los pocos, se han de disimular muchas veces las cosas que en otras partes sería delito no castigarse. Cuando más debe mirar esto el prudente capitán que otro ninguno, pues está escrito: Constituyéronte por caudillo, no te quieras ensalzar; más serás en ellos así como uno de ellos. Autores son de estas palabras santas Salomón y San Pablo. El Almirante era culpado de crudo en la opinión de aquel religioso, el cual como tenía las veces del Papa, íbale a la mano; y así como Colón hacía alguna cosa que al fraile no pareciese justa, en las cosas de la justicia criminal, luego ponía entredicho y hacía cesar el oficio divino. Y en esa hora el Almirante mandaba cesar la ración, y que no se le diese de comer al fray Buyl ni a los de su casa.

3.12.10. Mosén Pedro Margarite y los otros caballeros entendían en hacerlos amigos y tornábanlo a ser, pero para pocos días. Porque así como el Almirante hacía alguna cosa de las que es dicho, aquel padre le iba a la mano y tornaba a poner entredicho y a hacer cesar las horas y oficio divino, y el Almirante también tornaba a poner su estanco y entredicho en los bastimentos, y no consentía que le fuesen dados al fraile ni a los clérigos, ni a los que los servían. Dice el glorioso San Gregorio: "Nunca la concordia puede ser guardada, sino por sola la paciencia; porque continuamente nace en las obras humanas por donde las ánimas de los hombres sean de su unidad y amor apartadas".

3.12.11. A estas pasiones respondían diversas opiniones, aunque no se publicaban; pero cada parte tuvo manera de escribir lo que sentía en ellas a España. Por lo cual, informados en diferente manera los Reyes Católicos de lo que acá pasaba, enviaron a esta isla a Juan Aguado, su criado, que ahora vive en Sevilla. Y así se partió con cuatro carabelas y vino acá por capitán de ellas, como parece por una cédula que yo he visto de los Reyes Católicos, hecha en Madrid, a cinco de mayo, año de mil y cuatrocientos y noventa y cinco. Y por otra cédula mandaron a los que estaban en las Indias que le diesen fe y creencia, la cual decía así: "El Rey, la Reina: caballeros y escuderos, y otras personas que por nuestro mandado estáis en las Indias, allá vos enviamos a Juan Aguado, nuestro repostero, el cual de nuestra parte os hablará. Nos vos mandamos que le deis fe y creencia. De Madrid, a nueve de abril de noventa y cinco años Yo el Rey. Yo la Reina". Y de Fernán Alvarez, secretario, refrendada.

3.12.12. Este capitán hizo pregonar en esta isla Española esta creencia, y por ella todos los españoles se le ofrecieron en todo lo que les dijese de parte de los Reyes Católicos. Y así, desde a pocos días, dijo al Almirante que se aparejase para ir a España, lo cual él sintió por cosa muy grave, y vistióse pardo, como fraile, y dejóse crecer la barba.

3.12.13. Esta vuelta del Almirante a España fue año de noventa y seis, puesto que no fue mandado prender. Y mandaron llamar el Rey y la Reina a fray Buyl y a mosén Pedro Margarite, y fueron a España en la misma flota; y asimismo el comendador Gallego, y el comendador Arroyo, y el contador /20 recto/ Bernal de Pisa, y Rodrigo Abarca, y micer Girao, y Pedro Navarro, que todos éstos eran criados de la casa real. Y llegados todos en España, cada uno se fue por su parte a la corte a besar las manos a los Católicos Reyes. Y aunque por cartas desde acá, y después personalmente allá, oyeron a fray Buyl y otros quejosos, y fueron aquellos bienaventurados príncipes informados de las cosas del Almirante (y por ventura haciéndolas más criminales de lo que eran), después que a él le oyeron, habiendo respeto a sus grandes servicios, y por su propia y Real clemencia, no solamente le perdonaron, pero diéronle licencia que tornase a la gobernación de estas tierras. Y mandaron que continuase el descubrimiento de lo restante de estas Indias, y encargáronle mucho aquellos cristianísimos reyes el buen tratamiento de sus vasallos españoles y de los indios, y que él fuese más moderado y menos riguroso, como era razón. Y el Almirante así lo prometió, no obstante que los más de los que de acá fueron, hablaron mal en su persona. De lo cual no me maravillo, aunque él no tuviera culpa alguna; porque como a algunos de los que a estas partes vienen, luego el aire de la tierra los despierta para novedades y discordias, que es cosa propia en las Indias; así, naturalmente, están los indios y gentes naturales de ellas my diferentes de continuo; y no sin causa, por este pecado y otros muchos que entre ellos abundan, los ha Dios olvidado tantos siglos.

3.12.14. A esto, también, de las discordias que entre los cristianos ha habido en los tiempos pasados, o primeros años que acá pasaron, dieron mucha ocasión los ánimos de los españoles, que de su inclinación quieren antes la guerra que el ocio, y si no tienen enemigos extraños, búscanlos entre sí, como lo dice Justino; porque su agilidad y grandes habilidades los hacen muchas veces mal sufridos. Cuanto más que han acá pasado diferentes maneras de gentes; porque, aunque eran los que venían vasallos de los reyes de España, ¿quién concertará al vizcaíno con el catalán, que son tan diferentes provincias y lenguas? ¿Cómo se avendrán el andaluz con el valenciano, y el de Perpiñán con el cordobés, y el aragonés con el guipuzcoano, y el gallego con el castellano (sospechando que es portugués), y el asturiano y montañés con el navarro, etc. Y así, de esta manera, no todos los vasallos de la corona real de España son de conformes costumbres ni semejantes lenguajes. En especial que en aquellos principios, si pasaba un hombre noble y de clara sangre, venían diez descomedidos y de otros linajes oscuros y bajos. Y así, todos los tales se acabaron en sus rencillas

3.12.15. Mas como la cosa ha sido tan grande, nunca han dejado de pasar personas principales en sangre, y caballeros e hidalgos. que se determinaron de dejar su patria de España para se avecindar en estas partes, y especial y primeramente en esta ciudad, como sea lo primero de partes, y Indias donde se plantó la sagrada religión cristiana, como se dirá más adelante.

3.12.16. Más porque me parece que se me podría notar a descuido dejar de decir dos plagas nuevas que los cristianos, en este segundo viaje del Almirante (entre otras que he dicho y muchas que se dejan de decir), padecieron, las diré en el siguiente capítulo. porque fueron de mucha admiración y peligrosas. Y una de ellas fue transferida, con esta vuelta de Colón a España y de allí a todas las provincias del mundo todo, según se cree.

[3.13] Libro II, cap. xiv: De dos plagas o pasiones notables y peligrosas que los cristianos y nuevos pobladores de estas Indias padecieron y hoy padecen algunos. Las cuales pasiones son naturales de estas Indias, y la una de ellas fue transferida y llevada a España, y desde allí a las otras partes del mundo.[19]

3.13.1. Pues que tanta parte del oro de estas Indias ha pasado a Italia y Francia, y

[19]Oviedo 1535: fols. 20 recto–21 recto / Oviedo 1959: 1.53–55.

aun a poder asimismo de los moros y enemigos de España, y por todas así partes del mundo, bien es que, como han gozado de nuestros sudores, les alcance parte de nuestros dolores y fatigas, porque de todo, a lo menos por la una o por la otra manera, del oro o del trabajo, se acuerden de dar /20 verso/ muchas gracias a Dios. Y en lo que les diere placer o pesar, se abracen con la paciencia del bienaveturado Job, que ni estando rico fue soberbio, ni siendo pobre y llagado impaciente: siempre dio gracias a aquel soberano Dios nuestro.

3.13.2. Muchas veces en Italia me reía oyendo a los italianos decir el mal *francés*, y a los franceses llamarle el mal de *Nápoles*; y en la verdad, los unos y los otros le acertaran el nombre si le dijeran el mal de *las Indias*. Y que esto sea así la verdad, se entenderá por este capítulo y por la experiencia grande que ya se tiene del palo santo y del guayacán, con que especialmente esta terrible enfermedad de las búas, mejor que con ninguna otra medicina se cura y guarece. Porque es tanta la clemencia divina que adonde quiera que permite por nuestras culpas nuestros trabajos, allí, a par de ellos, quiere que estén los remedios, con su misericordia. De estos dos árboles se dirá en el libro X, capítulo ii: ahora sépase cómo estas búas fueron con las muestras del oro de estas Indias, desde esta isla de Haití o Española.

3.13.3. En el precedente capítulo dije que volvió Colón a España el año de mil y cuatrocientos y noventa y seis, así es la verdad. Después de lo cual vi y hablé a algunos de los que con él tornaron a Castilla, así como al comendador mosén Pedro Margarite, y a los comendadores Arroyo y Gallego, y a Gabriel de León, y Juan de la Vega, y Pedro Navarro, repostero de camas del príncipe don Juan, mi señor, y a los más de los que se nombraron donde se dijo de algunos criados de la Casa Real que vinieron en el segundo viaje y descubrimiento de estas partes. A los cuales y a otros oí muchas cosas de las de esta isla, y de lo que vieron y padecieron y entendieron del segundo viaje, además de lo que fui informado de ellos, y otros del primero camino, así como de Vicente Yáñez Pinzón (que fue uno de los primeros pilotos de aquellos tres hermanos Pinzones de quien queda hecha mención), porque con éste yo tuve amistad hasta el año de mil y quinientos y catorce que él murió. Y también me informé del piloto Hernán Pérez Mateos, que al presente vive en esta ciudad, que se halló en el primero y tercero viajes que el Almirante primero, don Cristóbal Colón hizo a estas Indias. Y también he habido noticia de muchas cosas de esta isla de dos hidalgos que vinieron en el segundo viaje del Almirante, que hoy día están aquí y viven en esta ciudad, que son Juan de Rojas y Alonso de Valencia, y de otros muchos que, como testigos de vista en lo que es dicho tocante a esta isla y a sus trabajos, me dieron particular relación. Y más que ninguno de todos los que he dicho, el comendador mosén Pedro Margarite, hombre principal de la Casa Real, y el Rey Católico le tenía en buena estimación.

3.13.4. Y este caballero fue el que el Rey y la Reina tomaron por principal testigo; y a quien dieron más crédito en las cosas que acá habían pasado en el segundo viaje, de que hasta aquí se ha tratado. Este caballero mosén Pedro andaba tan doliente y se quejaba tanto, que también creo yo que tenía los dolores que suelen tener los que son tocados de esta pasión, pero no le vi búas algunas. Y desde a pocos meses, el año susodicho de mil y cuatrocientos y noventa y seis, se comenzó a sentir esta dolencia entre algunos cortesanos. Pero en aquellos principios era este mal entre personas bajas y de poca autoridad, y así se creía que le cobraban allegándose a mujeres públicas, y de aquel maltrato libidinoso, pero después extendióse entre algunos de los mayores y más principales.

3.13.5. Fue grande la admiración que causaba en cuantos lo veían, así por ser el mal contagioso y terrible, como porque se morían muchos de esta enfermedad. Y como la dolencia era cosa nueva, no la entendían ni sabían curar los médicos, ni otros, por experiencia, aconsejar en tal trabajo.

3.13.6. Siguióse que fue enviado el Gran Capitán Gonzalo Fernández de Córdoba a Italia, con una hermosa y gruesa armada, por mandado de los Católicos Reyes y como su capitán general, en favor del rey Fernando, segundo de tal nombre en Nápoles, contra el rey Carlos de Francia, que llamaron de la Cabeza Gruesa; y entre aquellos españoles fueron algunos tocados de esta enfermedad, y por medio de las mujeres de mal trato y vivir se comunicó con los italianos y franceses. Pues como nunca tal enfermedad allá se había visto por los unos ni por los otros, /21 recto/ los franceses comenzáronla a llamar mal de Nápoles, creyendo que era propio de aquel reino; y los napolitanos, pensando que con los franceses había ido aquella pasión, llamáronla mal francés. Y así se llama, después acá en toda Italia, porque hasta que el rey Charles pasó a ella, no se había visto tal plaga en aquellas tierras.

3.13.7. Pero la verdad es que de esta isla de Haití o Española pasó este trabajo a Europa, según es dicho; y es acá muy ordinario a los indios, y sábense curar, y tienen muy excelentes hierbas y árboles y plantas apropiadas a ésta y otras enfermedades, así como el guayacán (que algunos quieren decir que es hebeno), y el palo santo, como se dirá cuando de los árboles se tratare.

3.13.8. Así que, de las dos plagas peligrosas que los cristianos y nuevos pobladores de estas Indias padecieron y hoy algunos padecen, que son naturales pasiones de esta tierra, ésta de las búas es la una, y la que fue transferida y llevada a España y de allí a las otras partes del mundo, sin que acá faltase la misma. Así que, continuando el propósito de los trabajos de Indias, dígase la otra pasión, que se propuso, de las niguas.

3.13.9. Hay en esta isla y en todas estas Indias, islas y Tierra Firme, el mal que he dicho de las búas, y otro que llaman de las niguas. Esto de las niguas no es enfermedad, pero es un mal acaso, porque la nigua es una cosa viva y pequeñísima, mucho menor que la menor pulga que se puede ver. Pero, en fin, es género de pulga, porque, así como ella, salta, salvo que es más pequeña. Este animal anda por el polvo, y donde quiera que quisieren que no le haya hase de barrer a menudo la casa, entrase en los pies y en otras partes de la persona, y en especial, las más veces, en las cabezas de los dedos, sin que se sienta hasta que está aposentada entre el cuero y la carne y comienza a comer de la forma que un arador y harto más. Y después, cuanto más allá está, más come. De manera que, como acuden las manos rascando, este animal se da tanta prisa a multiplicar allí otros sus semejantes que, en breve tiempo hace muchos; porque luego que entra el primero se anida, y hace una bolsita, entre cuero y carne, tamaña como una lenteja (y algunas como garbanzo), llena de liendres, las cuales todas se tornan niguas. Y si con tiempo no se sacan con un alfiler o aguja, de la forma que se sacan los aradores, son malas; y en especial que después que están criadas (que es cuando comienzan mucho a comer), de rascarlas, se rompe la carne; y espárcense de manera que si no las saben agotar, siempre hay en qué entender.

3.13.10. En fin, como en esto tampoco eran diestros los cristianos, como en el curarse de las búas, muchos perdían los pies por causa de estas niguas, o a lo menos algunos dedos de ellos, porque después se enconaban y hacían materia, y era necesario curarse con hierro o con fuego. Pero esto es fácil de remediar presto, sacándolas al principio; pero en algunos negros bozales son peligrosas, porque o por su mala carnadura, o ser bestiales y no saberse limpiar, ni decirlo con tiempo, vienen a mancarse de los pies, y así otros muchos que se quejan. Y yo las he tenido en mis pies, en estas islas y en la Tierra Firme, y no me parece que en hombres de razón es cosa para temerse, aunque es enojo en tanto que dura o está la nigua dentro; más fácil cosa es sacarla al principio. Yo tengo averiguado, y así lo dirán las personas que tienen experiencia en sacar estas niguas, que es menester tener aviso, cuando las sacan para las matar, porque alguna vez, así como con el alfiler o aguja la descubren, rompiendo el cuero del pie, así salta, y se va la nigua como una pulga. Esto acaece si ha poco que allí entró, y por esto se cree que la que entra en el pie, después que ha hecho su mala simiente, se va, así como vino, a otra parte a hacer más mal; o por ventura, por si se despide del pie, después de haber dejado en él una mala enjambre de innumerable simiente y generación.

[3.14] Comienza el libro tercero de la *Natural General Historia de las Indias*: Proemio[20]

3.14.1. /21 verso/ En este tercero libro se tratará de la guerra que los cristianos tuvieron, y el capitán Alonso de Hojeda, en nombre del Almirante don Cristóbal Colón, con el rey Caonabo, y de su prisión y muerte. Y de las victorias que hubo el Adelantado don Bartolomé Colón, hermano del Almirante, contra el rey Guarionex y otros catorce caciques o reyes que con él se juntaron; y cómo se apartó Roldán Jiménez, con algunos cristianos de su opinión, de la obediencia del Almirante y Adelantado. Y también se dirá del tercer viaje y descubrimiento del Almirante primero, cuando halló y descubrió parte de la gran costa de la Tierra Firme, y descubrió la isla de las Perlas, llamada Cubagua. Y de la gobernación del Almirante, y qué reyes y señores principales había en esta isla; y del gran lago de Xaraguá, y de otro lago que hay en las sierras y cumbres más altas de esta isla. Y cómo y con qué armas peleaban los indios, y qué gentes son los caribes y flecheros. Y se dirá también de la milagrosa y devotísima Cruz de la Vega. Y de la venida del comendador Francisco de Bobadilla, el cual envió preso en grillos a España al Almirante y a sus hermanos, el Adelantado don Bartolomé y don Diego Colón. Y por qué causas se murieron los muchos indios que hubo en esta isla Española. Y de la venida del Comendador Mayor de Alcántara don fray Nicolás de Ovando, y partida del comendador Bobadilla (que se ahogó en la mar con muchos navíos y gentes y mucho oro), y de la buena gobernación del Comendador Mayor. Y cómo el Almirante viejo y

[20]Oviedo 1535: fol. 21 verso / Oviedo 1959: 1.55–56.

primero, don Cristóbal Colón, hizo el cuarto viaje y descubrimiento en estas Indias, cuándo descubrió a Veragua y otras provincias de la Tierra Firme; y de su muerte, después, en España. Y cómo se mudó esta ciudad de Santo Domingo adonde ahora está. Y de la nobleza y particularidades de esta ciudad e isla, y de las Villas y poblaciones, y otras cosas concernientes y necesarias a la prosecución de aquella *Historia Natural*, como se verá más particularmente en los capítulos siguientes.

[3.15] Libro III, cap. i: Que trata de la guerra que tuvo el capitán Alonso de Hojeda con el cacique Caonabo, y de su prisión y muerte.[21]

3.15.1. En el segundo libro se dijo cómo después que el comendador mosén Pedro Margarite dejó la fortaleza de Santo Tomás, mandó el Almirante que la tuviese el capitán Alonso de Hojeda, y le hizo alcalde de ella, y diole cincuenta hombres para que la guardase, porque estaba en parte que importaba mucho, así para lo que tocaba a las minas ricas de Cibao como para la reputación y fuerza de los cristianos.

3.15.2. Mas como el Almirante fue partido para España, los indios, con soberbia (y en especial Caonabo, de cuyo señorío era aquella provincia), no eran contentos de aquel nuevo señorío y vecindad de la fortaleza. Y determinado el Caonabo y los ciguayos (que así se llamaban los flecheros indios de la costa del Norte en esta isla), acordaron de dar en la fortaleza quemarla, o ponerla por el suelo, si pudieran. Y con mano armada, y siendo más de cinco o seis mil hombres, cercaron aquel castillo y tuviéronle en mucho aprieto hasta treinta días, sin dejar salir de la fortaleza a algún hombre de ellos. Pero como el alcalde era mañoso y esforzado caballero, resistió a los contrarios de tal forma que, al cabo del tiempo que he dicho, desviaron su campo, y como gentes salvajes y no guerreros, se descuidaron y dieron lugar que este alcalde /22 recto/ hiciese mucho daño en ellos. Y como era hombre mañoso y de mucha solicitud, continuó la guerra de todas las maneras que él pudo, así con las armas, cuando convino, como con las astucias y cautelas que suele haber en los capitanes de experiencia. Y no obstante que en la continuación de la guerra murieron algunos cristianos, muchos fueron los indios que mataron, y al cabo fue preso Caonabo, con mucha parte de los suyos principales. Puesto que se dijo que Hojeda no le había guardado la seguridad que el cacique decía que le fue prometida, o no lo habiendo entendido Caonabo.

3.15.3. Por manera que de esta prisión de Caonabo se causó la paz y sujeción de la isla toda. Pero como Caonabo tenía un hermano, hombre de mucho esfuerzo y bien quisto de los indios, luego se juntaron con él todos los de su señorío; el cual, no olvidando la prisión de su hermano, acordó de ir a redimirlo con fuerza de armas, llevando presupuesto de tomar todos los cristianos que él pudiese presos; creyendo que después, a trueco de ellos, podría haber y rescatar a su hermano Caonabo, y libertar asimismo otros indios principales que con el estaban presos en poder de los cristianos. Y juntó más de siete mil hombres para esto, y los más flecheros, y ordenadas cinco batallas se pusieron bien cerca de los españoles, el capitán de los cuales, Alonso de Hojeda, con algunos de caballo y con la gente que él pudo sacar de

[21]Oviedo 1535: fols. 21 verso–22 recto / Oviedo 1959: 1.56–57.

la fortaleza, dejándola guardada, y con alguna que el Adelantado don Bartolomé le había enviado en su socorro (que por todos no eran trescientos hombres), peleó contra los indios. Y quiso Dios favorecer los nuestros y darles victoria, y así como los jinetes dieron en la delantera o primera batalla de los indios, los pusieron en huida, porque hubieron mucho espanto de tal novedad, y nunca habían visto esta manera de hombres a caballo pelear con ellos ni con otros. Y así fue hecho mucho estrago en los contrarios, y fue preso su principal caudillo, hermano de Caonabo, y otros muchos indios. Este día hizo Hojeda el oficio de valiente soldado y esforzado caballero y no menos prudente capitán.

3.15.4. Después que este cacique o rey fue preso, y su hermano, acordó el Adelantado don Bartolomé de enviarlos a España, con otros indios, algunos de los principales prisioneros. Porque le pareció que en esta isla sería mucho inconveniente tener al dicho Caonabo detenido, ni dejarle en la tierra, así por ser tan principal señor en ella como porque siempre había novedades a su causa, porque era hombre de mucho esfuerzo y sabio en la guerra. Y en dos carabelas que estaban puestas para España, mandó el Adelantado que los llevasen. Pero así como Caonabo y su hermano supieron que habían de ir al Rey y la Reina Católicos, el hermano se murió desde a pocos días, y el Caonabo, entrado en la mar, desde a pocas jornadas que navegaron también se murió. Y de esta manera quedó pacificada toda la tierra de este Caonabo por los cristianos. Y su mujer Anacaona, hermana del cacique Behechio (que era señor en la parte occidental hasta el fin de esta isla), se fue de la tierra de su marido a vivir en la de su hermano, a la provincia que llaman de Xaraguá, y allí fue tan acatada y temida por señora como el mismo Behechio. De esta Anacaona se dirá adelante, porque fue gran persona y en mucho tenida en estas partes, por ser muy valerosa y de grande ánimo e ingenio; y sus cosas de esta mujer fueron notables en bien y en mal, como se dirá en su lugar.

[3.16] Libro III, cap. ii: De la batalla y victoria que hubo el Adelantado don Bartolomé contra el rey Guarionex y otros catorce caciques o reyes; y cómo se apartó Roldán Jiménez de la obediencia y compañía del Adelantado don Bartolomé y del Almirante primero.[22]

3.16.1. Casi en el tiempo que el cerco se tenía por Caonabo contra el capitán Hojeda (según algunos dicen), o después que fue descercado (según otros afirman), el cacique Guarionex convocó todos los indios caciques que él pudo, y se juntaron más de quince mil hombres para dar sobre el Adelantado don Bartolomé y los cristianos que estaban con él en la ciudad de la Vega y por aquella comarca. Porque, como tengo /22 verso/ dicho, los indios se iban enojando de esta vecindad de los cristianos, y no querían, por ningún caso que permaneciesen y quedasen en la isla, así porque su señorío no fuese turbado ni aniquilado (como les parecía que se les iba aparejando), como porque sus ritos y ceremonias y vicios no parecían bien a los cristianos, y decían mal de ellos. Y también porque les pareció el tiempo aparejado para su mal propósito, a causa de los pocos cristianos que habían quedado en la tierra toda, así por las

[22]Oviedo 1535: fols. 22 recto–23 recto / Oviedo 1959: 1.57–58.

enfermedades y trabajos pasados que he dicho, como porque antes que viniesen otros de nuevo con el Almirante (que de cada día se esperaba), pudiesen excluir y acabar los que parecía que tenían ya alguna noticia de la tierra, y podrían ser aviso y mucho provechosos, o parte para poderles dañar en compañía de los cristianos que de nuevo viniesen y para ejecución de esto, juntado su ejército, movieron a buscar a los cristianos.

3.16.2. El Adelantado, certificado de lo que es dicho, no esperó ni quiso atender a hacerse fuerte en aquel pequeño pueblo, ni dar causa a que de noche le pegasen fuego o le cercasen en él sino como buen caballero y diestro capitán, salió al campo y trasnochó y anduvo tanto que llegó cerca del real del rey Guarionex, y a la segunda guarda, o casi a medianoche, con hasta quinientos hombres (entre sanos y enfermos), dio con tanta furia e ímpetu, animosamente, en los enemigos, por dos partes, que los desbarató. Y como los indios eran gente salvaje y desarmada y no diestra en la guerra a respecto de los cristianos, mataron muchos de ellos, y los demás fueron presos, puesto que muchos escaparon por la oscuridad de la noche. Pero fue preso el mismo rey Guarionex con otros catorce reyes o caciques, los más principales que en esta batalla se hallaron, la cual fue cerca de donde es fundada la villa del Bonao.

3.16.3. Fue esta victoria tan señalada cosa y de tanto favor para los cristianos que demás de aumentarse su crédito y esfuerzo en la reputación y memoria de los indios, dio causa a que cesaran en sus ruindades y rebeliones, y comenzaron a ser más domésticos y a comunicarse más con los cristianos, y a desechar los pensamientos de la guerra; puesto que, en la verdad, la gente de esta isla es la que de menos ser y esfuerzo se ha visto en todas las Indias e islas y Tierra Firme, y la que más quieta y sosegada manera de vivir tenía, no obstante que, como tengo dicho, no faltaban algunas guerras y discordias entre estas gentes; pero no tan continuadas y sangrientas como en otras partes.

3.16.4. Tornando a la historia: es de saber que después que el Adelantado hubo este vencimiento, parecióle que sería mucha causa, para perpetuar la paz y amistad entre los cristianos y los indios, soltar a Guarionex con los mejores partidos que él entendiese. Y así se dio orden en ello y fue libre. De ahí adelante hacía buen acogimiento y trataba bien a los cristianos en su tierra, cuando por ella pasaban o a ella iban. Otros dicen que en esta batalla no se halló Guarionex, sino su gente, y que iba por su capitán general el cacique Máyobanex, y que éste fue después, con otros, suelto, pero que, continuándose la guerra, había sido presa la mujer de Guarionex, y que por redimirla había venido de paces a ser amigo de los cristianos.

3.16.5. Después que estas victorias hubo el Adelantado, parecía que se le había trocado la condición, porque se mostró muy riguroso con los cristianos de allí adelante, en tanta manera que no le podían sufrir algunos, en especial Roldán Jiménez, que había quedado por alcalde mayor del Almirante. Al cual el Adelantado no hacía la cortesía o tratamiento que él pensaba ser merecedor, ni el Roldán consentía que en las cosas de la justicia fuese el Adelantado tan absoluto como quería serlo. Y de esta causa hubieron malas palabras, y el Adelantado le trató mal y, según algunos dijeron, puso o quiso poner las manos en él. Por lo que él se indignó de manera que con setenta hombres se apartó de su compañía y se entró la tierra adentro, alzado y desviado de la conversación de los cristianos, pregonando y diciendo las sinrazones que el Adelantado y el Almirante habían hecho o que él, por su enojo, les quería imponer. Y con determinación de no apartarse del servicio de los Reyes Católicos, el dicho Roldán hacía sus protestaciones para no estar debajo de la gobernación del Almirante ni del Adelantado en ningún tiempo (como nunca lo quiso después /23 recto/ estar), sino fuese a la provincia de Xaraguá: la tierra y señorío del rey Behechio y por allá anduvo y estuvo hasta que después algún tiempo vino a gobernar esta isla y tierra el comendador Francisco de Bobadilla, como se dirá adelante.

[3.17] Libro III, cap. iii: Que trata de lo que en esta isla pasó en tanto que el Almirante fue a España. Y del tercero viaje y descubrimiento que él hizo, cuando halló la costa (y grandísima parte del mundo incógnita) llamada Tierra Firme generalmente, donde muy grandes reinos y provincias se incluyen. Y de cómo descubrió asimismo la isla de Cubagua, donde es la riquísima pesquería de las perlas; y de otras islas nuevas que halló; y del suceso de todo ello, con otras cosas adherentes a la historia.[23]

3.17.1. Así como el Almirante estuvo algunos días en la corte de los Católicos Reyes, satisfaciendo a las quejas e informaciones que contra él habían dado fray Buyl y otros, y fue con clemencia oído y absuelto, como se dijo en el segundo libro, diósele licencia que tornase a la gobernación de estas tierras, y mandáronle continuar el descubrimiento de ellas. Y para ponerlo en efecto partió de la bahía de Cádiz en el mes de marzo del año de mil y cuatrocientos y noventa y seis (aunque algunos dicen que era en el año de noventa y siete de la Natividad de Jesucristo, nuestro Redentor); y salió a la mar Océana con seis carabelas, muy bien armadas y proveídas de bastimentos y de todo lo necesario para su viaje. Y después que llegó a Canaria, envió las tres carabelas a esta isla Española, con bastimentos y alguna gente, y él siguió su camino con las otras tres carabelas que le quedaron la vuelta de las islas que llaman, entre los vulgares, islas de Antonio, y ahora se dicen de Cabo Verde, que son las mismas que los antiguos nombraban las Gorgades. Y desde allí corrió con sus navíos al Sudeste bien ciento y cincuenta leguas. Y tomóles una gran tormenta, y púsolos en tal necesidad, que cortaron los mástiles de las mesanas, y aliviaron mucha parte de la carga, y se vieron en grandísimo peligro. Pero esta tormenta que dice Hernán Pérez Mateos, piloto que hoy está en esta ciudad de Santo Domingo, no fue así, según dice don Fernando Colón, hijo del Almirante, que allí se halló, el cual afirma que fue de calmas y calor tanta, que las vasijas se les abrían y el trigo se podría. Y les fue necesario alijar y arredrarse de la Equinoccial, y corrieron al Oeste-Noroeste, y fueron a reconocer la isla de la Trinidad. El cual nombre le puso el Almirante porque llevaba pensamiento de poner, a la primera tierra que viese, la Trinidad. Y así, cuando vio la primera tierra firme y la dicha isla, vio tres montes aun tiempo o cercanos, y luego puso a aquella isla por nombre la Trinidad, y pasó por aquel embocamiento que llaman la Boca del Drago, y vióse la Tierra Firme: y mucha parte de la costa de ella. Pero como es de flecheros caribes, y la isla que he dicho, asimismo, y tiran con la hierba irremediable, y es gente muy fiera y salvaje, no pudieron haber lengua con los

[23]Oviedo 1535: fol. 23 / Oviedo 1959: 1.58–60.

indios, aunque vieron muchos de ellos con sus piraguas y canoas, en que navegan, de las cuales y de su forma se dirá adelante; y también vieron gente en tierra.

3.17.2. Está esta isla en nueve grados de nuestro polo ártico, de la banda que tiene esta isla hacia el Sur o Mediodía; y de la que tiene mirando al Septentrión o Norte, está en diez grados. Tiene de latitud dieciocho o veinte leguas, poco más o menos, y de longitud veinticinco o algo más.

3.17.3. La tierra que está opuesta a la parte del Sur de esta isla en la Tierra Firme, se llama el Palmar, porque allí vieron y hay grandes palmares. Y más al Levante, la costa arriba, está Río Salado. Y porque queriendo tomar agua en él le hallaron muy salobre, dio causa que el Almirante así le nombrase. Al Poniente de esta isla de la Trinidad, está la punta de las Salinas en Tierra Firme, diez o doce leguas. Y entre esta punta y la Tierra Firme (aunque también la misma punta es tierra firme), está un golfo al cual el Almirante llamó la Boca del Drago (porque parece algo la figura de este embocamiento boca de drago abierta), dentro del cual hay muchas isletas.

3.17.4. Y desde la punta de las Salinas, que está /23 verso/ en diez grados de la Equinoccial, discurrió el Almirante por la costa al Poniente, y reconoció otras islas y púsoles nombre los Testigos, y a otra isla llamó la Generosa. Y vio otras muchas islas que por allí hay. Y fue adelante y descubrió la rica isla llamada Cubagua, que ahora llamamos la isla de las Perlas, porque allí es la principal pesquería de ellas en estas Indias. Y junto con ella está otra isla muy mayor, mandóla el Almirante llamar la Margarita. La isla de Cubagua, o de las Perlas, está casi cincuenta leguas al Poniente de la punta de las Salinas que se dijo más arriba. Esta es una isla pequeña que tendrá de circuito tres leguas, poco más o menos, y desde ella a la Tierra Firme y cuadro leguas a la provincia que se dice Araya. Y allí descubrió los Testigos (que son isleos), e isla de Pájaros y otras islas. Y pasó el Almirante, con sus tres carabelas, la costa de Tierra Firme al Poniente, y halló la isla de Poregari, que está veintisiete o treinta leguas de Cubagua. Y más adelante descubrió otras islas que se llaman Los Roques, y la isla de la orchilla, que se dice Yaruma, donde hay mucha cantidad de ella, según fama. Esta isla está a doce leguas de otra que también descubrió el Almirante más al Oeste, que se llama Corazao. Y asimismo descubrió otras muchas islas e isleos, hasta que llegó al cabo de la Vela. Y porque allí se vio una gran canoa o piragua de indios que iba a la vela, púsole nombre a aquella tierra el cabo de la Vela, en Tierra Firme. Desde el cual cabo a la dicha punta de las Salinas y Boca del Drago, hay ciento y ochenta leguas, poco más o menos. Y desde aquel cabo de la Vela atravesó el golfo que hay entre Tierra Firme y esta isla Española, y vino a esta ciudad, que en aquel tiempo estaba de la otra parte de este río. Está aquel cabo de la Vela, Norte Sur con la isla Beata, que es una isleta acerca de esta isla de Haití o Española, al Poniente de esta ciudad treinta y cinco leguas.

3.17.5. Así que éste fue el tercer viaje y descubrimiento que hizo el primero Almirante de estas Indias. Mas porque se dijo más arriba que en Cubagua halló la pesquería de las perlas, y es cosa tan notable y rica, se dirá de qué manera supo que allí las había, cuando en particular trataremos de esta isla.

[3.18] Libro III, cap. iv: De lo que el Adelantado don Bartolomé hizo, en tanto que el

Almirante fue a España, hasta que tornó a esta ciudad después que descubrió parte de la Tierra Firme. Y de la gobernación del Almirante hasta su prisión, y de los reyes o señores que había en esta isla.[24]

3.18.1. En el capítulo anterior se dijo el tercer viaje del Almirante don Cristóbal Colón, hasta que volvió a esta ciudad de Santo Domingo. Y ahora es de saber que en tanto que él estuvo en España y en el descubrimiento de parte de la costa y tierra grande y firme, y de las otras islas que se dijo en el capítulo precedente, no venían navíos de España ni de acá iban a ella Y como los que habían ido de acá con el Almirante (y antes sin él), y habían padecido los trabajos que se han dicho, e iban enfermos y pobres, y de tan mala color que parecían muertos, infamose mucho esta tierra e Indias, y no se hallaba gente que quisiese venir a ellas.

3.18.2. Por cierto, yo vi muchos de los que en aquella sazón volvieron a Castilla, con tales gestos que me parece que aunque el rey me diera sus Indias, quedando tal como aquéllos quedaron, no me determinara de venir a ellas. Y no era de maravillar si tales quedaban algunos, sino cómo pudo vivir o escapar hombre de todos ellos, mudándose a tierras tan apartadas de sus patrias, y dejando todos los regalos de los manjares con que se criaron, y desterrándose de los deudos y amigos, y faltando las medicinas, y por otras causas y necesidades que no se podrían acabar de expresar sin prolija relación.

3.18.3. Y como faltaba ya la gente, y no dejaban irse a España sino los que no podían o por falta de navíos, y de la vuelta del Almirante ninguna certidumbre se tenía, estaba ya casi perdida esta tierra y tenida por inútil, y con mucho temor los que acá estaban. Y sin duda se perdieran, sino fueran socorridos de aquellas tres carabelas que vinieron de España con gente (que dije que el Almirante envió desde la isla de Canaria) y trajeron, más, trescientos hombres sentenciados y desterrados para esta isla, los cuales llegaron en tal sazón que así los tales como los /24 recto/ que los trajeron, juntados con esos pocos que acá estaban, fueron causa que la tierra no se despoblase y se sostuviese; pues los cristianos no osaban ya salir de esta ciudad ni pasar el río para esta otra parte o costa de él. Y puédese afirmar que por este socorro fue restaurada la vida de los que acá estaban, y se sostuvo y no se perdió totalmente esta isla; porque entre aquella gente hubo muchos hombres valientes y especiales personas.

3.18.4. Y así, luego que los indios descercaron la ciudad de la Concepción de la Vega, y a esta ciudad y su fortaleza (estando de la otra parte de este río, donde primero fue fundada), y los indios perdieron la esperanza que tenían de ver la tierra sin los cristianos. En especial viendo desde a poco tiempo después venir al Almirante con otras tres carabelas, y muy buena gente en ellas, dejando ya descubiertas las islas y parte de la Tierra Firme y las Perlas, según se dijo en el capítulo antes de éste. El cual, llegado a esta ciudad (que estaba, como he dicho, de la otra parte de este río, enfrente de donde ahora está), halló al Adelantado, su hermano, y a los otros cristianos que con él estaban en paz; pero no muy contentos algunos de ellos por la ausencia de Roldán Jiménez, y con las murmuraciones que suele haber en esta tierra, porque quedaban algunos aficionados o infeccionados de las pasiones viejas del tiempo de

[24]Oviedo 1535: fols. 23 verso–24 verso / Oviedo 1959: 1.60–62.

fray Buyl. Mas todos obedecieron y recibieron al Almirante con alegre semblante y le dieron la obediencia como a virrey y gobernador que en nombre de los Católicos Reyes venía.

3.18.5. Y ejerciendo su oficio y gobernación como él mejor podía, nunca faltaron quejosos de sus obras, porque les parecía que así como favorecía y ayudaba a unos, así ofendía o maltrataba a otros. Angélico ha de ser el gobernador que a todos contentare, y más que humano, porque unos hombres son inclinados a vicios, y otros a virtudes; unos a trabajar y ejercitar las personas, y otros al reposo y quietud; unos a gastar, y otros a guardar; y unos a una cosa, y otros a otra. Y así, el que gobierna no puede contentar a tantos géneros de inclinaciones, porque unos quieren la guerra y robar y no poblar la tierra, sino darle un repelón y volverse donde le esperan y desea acabar sus días. Otros que querrían lo contrario y asentar y arraigarse, no les dan con qué ni les favorecen. Y así como son diversos los fines de los hombres, y tan difícil cosa entenderlos, así el que gobierna es menester que tenga especial ventura y favor de Dios para ser amado; no obstante que mucho está en la mano del que puede mandar para que le quieran bien los gobernados. Y si uno estuviere desabrido, muchos estarán satisfechos con que solamente tenga tres cosas: recto en las cosas de justicia, liberal y sin codicia. Volvamos a nuestra historia.

3.18.6. En esta sazón dio orden en fundar, o mejor diciendo, reformar la ciudad de la Concepción de la Vega, y la villa de Santiago y la villa del Bonao. Estas tres poblaciones hizo el Almirante primer don Cristóbal Colón en esta isla; y primero que todas ellas la ciudad Isabela, de la cual se pasó la gente a dar principio a esta ciudad de Santo Domingo, como se dijo en el segundo libro. Y estando las cosas en este estado, tornó el Almirante don Cristóbal en España. Y los Reyes Católicos, teniéndose por muy servidos de él, le confirmaron otra vez sus privilegios, en la ciudad de Burgos, a veintitrés días de abril de mil y cuatrocientos y noventa y siete años.

3.18.7. Mas porque para lo que se espera proseguir adelante en la Historia, conviene que se diga qué reyes o príncipes tenían el señorío de esta isla de Haití, que ahora llamamos Española, digo que aquí hubo (según yo supe de los testigos que tengo alegado, y por las memorias que yo he compilado desde que en Barcelona, año de mil y cuatrocientos y noventa y tres, vi los primeros indios y a Colón en la corte de los Reyes Católicos), cinco prefectos o reyes, que los indios llaman caciques, que mandaban y señoreaban toda la isla. Debajo de los cuales había otros caciques de menor señorío, que obedecían a alguno de los cinco principales. Y así, todos cinco eran obedecidos de los inferiores que mandaban o eran de su jurisdicción y señorío, y aquellos menores venían a sus llamamientos de paz o de guerra, como los superiores ordenaban, y mandábanles lo que querían. Los nombres de los cinco eran éstos: Guarionex, Caonabo, Behechio, Goacanagari, Cayacoa.

3.18.8. Guarionex tenía todo lo llano y señoreaba más de sesenta leguas en el medio de la isla. Behechio tenía la parte occidental y la tierra y provincia de Xaraguá, en cuyo señorío cae aquel gran lago de que en /24 verso/ adelante se dirá. El cacique o rey Goacanagari tenía su señorío a la parte del Norte, donde y en cuya tierra el Almirante dejó los treinta y ocho cristianos, cuando la primera vez vino a esta isla Cayacoa tenía la parte del Oriente de esta isla, hasta esta ciudad y hasta el río de

Haina, y hasta donde el río Yuna entra en la mar, o muy poco menos. Y en fin, era uno de los mayores señores de toda esta isla, y su gente era la más animosa por la vecindad que tenía de los caribes. Y éste murió desde a poco que los cristianos comenzaron a hacerle la guerra, y su mujer quedó en el estado y fue después cristiana, y se llamó Inés de Cayacoa. El rey Caonabo tenía su señorío en las sierras, y era gran señor y de mucha tierra. Este tenía un cacique por su capitán general en toda su tierra, y la mandaba en su nombre, que se decía Uxmatex el cual era bizco o bisojo, y era tan valiente hombre que le temían todos los otros caciques e indios de la isla. Este Caonabo casó con Anacaona, hermana del cacique Behechio, y siendo un caribe principal se vino a esta isla como capitán aventurero, y por el ser de su persona se casó con la susodicha e hizo su principal asiento donde ahora esta la villa de San Juan de la Maguana, y señoreó toda aquella provincia.

3.18.9. Nunca había ni acaecían guerras o diferencias entre los indios de esta isla sino por una de estas tres causas: sobre los términos y jurisdicción, o sobre las pesquerías, o cuando de las otras islas venian indios caribes flecheros a saltear. Y cuando estos extraños venían no eran sentidos, por muy enemigos y diferentes que los príncipes o principales caciques de esta isla estuviesen, luego se juntaban y eran conformes, y se ayudaban contra los que de fuera venían.

[3.19] Libro III, cap. vi: /26 recto/ De la venida del comendador Francisco de Bobadilla a gobernar esta isla Española, y de cómo envió preso en grillos al Almirante don Cristóbal Colón y al Adelantado don Bartolomé y don Diego, sus hermanos, con él. Y de los muchos indios que hubo en esta isla y las causas por qué se murieron o son casi acabados.[25]

3.19.1. Estuvo el Almirante en esta gobernación hasta el año de mil y cuatrocientos y noventa y nueve, que los Católicos Reyes don Fernando y doña Isabel, muy enojados, informados de lo que pasaba en esta isla y de la manera que el Almirante don Cristóbal Colón y su hermano el Adelantado don Bartolomé tenían en la gobernación, acordaron de enviar por gobernador de esta isla a un caballero, antiguo criado de la Casa Real, hombre muy honesto y religioso, llamado Francisco de Bobadilla, caballero de la orden militar de Calatrava. El cual, llegado a esta ciudad, luego prendió al Almirante y a sus hermanos, el Adelantado don Bartolomé y don Diego Colón, y los hizo embarcar en sendas carabelas. Y en grillos fueron llevados a España y entregados al alcaide o corregidor de la ciudad de Cádiz, hasta tanto que el Rey y la Reina mandasen lo que fuese su servicio cerca de su prisión y méritos. Quieren decir que al comendador Bobadilla no le mandaron prender al Almirante, ni había venido sino por juez de residencia, y para se informar del alzamiento de Roldán y sus consortes; pero en fin, mandándoselo o no, él prendió al Almirante y sus hermanos y los envió a España. Y quedó en el cargo y gobernación de esta isla este caballero, y la tuvo en mucha paz y justicia hasta el año de mil y quinientos y dos años, que fuere movido y se le dio licencia para tornar a España, aunque no fue su ventura de llegar a Castilla.

[25]Oviedo 1535: fol. 26 / Oviedo 1959: 1.65–67.

3.19.2. Y así como este caballero llegó a esta isla, luego el Roldán, que estaba apartado del Almirante, escribió al comendador, y se vinieron él y los otros cristianos que con él estaban en la provincia de Xaraguá, a servirle y estar en la obediencia que debían a los Reyes Católicos, cuyos vasallos eran. Y este Bobabilla envió muchas quejas e informaciones contra el Almirante y sus hermanos, significando las causas que le movieron a prenderlos; pero las más verdaderas quedábanse ocultas, porque siempre el Rey y la Reina quisieron más verle enmendado que maltratado. Pero diré lo que entonces algunos le oponían para culparle. Decíase que había querido tener secreto el descubrimiento de las perlas, y que nunca lo escribió hasta que él sintió que en España se sabía, y habían ido a la isla de Cubagua ciertos marineros llamados los Niños, y que esto lo hacía a fin de capitular de nuevo. Decían, asimismo, que era muy soberbio y ultrajoso, y que trataba mal a los servidores y criados de la Casa Real, y que mostraba ser absoluto, y que no obedecía, de las cartas y mandamientos de sus reyes, sano aquello que él quería, y que con lo de demás disimulaba y hacía su voluntad.

3.19.3. Todo esto cuentan otros de otra manera, y dicen que la muestra de las primeras perlas que se hubieron la envió el Almirante a los Reyes Católicos, luego que las descubrió, con un hidalgo dicho Arroyal. Y lo más cierto de todo fue que nunca faltaron en el mundo murmuradores y envidiosos. Y como esta tierra está lejos de su rey, y los que acá vienen son hijos de diferentes provincias y contrarios deseos y opiniones, así sienten las cosas diferenciadamente: unos con buen celo del servicio de Dios y del rey, pareciéndoles que el Almirante usaba absolutamente en la justicia y en todo lo demás, aunque la voz fuese en nombre de los Católicos Reyes, no quisieran tanta rigurosidad. Otros, por diversos fines o pasiones, pintáronle de tal manera con sus cartas, que, por ordenarlo así Dios, se efectuó la prisión del Almirante y de sus hermanos, y los llevaron a España, según he dicho. A esto dio mucho lugar la poca paciencia del Almirante y estar muy mal quisto y en posesión de crudo.

3.19.4. Llegado en España, así como el Rey y la Reina lo supieron, /26 verso/ enviaron a mandar que lo soltasen a él y a sus hermanos, y que se fuesen a la corte, y así lo hicieron. Y así como fue suelto el Almirante fue a besar las manos al Rey y a la Reina, y con lágrimas refirió sus disculpas lo mejor que él pudo. Y después que le oyeron, con mucha clemencia le consolaron y le dijeron tales palabras que él quedó algo contento. Y como sus servicios eran tan señalados, aunque en algo se hubiese desordenado, no pudo comportar la Real Majestad de tan agradecidos príncipes que el Almirante fuese maltratado. Y por tanto, le mandaron luego acudir con todas las rentas y derechos que acá tenía, que se los habían embargado y detenido cuando fue preso. Pero nunca más dieron lugar que tornase al cargo de la gobernación.

3.19.5. Mas como era prudente hombre, luego que a España fue con las nuevas del primer descubrimiento, suplicó a los Reyes Católicos que hubiesen por bien que sus hijos el príncipe don Juan los recibiese por pajes suyos. Los cuales eran don Diego Colón, hijo legítimo y mayor del Almirante, y otro su hijo don Fernando Colón, que hoy vive. El cual es virtuoso caballero, y demás de ser de mucha nobleza y afabilidad y dulce conversación, es docto en diversas ciencias, y en especial en cosmografía, y de quien la Católica Majestad hace cuenta, méritamente, como de tan buen criado y servidor, porque los servicios del Almirante, su padre, así lo piden. Y así, el príncipe don Juan trató bien a estos sus hijos, y eran de él favorecidos, y anduvieron en su casa hasta que Dios le llevó a su gloria en la ciudad de Salamanca, año de mil y cuatrocientos y noventa y siete.

3.19.6. Así que, tornando a la historia, después que el Almirante fue perdonado no le trataron menos bien el Rey y la Reina que primero. Y como era sabio procuró, por todas las vías que él pudo, de tornar a la gracia de aquellos buenos príncipes, y que le diesen licencia de volver a estas Indias. Pero como eran muchas las quejas que hubo contra él no lo pudo acabar tan pronto; y en tanto gobernó esta isla el comendador Bobadilla hasta el año de mil y quinientos y dos, según he dicho. En el cual tiempo se sacó mucho oro en las minas de esta isla, porque había muchos indios que andaban en ellas sacándolo para los cristianos y para los Reyes Católicos, que también mandaban tener sus propias haciendas y granjerías en su real nombre.

3.19.7. Todos los indios de esta isla fueron repartidos y encomendados por el Almirante a todos los pobladores que a estas partes se vinieron a vivir. Y es opinión de muchos que lo vieron y hablan en ello como testigos de vista, que halló el Almirante, cuando estas islas descubrió, un millón de indios e indias, o más, de todas edades, o entre chicos y grandes. De los cuales todos, y de los que después nacieron, no se cree que hay al presente en este año de mil y quinientos y cuarenta y ocho,[26] quinientas personas, entre chicos y grandes, que sean naturales y de la progenie o estirpe de aquellos primeros. Porque los más que ahora hay son traídos por los cristianos de otras islas, o de la Tierra Firme, para servirse de ellos. Pues como las minas eran muy ricas y la codicia de los hombres insaciable, trabajaron algunos excesivamente a los indios; otros no les dieron tan bien de comer como convenía; y junto con esto, esta gente, de su natural, es ociosa y viciosa, y de poco trabajo, y melancólicos, y cobardes, viles y mal inclinados, mentirosos y de poca memoria, y de ninguna constancia. Muchos de ellos, por su pasatiempo, se mataron con ponzoña por no trabajar, y otros se ahorcaron por sus menos propias, y a otros se les recrecieron tales dolencias, en especial de unas viruelas pestilenciales que vinieron generalmente en toda la isla, que en breve tiempo los indios se acabaron (. . .).

[3.20] Libro III, cap. vii: /27 verso/ De la venida del Comendador Mayor de Alcántara, don fray Nicolás de Ovando, el cual gobernó esta isla, y de la partida del comendador Francisco de Bobadilla, el cual con toda la flota se perdió en la mar con mucho oro. Y del aviso que dio el Almirante al Comendador Mayor para que no dejase salir la flota de este puerto, como hombre que conocía la disposición del tiempo, y por no creerle ni dejar entrar aquí, se perdió el armada y mucha gente.[27]

3.20.1. A la sazón que el Comendador de Jerez, don fray Nicolás de Ovando, de la

[26]In fol. 26 verso of the Seville edition Oviedo gives the date 1535 as the moment of writing. According to Muñoz (Oviedo ca. 1780) this section of the original manuscript with the later additions was already lost when they saw it. However, both Amador and Pérez Tudela (Oviedo 1851–1855: 1.71 / Oviedo 1959: 1.66) give the date 1548 instead of 1535. Their source has not been found yet, and the new date may well be a mistake of Amador de los Ríos.

[27]Oviedo 1535: fols. 27 verso–28 verso / Oviedo 1959: 1.69–70.

Orden y caballería militar de Alcántara, pasó a esta ciudad e isla, no era Comendador Mayor de su Orden, que después, estando acá, vacó la Encomienda Mayor de Alcántara por muerte de don Alonso de Santillán, y el Rey Católico le envió el título y merced de la Encomienda Mayor al dicho Comendador de Jerez, que acá estaba algunos años había. Y por tanto, no le llamaré en todo lo que de él tratare sino Comendador Mayor. El cual, por mandado del Rey y Reina Católicos, vino a esta isla con treinta naves y carabelas, y muy hermosa armada. Y vinieron con él muchos caballeros e hidalgos, y gente noble de diversas partes de los /28 recto/ reinos de Castilla y de León. Porque en tanto que la Católica Reina doña Isabel vivió, no se admitían ni dejaban pasar a las Indias sino a los propios súbditos y vasallos de los señoríos del patrimonio de la Reina, como quiera que aquéllos fueron los que las Indias descubrieron, y no aragoneses, ni catalanes, ni valencianos, o vasallos del patrimonio real del Rey Católico; salvo, por especial merced, a algún criado y persona conocida de la Casa Real, se le daba licencia, no siendo castellano. Porque como estas Indias son de la corona y conquista de Castilla, así quería la serenísima reina que solamente sus vasallos pasasen a estas partes y no otros algunos, si no fuese por hacerles muy señalada merced. Y así se guardó hasta el fin del año del mil y quinientos y cuatro que Dios la llevó a su gloria. Mas después el Rey Católico, gobernando los reinos de la serenísima reina doña Juana, su hija, nuestra señora, dio licencia a los aragoneses y a todos sus vasallos, que pasasen a estas partes con oficios y como le plugo. Y después la Cesárea Majestad extendió más la licencia, y pasan ahora de todos sus señoríos, y de todas aquellas partes y vasallos que están debajo de su monarquía.

3.20.2. Partió, pues, el Comendador Mayor desde España, año de mil y quinientos y dos años, y llegó a esta ciudad de Santo Domingo a quince de abril de aquel año, estando poblada esta vecindad de la otra parte de este río Ozama. Y luego fue obedecido por gobernador y el comendador Bobadilla, que lo había sido, dio orden en su partida, porque los Reyes Católicos le removieron del cargo y le dieron licencia que se fuese a España, teniéndose muy servidos de él en el tiempo que acá estuvo, porque había rectamente y como buen caballero hecho su oficio en todo lo que le tocó a su cargo. Y así se partió para Castilla en la flota y armada en que había venido el Comendador Mayor. Mas como habían sacado mucho oro, llevábanse en aquel viaje sobre cien mil pesos de oro fundido y marcado, y algunos granos gruesos por fundir para que en España se viesen. Porque aunque ya otras veces se había llevado oro para los Reyes Católicos, y de personas particulares, nunca hasta entonces en un viaje había ido tanto oro, juntamente fundido y por fundir y en algunos granos señalados. Entre los cuales iba un grano que pesaba tres mil y seiscientos pesos de oro, y al parecer de hombres entendidos y expertos mineros, decían que no tenía de piedra tres libras, que son seis marcos, que montan trescientos pesos. Así que, descontado lo que podría haber de piedra, quedaría el grano en tres mil y trescientos pesos de oro, y era tan grande como una hogaza de Utrera. Y porque dije en la memoria que escribí en Toledo, año de mil y quinientos y veinticinco años, que este grano pesaba tres mil y doscientos pesos, y aquello se escribió sin ver mis memoriales y teniéndome atrás de lo que pudiera decir en muchas cosas, ahora digo (pues estoy donde hay muchos testigos vivos que vieron aquel grano), que pesaba algo más de tres mil y seiscientos pesos según que dije más arriba, con piedra y oro. El cual halló una india de Miguel Díaz, del cual se dijo que fue causa que esta ciudad se poblase aquí, de la otra parte de este río. Y porque éste tenía compañía con Francisco de Garay, quedó el grano de ambos, y sobre lo que montó el quinto que perteneció al rey, sacados los derechos, se les pagó la demasía y quedó el grano para el Rey y la Reina, y llevándole aquella armada, se perdió. Y era tan grande, que así como la india que lo halló lo enseñó a los cristianos mineros, ellos, muy alegres, acordaron de almorzar o comer un lechón bueno y gordo, y dijo el uno de ellos: "Mucho tiempo ha que yo he tenido esperanza que comeré en plato de oro, y pues de este grano se pueden hacer muchos platos, quiero cortar este lechón sobre él. Y así lo hizo; y sobre aquel rico plato lo comieron, y cabía el lechón entero en él, porque era tan grande como he dicho.

3.20.3. Tornando a la historia: partió el comendador Bobadilla en fuerte hora y con mala ventura, y con él Antonio de Torres, hermano del ama del príncipe, que era capitán general de la flota en que el Comendador Mayor había venido. Y estando para partir acaeció que uno o dos días antes que el armada saliese de este puerto, llegó el Almirante primero don Cristóbal Colón, con cuatro carabelas, que venía a descubrir por mandado de los Reyes Católicos, y traía consigo a don Fernando Colón, su hijo menor. Y como llegó a una /28 verso/ legua de este puerto de Santo Domingo, envió allá el Comendador Mayor un batel con ciertos marineros. Y créese que estaba avisado de su venida, y aun prevenido para que no entrase aquí. Y como el Almirante sintió esto, envió a decir al Comendador Mayor que, pues no quería que entrase en lo que había descubierto, que fuese como lo mandaba, que él no pensaba que de aquello se servían los Reyes Católicos. Mas que le pedía por merced al Comendador Mayor, que no dejase salir el armada de este puerto, porque el tiempo no le parecía bien, que él se iba a buscar puerto seguro, pues aquí no le hallaba ni le acogían. Y así se fue con sus carabelas a Puerto Escondido, que es en esta isla, a diez leguas de esta ciudad de Santo Domingo, en la costa o banda del Sur, al Occidente, y allí estuvo hasta que pasó la tormenta que adelante diré. Y después de pasada, atravesó desde allí para la costa de Tierra Firme, y descubrió lo que se dirá adelante en su lugar. Otros dicen que se fue a Azúa, y que allí estuvo el Almirante hasta que pasó la tormenta.

[3.21] Libro III, cap. viii: De lo que descubrieron en la costa de Tierra Firme los capitanes Alonso de Hojeda y Rodrigo de Bastidas.[28]

3.21.1. En el tiempo que estuvo en Espada el Almirante primero, se siguió que el capitán Alonso de Hojeda, con favor del obispo don Juan Rodríguez de Fonseca (que era el principal que entendía en la gobernación de estas Indias), vino a descubrir por la costa de Tierra Firme, y trajo su derrota a reconocer debajo del río Marañón, en la provincia de Paria, y llegó a tomar tierra ocho leguas encima de donde ahora está la población de Santa Marta, en una provincia que se decía Cinta. Y era allí cacique uno llamado Ayaro, el cual quedó de paces y muy amigo de los cristianos, al cual después tomó por engaño, y no bien haciéndolo, otro capitán dicho Cristóbal Guerra. Esto fue

[28]Oviedo 1535: fols. 28 verso–29 recto / Oviedo 1959: 1.70–72.

año de mil y quinientos y uno.

3.21.2. Pero no fueron solos estos armadores, porque el capitán Rodrigo de Bastidas corrió desde el cabo de la Vela (donde el Almirante había llegado cuando descubrió la costa de la Tierra Firme), y pasó adelante al Poniente, como se dirá en su lugar. Porque sin culpa mía no podría callar lo que a mi noticia ha venido de lo que señaladamente ha hecho cada uno en estas partes, que sea digno de acuerdo. Por tanto, digo que Rodrigo de Bastidas salió de España año de mil y quinientos y dos, con dos carabelas, desde el puerto o bahía de la ciudad de Cádiz, a su costa y de Juan de Ledesma y otros sus amigos. Y la primera tierra que tomaron fue una isla, que por ser muy fresca y de muy grandes arboledas, la llamaron Isla Verde; la cual isla está a la banda o parte que hay desde la isla de Guadalupe hacia la Tierra Firme, y cerca de las otras islas que en aquel paraje hay. Y de allí, levantados estos navíos, fueron por la costa de la Tierra Firme, y platicando con los indios en diversas partes de ella, hubieron hasta cuarenta marcos de oro. Y discurrieron por la costa, la vía del Poniente, por delante del puerto de Santa Marta, desde el cabo de la Vela, y por delante del río Grande. Y más adelante descubrió el mismo capitán Rodrigo de Bastidas el puerto de Zamba, y los Coronados, que es una tierra donde todos los indios de ella traen muy grandes coronas. Y más al Occidente descubrió el puerto que llaman de Cartagena, y descubrió las islas de San Bernardo y las de Baru, y las que llaman islas de Arenas, que están enfrente y cerca de la dicha Cartagena. Y de ahí pasó adelante y descubrió a Isla Fuerte, que es una isla llana, dos leguas de la costa de Tierra Firme, donde se hace mucha sal y buena. Y más adelante está la isla de la Tortuga; ésta muy pequeña y no poblada. Y más adelante descubrió el puerto de Cení; y pasó más adelante y descubrió la punta de Caribana, que está a la boca del golfo de Urabá, y entró dentro del mismo golfo y vio los isleos o farallones que están en la otra costa frontera, junto a tierra, en la provincia del Darién. Y como allí llegó, acabó de descubrir las ciento y treinta leguas que he dicho, poco más o menos, que hay desde el cabo de la Vela hasta allí. Y cuando el agua fue de bajamar, hallóla dulce en cuatro brazas donde pudo estar surgido, y llamó golfo Dulce aquel que se llama de Urabá. Pero no vio el río de San Juan, que también le llaman río Grande, que entra por siete bocas o siete brazos en el dicho golfo, el cual es causa que se torne dulce el agua de la mar, y en más espacio de doce leguas de largo y otras cuarenta y cinco, y en partes seis, de ancho que hay de costa a costa, dentro en el dicho golfo de Urabá; de lo cual y del dicho río se dirán más particularidades adelante, porque yo he estado algunos años en aquella tierra. En este viaje iba por piloto principal Juan de la Cosa, que fue muy, excelente hombre de la mar.

3.21.3. En aquel golfo estuvieron estos armadores algunos días, y como sus navíos estaban muy bromados y hacían mucha agua, acordaron de dar la vuelta y atravesaron a la isla de Jamaica, donde tomaron refresco. Y de allí fueron a la isla Española, y entraron en el golfo de Xaraguá, y allí perdieron los navíos, que no los podían sostener. Y salió la gente en tierra y fuéronse a la ciudad de Santo Domingo, donde hallaron al comendador /29 recto/ Bobadilla, que ya tenía preso al Almirante. Y también prendió al dicho capitán Bastidas porque había rescatado con los indios de la misma isla Española, y envióle preso a España en el mismo navío que el Almirante fue llevado, porque la una prisión y la otra fueron casi a un tiempo. Pero luego el Rey y la Reina le mandaron soltar, y por este servicio, que fue grande y hecho a propia costa del mismo capitán Rodrigo de Bastidas, y otros sus amigos, como he dicho, los Católicos Reyes le hicieron merced de cincuenta mil maravedís de juro de por vida en aquella tierra y provincia del Darién.

3.21.4. Todo lo que descubrió Bastidas en este viaje, hasta la punta de Caribana, es de indios flecheros y de la más recia gente de la Tierra Firme, y tales son desde el cabo de la Vela al Oriente, hasta la punta de las Salinas y Boca del Dragón, y todo lo que el primero Almirante había descubierto en Tierra Firme. Y tiran, en toda la dicha costa e islas de ella, con hierba muy mala e irremediable, y si hay remedio, los cristianos no le saben. En su lugar se dirá de qué manera o con qué materiales hacen los indios esta ponzoñosa hierba; y por no detenerme ahora en esto, tornaré al Almirante y a su descubrimiento.

[3.22] Libro III, cap. ix: Que trata de cómo se perdió el armada con el comendador Bobadilla, y del último viaje y descubrimiento que hizo el Almirante don Cristóbal Colón en la Tierra Firme.[29]

3.22.1. Dicho tengo en el capítulo vii de este libro, cómo el Almirante llegó cerca del puerto de esta ciudad, viniendo de España para ir a descubrir lo que descubrió en su último viaje de la Tierra Firme, yendo a buscar el estrecho que él decía que había de hallar para pasar a la mar Austral (en lo cual se engañó, porque el estrecho que él pensaba ser de mar, es de tierra, como se dirá delante). Pero no le fue dado lugar por el Comendador Mayor para que entrase en este puerto de esta ciudad de Santo Domingo. Por lo cual, después, el Almirante envió a avisar que el tiempo estaba de manera que le parecía que el comendador Bobadilla y la armada que con él estaba aparejada para ir a España, en ninguna manera debía partir de esta ciudad. Mas, como no se le dio crédito, sucedió de ello lo que aquí diré. Y el Almirante, como prudente nauta, se cogió a Puerto Escondido, y pasada la tormenta tiró para el descubrimiento de la Tierra Firme. Y como ya él tenía noticia que el capitán Rodrigo de Bastidas había descubierto hasta el golfo de Urabá (que está en nueve grados y medio la punta de Caribana, que es a la boca de aquel golfo), pasóse adelante a descubrir la costa de Tierra Firme más al Poniente. Lo cual en este capítulo se dirá, porque no quiero olvidar la muerte del comendador Bobadilla y del capitán de la flota, Antonio de Torres, hermano del ama del príncipe, lo cual pasó de esta manera.

3.22.2. Partieron estos caballeros de este río y puerto de esta ciudad de Santo Domingo, por no haber tomado el consejo del Almirante. Y salida el armada a la mar, ocho o diez leguas de aquí, dioles tal tiempo que de treinta naos y carabelas no escaparon más de cuatro o cinco, y dieron al través todas las de demás por estas costas, y muchas se hundieron y las tragó la mar, que jamás parecieron. Y anegáronse más de quinientos hombres, entre los cuales eran los más principales los que tengo dicho, y asimismo aquel Roldán Jiménez, que se había alzado contra el Almirante y Adelantado, su hermano. Y se ahogaron asimismo otros gentiles hombres, hidalgos y

[29]Oviedo 1535: fols. 29 recto–30 verso / Oviedo 1959: 1.72–75.

muy buena gente. Y allí se perdió aquel grano de oro que dije que pesaba tres mil y seiscientos pesos, con más de otros cien mil pesos de oro y otras muchas cosas. Así que fue muy gran pérdida y mala jornada.

3.22.3. El Almirante, como conoció el tiempo, recogióse al Puerto Escondido, el cual nombre él le puso. Y desde allí, así como fue pasada la tormenta, atravesó la vuelta de Tierra Firme, y no corrió riesgo, según pareció por el efecto, porque descubrió, debajo de lo que tengo dicho que costeó Bastidas, según yo oí a los pilotos Pedro de Umbría y Diego Martín Cabrera y Martín de los Reyes, y a otros que se hallaron en ello, lo que ahora diré. El Almirante fue a reconocer la isla de Jamaica, y de allí pasó y fue a reconocer el cabo de Higueras y las islas de los Guanajes (una de las cuales se dice Guanaja), y fue a Puerto de Honduras, a la cual tierra llamó y puso nombre Punta de Cajines, y de allí fue al cabo de Gracias a Dios, y tiró la vuelta del Levante, la costa arriba de Tierra Firme, y descubrió la provincia y río de Veragua, y pasó a otro río grande, que está más al Oriente, y llamóle río de Belén. Este está una legua del río que los indios llaman Yebra, que es el mismo de Veragua: la cual se cree que es una de las más ricas cosas que hay en todo lo descubierto. Y de ahí, subiendo la costa al Oriente, llegó a un gran río, y llamóle río de Lagartos. Este es el que los cristianos ahora llaman Chagre, que nace cerca de la mar del sur, aunque viene a fenecer en la del Norte, y pasa a cuatro leguas de Panamá. Y de allí, discurriendo, llegó a una isla que está junto a la costa de la Tierra Firme, y llamóla isla de Bastimentos, y a Puerto Bello. /29 verso/ Y de allí pasó por delante del Nombre de Dios (el cual nombre puso después a aquel puerto el capitán Diego de Nicuesa, como se dirá en su lugar). Y pasó el Almirante al río de Francisca y al puerto del Retrete; y de allí subió hasta el golfo de Secativa, y llamólo golfo de San Blas; y subió más por la costa, hasta las islas de Pocorosa, y allí llamó el Almirante a aquel lo el cabo del Mármol. Por manera que de este camino, que fue el último que el Almirante hizo a estas partes, descubrió de la Tierra Firme ciento y noventa o doscientas leguas de costa, poco más o menos.

3.22.4. Y desde allí atravesó a la isla de Jamaica, la cual está, del cabo de Gracias a Dios, la vuelta del Nordeste, cien leguas. Y allí se le perdieron los dos navíos, que los traía ya muy cansados y bromados; y de cuatro que había llevado, el uno dejó perdido en el río de Yebra (que es en la provincia de Veragua), y el otro le dejó en la mar, porque no se podía tener sobre el agua, porque en aquellas costas de Tierra firme, como hay muchos y grandes ríos, así hay mucha broma en ellos, y presto se pierden los navíos. Pero en treinta días que atravesaron, fue a reconocer la tierra de Omohaya, que es en la isla de Cuba, de la banda del Sur, casi al fin de la isla, donde ahora está poblada la villa de la Trinidad. Y desde allí fue a Jamaica, donde, como es dicho, perdió los otros dos navíos, y dio con ellos, zabordando en la costa, donde ahora dicen Sevilla. Y desde allí dio noticia de su venida al Comendador Mayor (que estaba en esta ciudad de Santo Domingo) con una canoa que envió de indios, y en ella a Diego Méndez, su criado, que es un hidalgo, hombre de honra, vecino de esta ciudad, que hoy día vive. El cual se atrevió a mucho, por ser la canoa muy pequeña, y porque fácilmente se trastornan en la mar tales canoas, y no son para engolfarse ninguno que ame su vida, sino para la costa y cerca de tierra. Pero él, como buen criado y hombre animoso, viendo a su señor en tanta necesidad, se aventuró y determinó y pasó toda la mar que hay desde aquella isla a ésta, con las cartas del Almirante para que el Comendador Mayor le socorriese y enviase por él. Por el cual servicio (que en la verdad fue muy señalado, cuanto se puede encarecer) el Almirante siempre le tuvo mucho amor y le favoreció. Y sabido por el Rey Católico, le hizo mercedes, y le dio por armas la misma canoa, por ejemplo de su lealtad. Y sin duda, en aquellos principios, meterse un hombre en la mar con sus enemigos, siendo como son tan grandes nadadores, y en barca o pasaje tan peligroso e incierto, fue cosa de grande ánimo y de señalada lealtad y amor que a su señor tuvo.

3.22.5. Y como el Comendador Mayor vio las cartas del Almirante, envió luego una carabela a saber si era verdad, y para ver de la manera que estaba el Almirante y sentir la cosa, y no para traerlo. Pero el Diego Méndez compró un navío de los dineros del Almirante y abasteciόle, y envió por su señor, en que vino a esta isla, en tanto fue el Diego Méndez fue a Castilla a dar la noticia al Rey y Reina Católicos de lo que el Almirante había hecho en aquel viaje.

3.22.6. No es razón de dejar en silencio lo que al Almirante intervino en aquella isla, después de haber enviado a Diego Méndez a ésta como es dicho, a dar noticia de su quedada allí, porque es cosa memorable y para ser notado lo que ahora diré. Es de saber que, así de los trabajos que su gente y marineros habían pasado en este descubrimiento, como en haber pasado por tan diferentes regiones, y con tan malas comidas y falta de reposo, había muchos enfermos. Y los que estaban sanos se le amotinaron, inducidos a ello por dos hermanos que allí iban, llamados Francisco de Porras, capitán de un navío de aquéllos, y Diego de Porras, contador de aquella armada. Los cuales tomaron todas las canoas que los indios tenían, y publicaron que el Almirante no quería ir a Castilla, porque les había dicho que esperasen la respuesta de Diego Méndez y que enviase navíos que los llevasen a todos. Pero ellos, mal aconsejados, no queriendo obedecer su mandado, se fueron y metieron en la mar, pensando atravesar y venir en las canoas a esta isla Española. Y aunque muchas veces lo tentaron, no pudieron salir con su intención, antes, porfiándolo, se anegaron algunos de los compañeros que a éstos seguían. Por lo cual acordaron, los que de ellos quedaron, de volver donde el Almirante quedaba, con determinación de tomarle los navíos que se hubiesen venido. Mas en tanto que los alzados /30 recto/ y desobedientes entendían en lo que es dicho, cobraron salud los que habían quedado enfermos, y en compañía del Almirante, aunque eran pocos en número. Y como fue entendida la malicia, mandó el Almirante al Adelantado don Bartolomé, su hermano, que saliese al campo a resistir el mal propósito de los contrarios. Y peleó con ellos y los desbarató y venció, y mató tres o cuatro de ellos, y otros muchos quedaron heridos. Y ésta fue la primera batalla que se sabe haber habido entre cristianos en estas partes e Indias. Y el Francisco y Diego de Porras fueron presos.

3.22.7. Antes que esta batalla y diferencias sucediesen, como los indios vieron que los que estaban sanos de los cristianos se habían ido y dejado al Almirante, y que los que con él habían quedado eran pocos y enfermos, no les querían dar de comer ni otra cosa alguna. Y viendo esto el Almirante, hizo juntar a muchos de los indios y díjoles que si no le daban de comer a él y a los cristianos, que tuviesen por cierto que había de venir muy presto una pestilencia tan grande que no quedase indio alguno de ellos, y que por señal de esto, y de la pestilencia; y vertimiento de sangre que habría en ellos, verían tal día (que él las señaló) y a tal hora, la luna hecha sangre. Esto dijo él porque, como era gentil astrólogo, sabía que había de ser eclipse de la luna cuando les había dicho. Llegado, pues, el tiempo, como vieron los indios eclipsada la luna, creyeron lo que el Almirante les había dicho, y muchos de ellos fueron dando voces y llorando a pedir perdón y rogar al Almirante que no estuviese enojado. Y diéronle a él y a los que con el estaban cuanto querían y habían menester de sus mantenimientos, y sirviéronle muy bien.

3.22.8. En esta manera de vida trabajosa estuvo el Almirante y los cristianos que le quedaron, un año, durmiendo y habitando en los navíos que estaban al través, anegados hasta la cubierta, dentro del agua de la mar, junto a tierra, y dentro del puerto donde ahora está la villa de Sevilla, que es la principal población de aquella isla. Y allí cerca fue la batalla que es dicho, y el puerto se dice Santa Gloria.

3.22.9. Pasado lo que es dicho, llegó la carabela que Diego Méndez envió por el Almirante, y cuando se embarcaba en ella, lloraban los indios porque se iba, porque pensaban que él y los cristianos eran gentes celestiales.

3.22.10. Llegado el Almirante a esta ciudad de Santo Domingo, estuvo algunos días descansando aquí. Y festejóle el Comendador Mayor y túvole en su posada, hasta que después se partió el Almirante, en los primeros navíos que fueron a España, a dar cuenta al Rey Católico de lo que él había hecho en este su postrero descubrimiento de parte de la Tierra Firme. Y de aquel camino, después que volvió a Castilla, como ya era viejo y enfermo, y muy apasionado de gota, murió en Valladolid, año de la Natividad de Cristo de mil y quinientos y seis años, en el mes de mayo, estando el Rey Católico en Villafranca de Valcázar, a la sazón que el serenísimo rey don Felipe y la serenísima reina doña Juana venían a reinar en Castilla.

3.22.11. Así que, muerto el Almirante donde es dicho, fue llevado su cuerpo a Sevilla, al monasterio que está a la otra parte del Guadalquivir, llamado las Cuevas, de la Orden de la Cartuja, y allí se puso en depósito. ¡Plegue a Dios de tenerle en su gloria! (. . .) porque, demás de lo que sirvió a los reyes de Castilla, mucho es lo que todos los españoles le deben; porque, aunque en estas partes han padecido y muerto muchos de ellos en las conquistas y pacificación de estas Indias, otros muchos quedaron ricos y remediados. Y lo que mejor es, que, en tierras tan apartadas de Europa, y donde el diablo era tan servido y acatado, le hayan los cristianos desterrado de ella, y plantado y ejercitado la sagrada fe católica nuestra e Iglesia de Dios en partes tan remotas y extrañas, y de tan grandes reinos y señoríos, por medio e industria del Almirante don Cristóbal Colón. Y que, demás de esto, se hayan llevado y llevarán tantos tesoros de oro, y plata, y perlas, y otras muchas riquezas y mercaderías a España. Por lo cual ningún virtuoso español se desacordará de tantos beneficios como su patria recibe y han resultado, mediante Dios, por la mano de este primero Almirante de estas Indias.

3.22.12. Al cual sucedió en su título y casa y estado el Almirante don Diego Colón, su hijo; el cual casó con doña María de Toledo, /30 verso/ sobrina del ilustre don Fadrique de Toledo, Comendador Mayor de León en la Orden militar de Santiago. En la cual hubo el Almirante don Diego Colón al Almirante don Luis Colón, que después heredó su casa y estado, y al presente lo tiene, y hubo otros hijos en esta señora.[30]

[3.23] Libro III, cap. xi.[31]

3.23.1. Ninguna cosa de esas e de otras muchas que se pueden decir en loor de Sicilia e de Inglaterra, no contradigo; pero ha de considerar el lector que todas esas cosas hacen a mi propósito, pues de tantos años aquellas islas están pobladas de gente de razón e con corte de príncipes e reyes tan señalados como en la una y en la otra ha habido; que tanto más se debe estimar nuestra isla (La Española) pues siempre ha estado en poder de gente salvaje y bestial e que su principio se puede contar desde el año de mil e cuatrocientos e noventa y dos años que los primeros cristianos aquí vinieron con el primero Almirante don Cristóbal Colón (que en este de mil e quinientos e cuarenta y siete, son cincuenta y cinco años).[32] Y en tan breve tiempo estar las cosas de esta isla en el estado que es dicho, hase de tener en mucho, e atribuirse solo a Dios e a la buena ventura de los Reyes Católicos de España y al invictísimo emperador don Carlos su nieto, nuestros príncipes e a la diligencia e virtud de sus milites y vasallos castellanos, con cuya industria e armas se ha poblado e, mediante Nuestro Señor, siempre se va más ennobleciendo.

[3.24] Libro IV, cap. i: /36 verso/ Donde se trata de la venida del segundo Almirante don Diego Colón, a esta ciudad de Santo Domingo, puerto de la isla Española, y de las mudanzas que ha habido en la gobernación de ella y otras cosas.[33]

3.24.1. Lo que dijo aquella serenísima Reina doña Isabel fue esto: cuando el primero Almirante, don Cristóbal Colón, hubo descubierto estas Indias, estando un día dando particular razón al Rey y a la Reina de las cosas y particularidades, que los árboles en esta tierra, por grandes que sean, no meten hondas debajo de tierra sus raíces, sino poco debajo de la superficie.

3.24.2. Y así es la verdad, porque además de aquella corteza o temple: que tiene la superficie del terreno (que puede ser medio estado, o poco más) poquísimos y raros árboles llegan las raíces un estado de hondo; porque allí adelante, o antes, hallan la tierra seca y cálida cuanto más ahondan; y como en lo alto está húmeda, en aquel lo poco se sustentan las árboles y se extienden y multiplican, y esparcen tantas raíces, o más, que tienen ramas, pero, como es dicho, no entran en lo hondo de la tierra. Verdad es que al árbol de la cañafístola sólo en estas partes llega hasta el agua con sus raíces; pero tales árboles no los vio Colón ni los había de esta cañafístola que se trajo para medicina, no obstante que en la mayor parte de las Indias hay cañafístolas salvajes,

[30]From bk. 3, chap. 11; Amador/Pérez de Tudela's text refers to the complete and revised edition which Oviedo was preparing and was never published.

[31]Oviedo ca. 1535–1549: Library of the Royal Academy of History of Madrid MS 9/551, fol. 5 verso / Oviedo 1959: 1.82. This passage appears in the manuscript as an addition to the core text. It was added, however, a bit later than the writing of the original text, sometime before the end of 1539.

[32]The figures deleted in the manuscript refer to a primitive version drafted in the late thirties which was updated three times: in the early forties (illegible), in 1545, and finally in 1547.

[33]Oviedo 1535: fols. 36 verso–37 recto / Oviedo ca. 1535–1549: Huntington Library MS HM 177, vol.2, fol. 14 verso / Oviedo 1959: 1.91.

como se dirá en su lugar.

3.24.3. Así que, tornando a la historia, como la Reina oyó lo que el Almirante había dicho, preguntóle que a qué atribuía el no meter los árboles /37 recto/ sus raíces en la tierra, sino tan poco como decía. Y él replicó que como en estas Indias llueve mucho y hay muchas aguas que templan la faz y superficie de la tierra, que aquello era la causa que los árboles, con poca hondura, se extendiesen en raíces y no las metiesen en la calor de lo muy bajo de la tierra, que de necesidad hallarían en lo hondo, por estar en tal clima esta tierra, y por eso había de ser más caliente en lo hondo y quemar las raíces que allá bajasen; las cuales, sintiendo esto, naturalmente se extendían por donde esta misma naturaleza las guía y les conviene extenderse para su nutrimiento. Después que la Reina le hubo escuchado, mostró haberle pesado lo que había oído y dijo estas palabras: En esa tierra donde los árboles no se arraigan, poca verda y menos constancia habrá en los hombres.

Por cierto, quien conociere, no podrá negar que la Reina Católica habló de lo que es dicho sino como más que filósofo natural y no adivinando, sino diciendo la misma verdad y como pasa. Porque esta generación de los indios es muy mentirosa y de poca constancia como son los muchachos de seis o siete años, e aun no tan constantes.[34]

[3.25] Libro V, cap. iii: /49 recto/ De los matrimonios de los indios, y cuántas mujeres tienen, en qué grados no toman mujeres ni las conocen carnalmente, y de sus vicios o lujuria, y con qué manera de religiosidad cogían el oro, y de la idolatría de estos indios y otras cosas notables.[35]

3.25.1. El Almirante don Cristóbal Colón, primero descubridor de estas partes, como católico capitán y buen gobernador, después que tuvo noticia de las minas de Cibao y vio que los indios cogían oro en el agua de los arroyos y ríos, sin cavarlo, con la ceremonia y religión que es dicho, no dejaba a los cristianos ir a coger oro sin que se confesasen y comulgasen. Y decía que, pues los indios estaban veinte días primero sin llegar a sus mujeres (ni otras), y apartados de ellas, y ayunaban, y decían ellos que cuando se veían con la mujer, que no hallaban el oro, por tanto que, pues aquellos indios bestiales hacían aquella solemnidad, que más era que los cristianos se apartasen de pecar y confesasen sus culpas, y que estando en gracia de Dios, nuestro Señor les daría más cumplidamente los bienes temporales y espirituales. Esta santimonia no placía a todos, porque decían que, cuanto a las mujeres, más apartados estaban que los indios los que las tenían en España. Y cuanto al ayunar, que muchos de los cristianos se morían de hambre y comían raíces /49 verso/ y otros malos manjares, y bebían agua. Y que cuanto a la confesión, que la Iglesia no los constreñía sino una vez en el año, por Pascua de Resurrección, y que así lo hacían todos, y algunos más veces; y que pues Dios no les pedía más, que le debía al Almirante bastar lo mismo y dejarlos

[34]In Oviedo 1535: "es la que más miente y en la que ninguna constancia se halla y más incapaces son que muchachos de seys o siete años y aun no tan ábiles." The correction moderating the terms in which the intellectual proficiency of the Indians was evaluated was made probably after 1541. The primitive draft of the manuscript still bears the 1535 version of the passage which was deleted and corrected at a later stage.

[35]Oviedo 1535: fol. 49 recto / Oviedo ca 1535–1549: Library of the Royal Academy of History of Madrid MS 9/551 / Oviedo 1959: 1.120–121. The manuscript does not present in this passage any addition or modification with respect to the 1535 edition.

buscar su vida, y no usar con ellos de tales cautelas. Y así lo atribuían a otros fines que por aventura sería bien posible no pasarle por pensamiento. Pero a los que se confesaban y comulgaban, no les negaba la licencia para ir a coger oro; mas a los otros no les consentía ir a las minas, antes los mandaba castigar si iban sin expresa licencia suya.

[3.26] Libro VI, cap. viii: /68 recto/ El cual trata de los metales y minas que hay de oro en esta isla Española; el cual se divide en once párrafos o partes. Y decirse ha así mismo, de la manera que se tiene en el coger del oro y otras particularidades notables y concernientes a la historia.[36]

3.26.1. (. . .) Quiero acordar al que me oye que, como prudente lector, quiera colegir de este capítulo y lo que contiene, qué grandísimo tesoro habrá ido a España de esta isla y de las otras que están pobladas de cristianos, y de la Tierra Firme, después que estas tierras se descubrieron, en oro puro y virgen, sin haber en otra nación alguna, primero que en españoles, entrado. Y no tan solamente para los reyes de España (cuyo es este Imperio y riquísimo señorío), sino mucho más para sus vasallos y súbditos; porque el Rey no lleva sino el quinto de sus derechos, y en algunas provincias, por hacer merced a sus vasallos, no lleva sino diezmo o menos; allende los muchos quintales de plata que del Perú y de la Nueva España se han llevado, y sin innumerables marcos de perlas y aljófar, y sin otras granjerías grandes y de mucha importancia que hay en estas tierras, de que tantos provechos resultan en el mundo todo.

3.26.2. Por cierto, aquella estatua llamada *Holosphiraton*, y la otra de Leonino, que fue el primero de los hombres que en el templo de Delfos puso asimismo una estatua de oro maciza (que fue en la septuagésima olimpíada), muy mejor la merece don Cristóbal Colón, primero descubridor e inventor de estas Indias, y primero Almirante de ellas en nuestros tiempos;[37] pues no como Leonino, que mostrando arte oratorio allegó el oro de su estatua, sino como animoso e sabio nauta y valeroso capitán nos enseñó este Nuevo Mundo,[38] tan colmado de oro, que se podrían haber hecho millares de tales estatuas con el que ha ido a España y continuamente se lleva. Pero más digno es de fama y gloria por haber traído la fe católica donde estamos, y a todos estos indios en que, por la gracia de Dios Nuestro Señor, cada día se aumenta la religión cristiana. Ved de cuánto mérito e inmortalidad es el nombre y ánima de aquel cuya industria fue principio de tanto bien.[39]

[3.27] Libro VI, cap. xliii: En el cual se trata de la diversidad de las lenguas de estas

[36]Oviedo 1535: fol. 68 / Oviedo ca 1535–1549: Huntington Library MS HM 177, vol. I, fols. 22 verso–23 recto / Oviedo 1959: 1.167. The manuscript follows the printed edition except for the last sentence of the chapter. At a later stage, however, Oviedo added slight modifications.

[37]The "en nuestros tiempos" was added sometime after the first draft of the manuscript.

[38]The adjective "e sabio" was also added to the primitive draft.

[39]The last sentence, "Ved de cuánto mérito e inmortalidad es el nombre y ánima de aquel cuya industria fue principio de tanto bien," does not appear in the 1535 edition.

Indias, islas y Tierra Firme del mar Océano.[40]

3.27.1. La primera lengua con que el primero Almirante, don Cristóbal Colón, descubridor de estas partes, topó, fue la de las islas de los Lucayos; y la segunda la de la isla de Cuba; y la tercera la de ésta de Haití o Española. De las cuales, ninguna se entiende con la otra. Esto en el primero viaje y en el segundo que el Almirante hizo a las Indias. Después, cuando descubrió la gran costa de la Tierra Firme y de los caribes, topó y vio otras lenguas muchas y muy diferentes entre sí, así como las de los caribes flecheros, y otras naciones que allí hay, diferentes en las lenguas y en los ritos y ceremonias y en sus creencias y costumbres, en tanta manera y en tantas partes, que lo que está visto hasta el tiempo presente es incontable, y lo que está por ver y saberse es muy a la larga, y para que los venideros tengan mucho más que escribir que lo que yo he podido comprender de estas materias.

[3.28] Libro VI, cap. xlvi: de un notable, mucho de notar, de la mudanza de los tiempos en esta ciudad de Santo Domingo e isla Española, y aun en las otras partes de estas Indias que se han poblado de los cristianos.[41]

3.28.1. Estas tierras que los cristianos en estas Indias han poblado, habitándolas, como es notorio a todos los que ha algún tiempo que por ellas andamos (puesto que desde el año de mil y quinientos cuarenta y ocho,[42] no son más de cincuenta y seis años, y yo vi a Colón, primero Almirante y descubridor de estas partes y a los más de los primeros pobladores, digo de los principales hombres que acá pasaron entonces, y aun de los que han venido después con cargos y oficios más señalados), muy trocadas las veo en aquellas provincias por donde yo he andado, y cada día lo están más, en cuanto a los temporales del frío y de la calor, y cada día, cuanto más van y más corre el tiempo, tanto más templada o menos calor hallamos; y en esta opinión todos, comúnmente los españoles que algún tiempo por acá viven, son conformes y lo dicen.

[3.29] Libro IX, Proemio.[43]

3.29.1. /87 verso/ Aunque ha pocos años que los primeros cristianos vinieron a esta partes (pues mis ojos vieron y conocieron los primeros, y yo vi mucha veces al primero Almirante don Cristóbal Colón, y a su hermano el Adelantado don Bartolomé Colón,[44] y al piloto Vicente Yáñez, y a otros los que con él vinieron en el primer viaje y descubrimiento de esta tierra), no me maravillo de lo que no se ha podido alcanzar, sino de lo mucho que se sabe y tiene noticia en tan poca edad.

[40]Oviedo ca 1535–1549: Huntington Library MS HM 177 vol. I, fol. 51 / Oviedo 1959: 1.203. This passage diverts from the text of 1535. It may have been written around 1541–1542 since by then Oviedo had already received Pedro Mexia's *Silva de Varia Lección*, published in Seville in 1540.

[41]Oviedo ca. 1535–1549: Huntington Library MS HM 177 vol. I, fol. 55 recto / Oviedo 1959: 1.206. This passage was written in 1542, as it appears in the autograph manuscript. Amador de los Ríos arbitrarily transcribed 1548.

[42]1542 in the manuscript.

[43]Seville, 1535, fol. 87 verso / Huntington Library HM 177 vol. II, fol. 50v / Pérez de Tudela: 1.278–279.

[44]The sentence "y a su hermano el Adelantado don Bartolomé Colón" does not appear in the 1535 edition.

[3.30] Libro XII, Proemio.[45]

3.30.1. Por manera que infiero de este número duodécimo, que es hermoso santo y digno de no olvidarle algún católico, y que cuadra al libro animales; pues que estas gentes de estas Indias, aunque racionales y la misma estirpe de aquellas ocho personas de aquella santa arca y compañía de Noé, estaban ya hechas irracionales y bestiales con sus idolatrías y sacrificios y ceremonias infernales, y gozaba el diablo sus ánimas tantos siglos ha. Y por medio de la real silla de Castilla y bienaventurados Reyes Católicos, don Fernando V de tal nombre, y de doña Isabel, de gloriosa memoria, y de la Cesárea Majestad del Emperador Rey don Carlos, nuestro señor, su nieto, y en virtud de la doctrina y armas de sus ínclitos españoles (espirituales y temporales, o eclesiásticos y seglares) esta doctrina evangélica de los doce apóstoles se ha ejercitado y traído a estas partes con la industria y guía del Espíritu Santo, cuyo ministro y adalid fue el memorable don Cristóbal Colón, primero descubridor de estas Indias.

[3.31] Libro XII, cap. x: De los animales que en la Tierra Firme llaman los españoles tigres, y los indios los llaman en diversa manera, según la lengua de aquellas provincias donde los hay.[46]

3.31.1. Para mi opinión, dicho he lo que siento de ser o no ser tigres estos ochis; mas sea cualquiera de los que se notan en el número de la piel maculada, o por ventura otro nuevo animal que asimismo la tiene y no está en la cuenta de los que están escritos, porque de muchos animales que hay en la Tierra Firme, y entre ellos éstos que yo aquí pondré (o los más de ellos), ningún escritor de los antiguos hace memoria de ellos, como quiera que están en provincias que ignoraban, y que la cosmografía de Tolomeo ni de otros autores no se lo acordaba ni lo dijo, hasta que el Almirante don Cristóbal Colón nos la enseñó. Cosa por cierto más digna y sin comparación capacísima de memoria y grande, que no fue dar Hércules entrada al mar Mediterráneo en el Océano pues los griegos hasta él, nunca le supieron, y de aquí viene aquella fábula que dice que los montes Calpe y Abila (que son los que en el estrecho de Gibraltar, el uno en España y el otro en África, están enfrente uno de otro) eran juntos, y que Hércules los abrió y dio por allí entrada al mar Océano, y puso sus columnas en Cádiz y Sevilla, las cuales César méritamente trae por divisa con aquella su letra de *Plus Ultra*. Palabras en verdad a solo tan universal Emperador, y no a otro príncipe alguno convenientes, pues en partes tan apartadas de donde Hércules llegó (y donde después ningún otro príncipe ha llegado), las ha puesto su Cesárea Majestad. Y pues Hércules tan poco navegó como de Grecia hasta Cádiz hay, y por eso los poetas o historiadores dicen que dio puerta al Océano, sin duda la memoria de Colón de más alto premio es, y muy sin comparación el mérito y ventaja que a Hércules tiene.

[3.32] Libro XVII, Proemio.[47]

3.32.1. /129 recto/ En el primero viaje que el Almirante primero, don Cristóbal

[45]Oviedo 1959: 2.28. Passage added to the 1535 edition. The original manuscript has been missing since the beginning of this century.

[46]Oviedo 1959: 2.40–41. The same case.

[47]Oviedo 1535: fol. 129 recto / Oviedo 1959: 2.109–110.

Colón, hizo a estas Indias, como ya lo tengo dicho en otras partes de esta historia, la primera tierra que descubrió fueron las islas Blancas y comenzáronlas a llamar así porque, como son de arena, parecían blancas. Pero el Almirante mandó que se llamasen las Princesas, porque fueron el principio de la vista y descubrimiento de estas islas y de todo lo de las Indias. Y arribó a la que llaman Guanahani, que está en medio de las isletas Blancas o Princesas, en el mes de noviembre de mil y cuatrocientos y noventa y dos años de la Natividad de Jesucristo, nuestro Redentor. Esta isla de Guanahani es una de las que los indios llaman de los Lucayos, que están de la isla de Cuba a la parte del Norte, opuestas. Y de allí pasó a la de Cuba, que está sesenta leguas de la que he dicho.

[3.33] Libro XVIII, cap. xx.[48]

3.33.1Pero después tornó el mismo Gonzalo de Guzmán a la misma gobernación e oficio, en nombre del Almirante don Luis Colón, hasta el año de mil e quinientos e treinta y siete, que se dio cierto asiento en los pleitos que el Almirante trataba sobre sus privilegios con el fiscal real mucho tiempo había. E el emperador nuestro Señor, como gratísimo príncipe, hubo por bien de mandar fenecer tales litigios, por respecto a los servicios del primero Almirante, don Cristóbal Colón.

[3.34] Libro XIX, Proemio.[49]

3.34.1. /153 recto/ Así, a este propósito hablaré en este libro XIX en la isla de Cubagua, la cual es muy pequeña y esterilísima y sin gota de agua de río ni fuente, ni lago o estaño; y con ésta y otras dificultades; sin haber en ella donde se pueda sembrar ni hacer mantenimiento alguno para servicio del hombre, ni poder criar ganados, ni haber algún pasto, está habitada y con una gentil república que se llama la Nueva ciudad de Cádiz. Y ha sido tanta su riqueza, que tanto por tanto no ha habido en las Indias cosa más rica ni provechosa en lo que está poblado de los cristianos. Y no tiene más espacio o territorio de tres leguas de circunferencia (poco más o menos). Y dicen muchos que lo pueden bien saber, que desde el año de mil y cuatrocientos y noventa y seis años, que fue por el primero Almirante don Cristóbal Colón descubierta hasta ahora, se ha habido de provecho en esta isla tanto valor de perlas y aljófar, que han montado los quintos y derechos reales y el valor que a personas particulares ha redundado de la abundancia y grandísima cantidad de ellas (que allí se han sacado), que es grandísima la estimación y precio que esta granjería ha tenido. El cual ejercicio allí se ejercita cotidianamente. Mas porque la historia lleve su orden, diré de su descubrimiento lo que he podido comprender y ha venido a mi noticia de esta isla.

[3.35] Libro XIX, cap. i: /153 verso/ Del descubrimiento de la isla de Cubagua, donde se pescan las perlas, y donde se vieron primero en estas Indias, y cómo tuvieron

[48]Oviedo 1959: 2.152. This passage does not appear in the 1535 edition. The original manuscript used by Amador is today missing. By means of textual references it can be dated in 1540.

[49]Oviedo 1535: fol. 153 recto / Oviedo 1959: 2.188.

noticia de ellas los españoles.[50]

3.35.1. El tercero viaje y descubrimiento que hizo el primero Almirante de estas Indias, don Cristóbal Colón, fue el año de mil y cuatrocientos y noventa y seis años, el cual, en el mes de marzo, partió de la bahía de Cádiz con seis carabelas muy bien armadas (como se dijo en el libro III), de las cuales en la prosecución de su camino, envió las tres de ellas a esta isla Española, y con las otras tres continuó su descubrimiento. Con esta armada, hecho el Almirante a la vela desde la isla de Cádiz, tomó puerto desde a pocos días en las islas de Canaria, donde se proveyó de agua y leña y otras cosas para su viaje, y desde allí corrieron en demanda de las islas de Antón, que comúnmente se llaman de Cabo Verde, que son las mismas que los antiguos cosmógrafos llaman las Gorgades, puesto que algunos dicen que se llaman las Hespérides, lo cual yo niego, afirmándome en aquella autoridad y autoridades que alegué en el libro II, capítulo III, por donde se prueba suficientemente que las Hespérides son estas islas de nuestras Indias. Pero dejemos eso aparte.

3.35.2. Tornando al propósito, digo que desde las islas de Cabo Verde el Almirante con sus tres navíos corrió al Sudoeste hasta ciento y cincuenta leguas (según dice el piloto Hernán Pérez Mateos, que hoy vive y está en esta ciudad); y tomóles después una tormenta que les puso en tanta necesidad, que cortaron los mástiles de las mismas y echaron a la mar mucha parte de la carga; y se vieron en tanto peligro que se pensaron perder, y corrieron al Nor-Noroeste y fueron a reconocer la isla de la Trinidad. Pero esta tormenta que el piloto Hernán Pérez cuenta, no la aprobaba así don Fernando Colón, hijo del Almirante, que se halló en el mismo viaje con su padre; el cual me dijo que el trabajo en que se vieron fue de calmas y calor tan grande que la vasija se les abría y el trigo que llevaban se les podría, y de necesidad alijaron e se arredraron de la Equinoccial.

Parece que quien oyere decir que se apartaron de la Equinoccial por la calor, que es aprobar la opinión falsa que los antiguos tuvieron, que decían que la tórrida zona (que es la misma equinoccial) es inhabitable por el excesivo calor del sol; y adelante, cuando se trate de la mar Austral, tengo de mostrar y escribir que debajo de la línea o tórrida zona y a par de ella, de ésta y de la otra parte, es habitada, pues cada día nuestros españoles pasan del un trópico al otro. Digo que don Fernando Colón decía bien, porque en la mar, por doquiera que pase la dicha Equinoccial y cerca de ella, de esta o de la otra parte, no hay duda sino que hay mucha calor; y así, por esta causa, como él decía, se apartarían de ella en este camino. Pero en tierra, por donde pasa la misma línea del Equinoccio, proveyó el que todo lo ordenó, que es Dios, de poner por allí tales montañas y sierras, que no solamente están, pero a causa de ellas y del aire, son templadas las provincias y regiones por donde pasa la tórrida zona. Más aún: no faltan hielos y nieves grandes en algunas partes de ella y de lo que le es circunstante. Y esto es lo que no entendieron los antiguos, por lo cual, fundándose como naturales, les parecía debidamente que no podía ser habitada la dicha Equinoccial por la mucha

[50]Oviedo 1535: fol. 153 verso / Oviedo 1959: 2.189–191. In this passage, the text shows important additions with respect to the 1535 edition which are undatable due to the loss of the manuscript after it was transcribed by Amador de los Ríos.

fuerza del sol.[51]

3.35.3. Tornemos a nuestra historia, porque en esa otra materia, como digo, cuando lleguemos a la Equinoccial, se dirá de ella más largamente lo que está visto y se ve cada día por nuestros españoles. Así que reconociendo la isla de la Trinidad, dice don Fernando que este nombre le puso el Almirante porque llevaba pensamiento de nombrar así la primera tierra que hallase, y siguióse que vieron a un tiempo tres montes cercanos, o al parecer poco distantes unos de otros, y llamó y nombró a la isla la Trinidad, y pasó por aquel embocamiento y llamóle Boca del Drago, y viose la Tierra Firme /154 recto/ luego y mucha parte de la costa de ella, como más largamente en otro lugar lo tengo dicho. Y desde la punta de las Salinas en Tierra Firme (donde está esta Boca del Drago, que está en diez grados de la línea equinoccial, a la parte de nuestro polo ártico) corrió el Almirante por la costa de Tierra Firme al Occidente y reconoció otras islas, como lo tengo dicho en el libro III. De allí pasó adelante y descubrió la isla Rica, llamada Cubagua (de la cual aquí se trata), que los cristianos al presente llaman isla de las Perlas, donde después de algunos años se fundó la Nueva ciudad de Cádiz, y allí es la pesquería de las perlas. Junto a esta isla está otra mayor, llamada la Margarita, porque así la nombró el Almirante.

3.35.4. Hay desde la punta de las Salinas hasta la isla de Cubagua cincuenta leguas al Poniente, y es pequeña isla, y tendrá, como tengo dicho, de circunferencia tres leguas, poco más o menos, y de longitud una y media, y de latitud una pequeña. Dista de la gran costa de Tierra Firme cuatro leguas a la primera tierra de la provincia que se dice Araya. Y porque en esta isla de Cubagua (como se dijo en el Proemio) no hay agua, los que allí viven pasan por ella a la Tierra Firme, al río que llaman Cumaná, que es a siete leguas de la Nueva Cádiz (çosa en la verdad trabajosa). Mas con la ganancia todas esas necesidades comportan los hombres a propósito de sus intereses.

3.35.5. Está Cubagua diez grados y casi medio más desviada de la Equinoccial en nuestro horizonte. Y desde ella a esta ciudad de Santo Domingo de esta isla Española puede haber ciento y setenta leguas o ciento y ochenta, pocas más o menos. Está Norte Sur con la isla de Santa Cruz de los Caribes a ciento y diez leguas, la cual isla de Santa Cruz está en la banda del Norte. Por la parte de Mediodía tiene la Tierra Firme cuatro leguas lo más cercano de ella y a veinticinco leguas al Poniente tiene la isla Poregari. Así que esto que he dicho es su asiento y límites y aledaños; pero la tierra más propíncua de Cubagua es la isla Margarita, que he dicho que está una legua de ella, a la banda del Norte.

3.35.6. Todo lo demás que en este tercero viaje descubrió el Almirante queda dicho en el libro III de esta primera parte, y no hay necesidad de tornarlo a repetir aquí, sino lo que hace al propósito de estas dos islas de Cubagua y Margarita, haciendo relación de la manera y ocasión por donde se supo que había perlas allí, lo cual fue de esta forma.

3.35.7. Así como el Almirante surgió a par de Cubagua con sus tres carabelas, mandó a ciertos marineros salir en una barca y que fuesen a una canoa que andaba pescando perlas, la cual, como vio que los cristianos iban a ella, se recogió hacia la

[51]The whole passage from “Parece” to “sol” was added to the 1535 edition.

tierra de la isla. Y entre otros indios vieron una mujer que tenía al cuello un gran cantidad de hilos de aljófar (porque de lo menudo no hacían caso los indios, ni tenían arte ni instrumento tan sutil con que horadarlo). Entonces uno de aquellos marineros tomó un plato de barro de los de Valencia (que también llaman de Málaga), que son labrados de labores que relucen las figuras y pinturas que hay en los tales platos, e hízole pedazos, y a trueco de los cascos del plato rescataron con los indios e india ciertos hilos de aquel aljófar grueso. Y como les pareció bien a aquellos marineros lleváronlo al Almirante, el cual, como entendió el negocio más profundamente, pensó de lo disimular, pero no le dio lugar el placer que hubo en verlo, y dijo: Dígoos que estáis en la más rica tierra que hay en el mundo, y sean dadas a Dios muchas gracias por ello. Y tornó a enviar la barca con otros hombres a tierra, y mandóles que rescatasen tanto aljófar o perlas cuanto cupiese en una escudilla, a trueco de otro plato hecho pedazos, como el que es dicho, y de algunos cascabeles. Y llegados a la isla, rescataron con aquellos pescadores hasta cinco o seis marcos de perlas y aljófar, todo mezclado de la forma que los indios lo pescan, grueso y menudo. Y tomó el Almirante aquellas perlas para llevarlas él o enviarlas a España a los Reyes Católicos don Fernando y doña Isabel, de gloriosa memoria. Y no se quiso detener allí por no dar ocasión que los marineros y la gente que con él iban se cebasen en el deseo y codicia de las perlas, pensando de tener la cosa secreta hasta en su tiempo y cuando conviniese. Y si quisiera pudiera rescatar entonces media fanega de perlas, según dice el piloto Hernán Pérez Mateos, que aquí está. El cual afirma que vio tanta o más cantidad de ella, pero no quiso el Almirante /154 verso/ dar lugar a ello.

3.35.8. Pero como en los marineros hay poco secreto, cuando después algunos de los que allí se acertaron volvieron a España, publicaron lo que es dicho en la villa de Palos, de donde a la sazón eran los más de los marineros que andaban en estas partes. Y súpose asimismo en Moguer, y salieron de allí ciertos armadores, vecinos de aquella villa, que lo alcanzaron a saber, llamados los Niños, entre los cuales era un Per Alfonso Niño. Y con una nao, tomando consigo para esto algunos de los que se hallaron con el Almirante cuando había descubierto aquella isla de las perlas, fuéronse a ella y rescataron muchas, y tornáronse ricos a España, si pudieran salir con su salto. Verdad es que este Per Alfonso tuvo licencia para venir a estas partes a descubrir; pero diosele con condición de que no se allegase a lo que el Almirante hubiese descubierto con cincuenta leguas, lo cual no guardó, antes se fue derechamente a lo que estaba ya sabido, e hizo su rescate. Y cuando dio la vuelta para Europa, aportó en Galicia, donde estaba por virrey Hernando de Vega, señor de Grajal (que después fue Comendador de Castilla de la Orden militar y caballería de Santiago), y entre los que iban con el Per Alfonso, tuvieron algunas diferencias con él y decían que no había partido bien con ellos el rescate y perlas, ni al Rey había dado el quinto suyo como se le había de dar. De forma que llegó a noticia del virrey y mandóle prender, y tomó a él y sus consortes las perlas y el navío, como a personas que no habían guardado la forma de la licencia, y envió le preso a la corte al Per Alfonso y algunos de los otros, donde con mucho trabajo hubieron su liberación. De ahí de en adelante se puso gran recaudo en la isla.

3.35.9. Quisieron algunos decir que para la autoridad y confianza del Almirante fue mucho desvío este descubrimiento de las perlas, porque dicen que se supo en España por los marineros que con él se hallaron cuando descubrió a Cubagua y las perlas, y por cartas de personas particulares antes que por las suyas, lo cual otros niegan.

[4] FROM *LA HISTORIA GENERAL Y NATURAL DE LAS YNDIAS* SEGUNDA PARTE, DEDICATORIA AL EMPERADOR[52]

[4.1]

4.1.1. /3 recto/ Dejemos esto y tornemos a nuestra historia y principal intento. Godos son y españoles los que estas nuestras Indias hallaron, vasallos de vuestra Majestad y de esta Corona Real de Castilla, guiados por la industria de aquel memorable Almirante primero de ellas, don Cristóbal Colón, cuya memoria no puede haber fin; porque aunque todo lo escrito y por escribir en la tierra perezca, en el cielo se perpetuará tan famosa historia, donde todo lo bueno quiere Dios que sea remunerado y permanezca para su alabanza y gloria de tan famoso varón.

4.1.2. De cuyos sucesores de este Almirante me parece y es razón que quede un continuo y perpetuo acuerdo en vuestra sagrada Majestad, y en todos los reyes de Castilla, para honrar y gratificar y conservar la sucesión de Colón y de su casa, y sostenerla y aumentarla y estimarla como joya propia y ornamento de sus reinos, pues fue causa de tantos bienes, y que Cristo y su fe católica en estas Indias se sirviese y aumentase y repredicase nuestra religión cristiana, que desde tiempo inmemorial no se conocía en tantos y tan extraños reinos. Y que desde ellos se llevasen tantos y tan innumerables tesoros a vuestra real cámara a España, y tan bien se empleasen por vuestra Majestad en servicio de Dios contra infieles y en tan santas empresas y obras pías como vuestra Cesárea Majestad se ejercita y los despende. Lo cual más puntualmente digan vuestros elegantes historiadores que asisten presencialmente cerca de vuestra Majestad, que yo desde tan lejos no puedo tan llenamente hablar como en cosas de estas partes e Indias.

[4.2] Libro XX, Proemio.[53]

4.2.1. /4 recto/ La conciencia me acusa e incita a que comience este segundo volumen de estas historias (tocantes a Tierra Firme), en el primero Almirante, don Cristóbal Colón, descubridor y autor y fundamento de todos los descubrimientos de las Indias, islas y Tierra Firme del mar Océano (y esta alabanza a él solo y no a otro hombre alguno se debe tal gloria); y la orden de la historia me requiere y pide que no en el Almirante, sino en el capitán Fernando de Magallanes que descubrió aquel grande y famoso estrecho austral en la misma Tierra Firme, tome principio este libro (. . .) Y para que al Almirante ni otro alguno no le quede escrito, ni haya de qué se pueda quejar de mí, cuando se hablare en otros capitanes y particulares personas que continuaron tras el loable y principal descubridor, a navegar y a acrecentar, sobre aquel principio primero, los otros descubrimientos, se dirán puntualmente en qué tiempo y en qué partes y provincias lo hizo cada uno. Y así, se le guardará al Almirante su preeminencia y superioridad en este caso de primero descubridor y autor de tan alta y ardua e importante memoria, y se dará de cada uno la noticia que le

[52]Oviedo 1557: fol. 3 recto / Oviedo ca. 1565: Library of the Royal Palace of Madrid MS II-3041, fols. 4 verso–5 recto / Oviedo 1959: 2.214. The texts of both the 1557 printed edition and the Truxillos manuscripts are dated in 1547. Probably through error, Amador's text records the date 1544 instead.

[53]Oviedo 1557: fol. 3 / Oviedo ca. 1565: Library of the Royal Palace of Madrid MS II-3041, fols. 6 recto–7 recto / Oviedo 1959: 2.216. Written sometime before 1542.

pertenece.

[4.3] Libro XX, cap. i: /5 verso/ En que se trata de la persona del capitán Fernando de Magallanes, y del famoso y grande estrecho austral que descubrió en la Tierra Firme, y del viaje que hizo por allí a la Especiería e islas del Maluco, y de la nao *Victoria* que bojó o circuyó y anduvo la redondez del Universo, etc.[54]

4.3.1. El camino que Fernando de Magallanes quería hacer era navegar derecho a Poniente, hasta que, circundado el orbe, llegase al Levante. Y esto era lo que parecía difícil poderse hacer y casi imposible, /6 recto/ no porque se juzgue difícil, midiéndolo por el aire, sino porque estaba en duda si la natura hubiese dado tal disposición o tal entrada en la Tierra Firme que, navegándose a Poniente, pudiesen ir a Levante. Y a este propósito muchos han tentado en la parte interior de la Tierra Firme buscar algún estrecho que pasase, por agua, de mar a mar, a causa que el Almirante primero, don Cristóbal Colón, dijo que le había, y aun hizo pintar algunas figuras de estas nuestras Indias en que le hizo pintar; pero no le hay, ni hasta ahora se sabe, en toda la costa interior de la Tierra Firme. Y porque el lector mejor entienda cuál es lo que llamo interior, digo que es lo que hay entre el cabo de Santo Agustín y el cabo del Labrador.

[4.4] Libro XXI, cap. v: En que se trata y declara qué cosa es la línea equinoccial.[55]

4.4.1. El descubridor primero y principal que lo enseñó a todos los que lo han querido imitar en nuestros tiempos, fue el memorable Almirante primero de estas Indias, don Cristóbal Colón. Y este loor suyo es, principalmente; puesto que los otros capitanes que le han seguido en tal ejercicio, merecedores son de fama y buen nombre por sus obras y gentiles deseos, con tanto que no desconozcan su preceptor y dechado de donde tomaron aliento y doctrina sus intentos, que es el mismo Colón, sin el cual aviso nunca lo comenzaron.

[4.5] Libro XXI, cap. vi: Prosiguiendo la continuación de la geografía de la Tierra Firme, en que declara lo que hay, costa a costa, desde la línea del Equinoccio o promontorio llamado cabo Blanco, por donde la línea entra en esta tierra, hasta el golfo de Urabá y los Farallones.[56]

4.5.1. Aquella mar que hay entre la Boca del Drago e isla de la Trinidad la Tierra Firme, descubrió el Almirante primero en el tercer viaje que hizo a estas partes, el año de mil cuatrocientos y noventa y seis, como más largamente se dijo en el tercero libro de la primera parte de esta *General Historia de Indias*. Y vio primero esta isla y nombróla Trinidad, porque mirándola a ella y a la Tierra Firme, se mostraron tres montes a un tiempo. Y entró por el embocamiento que es dicho, y llamóle Boca del Drago, y no hubo lengua con los indios, porque es gente feroz y flecheros, aunque vio muchos en canoas y piraguas grandes. La parte que esta isla tiene al Sur está en ocho grados y dos tercios, y tiene de longitud treinta leguas o más, y de latitud veinticinco.

[54]Oviedo 1557, fols. 5 verso–6 recto / Oviedo ca. 1565: Library of the Royal Palace of Madrid, MS II-3041 / Oviedo 1959: 2.218.

[55]Oviedo ca. 1565: Library of the Royal Palace of Madrid MS II-3041 / Oviedo 1959: 2.318.

[56]Oviedo ca. 1565: Library of the Royal Palace of Madrid MS II-3041 / Oviedo 1959: 2.321.

Y la Tierra Firme que le está a la parte del Sur, se llama el Palmar, y el Almirante primero le dio ese nombre; y la punta de las Salinas, que es en la Tierra Firme, en la Boca del Drago, o embocamiento entre esa punta de Salinas y la isla, aquella punta o promontorio fue la primera tierra que los cristianos vieron en la Tierra Firme, la cual ahora llaman punta de Paria, porque aquel golfete que se hace entre la isla y la Tierra Firme, le llaman el golfo de Paria.

4.5.2. Porque estos maestros que pintan las cartas de navegar, intitúlanlas como los que lo navegan se lo dicen, y cada día mudan, o quitan nombres a sabor de temerarios. Lo cual es muy gran desatino, y no guardar los nombres primeros es poner confusión en todo. A la que la carta llama Corazante, llaman los indios Corazao, y el Almirante, que la descubrió, la dejó con su nombre; a la que el Almirante llamo Poregari llaman ahora Yaruma o de Orchilla. Pasemos adelante. Desde el cabo de los Monjes corriendo cuarenta leguas del Este al Oeste, está el cabo de la Vela, el cual nombró así el Almirante primero porque vio allí una gran canoa o piragua de indios que iba a la vela, y por eso se le digo este nombre a aquel cabo o promontorio.

[4.6] Libro XXI, cap. vii: En continuación de la costa y geografía de la Tierra Firme, en que se dirá lo que hay, costa a costa, desde los tres Farallones del Darién, que están en el golfo de Urabá, hasta en fin del golfo que llaman de las Higüeras.[57]

4.6.1. Aquí conviene que vuelva nuestra historia al inventor de estos descubrimientos, que fue el primero Almirante de estas Indias, don Cristóbal Colón, y diráse lo que más descubrió de la Tierra Firme en el cuarto y último viaje que a estas partes hizo. El cual, desde España vino al puerto de esta ciudad de Santo Domingo de la isla Española; pero no le quiso dejar entrar aquí el Comendador Mayor de Alcántara, don fray Nicolás de Ovando, gobernador de estas partes, como se dijo en el libro III de la primera parte de esta General Historia. Y así, él se fue en su descubrimiento con cuatro carabelas que trajo, de las cuales eran pilotos Pedro de Umbría, y Diego Martín Cabrera y Martín del los Reyes. Y desde aquí fue a reconocer la isla de Jamaica, y de allí atravesó a la Tierra Firme y fue a reconocer el cabo de las Higüeras y las islas de los Guanajes, una de las cuales se llama Guanaja. Y fue al puerto de Honduras, la cual tierra llamó y puso nombre punta de Cajines; pero den la moderna carta de otra manera está; que yo lo oí a los pilotos que he dicho, como se dirá adelante.

4.6.2. Desde allí fue al cabo de Gracias a Dios, y tiró la costa del Levante, la costa arriba de Tierra Firme, y descubrió la provincia y río de Veragua. De la cual, el año que pasó de mil y quinientos y treinta y seis, el Emperador nuestro señor hizo merced, con título de duque de ella, al Almirante don Luis Colón, y le hizo merced asimismo de la isla de Jamaica, con título de marqués de ella, y le dio demás de eso diez mil escudos de oro, en cada un año, en las rentas y derechos reales de esta isla Española, y el alguacilazgo mayor de esta ciudad de Santo Domingo, con voto en el cabildo del Regimiento de esta rica república; todo esto perpetuo y mayorazgo indivisible para él y sus sucesores, confirmándole perpetuamente el título de Almirante primitivo de

[57]Oviedo ca. 1565: Library of the Royal Palace of Madrid MS II-3041 / Oviedo 1959: 2.325–327.

estas Indias en todo lo descubierto y por descubrir en ellas, habiendo respeto a los grandes y tan señalados servicios de su abuelo el Almirante primero, don Cristóbal Colón (de quien aquí se trata méritamente), como gratísimo príncipe. Porque hablando en verdad, los servicios del Almirante don Cristóbal fueron muy estimados y apartados de la costumbre por donde se adquieren nuevos estados; porque si traemos a la memoria el origen y principios que tuvieron las casas y estados de los Grandes de España y de otras partes, hallaremos que por algunos servicios notables o privanza particular los reyes hicieron señores y dieron rentas y títulos y dignidades a quien los mereció o les plugo. Pero no hallareis que ninguno de aquéllos, así medrados o sublimados, dieron a su rey el reino, como Colón, que no solamente en descubrir estas partes dio a la corona real de Castilla y de León y a los Reyes Católicos, de inmortal memoria, don Fernando y doña Isabel, y sus sucesores un reino, o dos o tres muy grandes, pero dióles una mitad del mundo universo, mayor que todas aquellas tres partes, Asia, África y Europa, en que los antiguos pensaron que el mundo todo se incluía; porque en estas nuestras Indias hay y caven muchos más reinos e imperios que no están escritos por ningún autor antiguo ni moderno, hasta que Colón nos lo enseñó a todos. Y que esto se crea ser así, tornad a leer lo que dije en el capítulo V que dice Plinio, en que confiesa que de cinco partes del mundo, las tres no son habitadas; y veremos, al contrario de su opinión, la bandera del país colocada por la industria del Almirante Colón, y enseñoreado el cetro castellano en la tórrida zona; y pasamos y volvemos del un trópico al otro, no obstante los inconvenientes que Plinio y otros hallaron para que tales tierras fuesen habitadas.

4.6.3. Dejemos ahora de hablar y de loar lo que el primero Almirante de estas Indias sirvió y mereció, pues que ni yo sabré tan suficientemente escribirlo como él lo supo obrar, ni hay ninguno tan ignorante ni de tan poco juicio que ignore sus méritos. Tornemos al camino.

4.6.4. Así que descubrió a Veragua y pasó a otro río grande que está más al Oriente, y llamóle río de Belén, el cual está una legua de otro río que los indios llaman Yebra, que es el mismo de Veragua. Y más al Este llegó a otro poderoso río, y púsole nombre río de Lagartos, porque hay muchos y muy grandes en él, o mejor diciendo, cocatrices. A este río le llaman los indios Chagre, y los cristianos asimismo le dicen Chagre; el cual nace a dos leguas de la mar del Sur, y pasa a cuatro de la ciudad de Panamá, en la provincia de Cueva, que ahora se llama Castilla del Oro, y viene a fenecer y lanzarse en esta otra mar y costa del Norte, donde el Almirante viejo le llamó río de Lagartos. De allí discurrió adelante, y halló una isla que está junto a la costa de Tierra Firme, y llamóla isla de Bastimentos, porque la halló toda cultivada y labrada de maizales, de yuca, e ajes, e batatas, y puso nombre de Puerto Bello. Allí, subiendo la costa arriba, pasó por delante del puerto del Nombre de Dios, pero no lo vio. Y llegó al río de Francisca, el cual nombre le puso el Almirante porque allí se tomó una india que quiso ser cristiana, y le llamaron Francisca. Más adelante halló un puerto que se llamó el Retrete, y subió hasta el golfo de Secativa, que es una ensenada en aquella costa, llena de muchas isletas. Y llamóle golfo de San Blas, porque el día de este santo obispo y mártir de Cristo, a los tres de febrero, llegó allí. Desde el golfo de Secativa o de San Blas subió por la costa hasta las islas de Pocacosi, y llamó aquello el cabo del Mármol, y desde allí atravesó a la tierra de la Jamaica.

4.6.5. Y esto fue lo que de la Tierra Firme descubrió el Almirante primero del cuarto viaje que hizo a esta parte. Y volvió a España, donde murió en Valladolid, año de mil y quinientos y seis años, desde a pocos días que se desembarcaron de La Coruña de Galicia, viniendo a reinar en Castilla los serenísimos príncipes el rey don, Felipe y la reina doña Juana, nuestros señores, padres de la Cesárea y Sagrada Majestad del Emperador Rey don Carlos, nuestro señor.

4.6.6. Ahora que está muy mejor entendida aquella costa de Tierra Firme y las cartas de navegar más apuntadas, y por la relación de los pasados se sabe que el Almirante don Cristóbal descubrió en este su último viaje hasta doscientas leguas de la costa de Tierra Firme, poco más o menos, y por esto no creen algunos que él pasase del cabo de Honduras abajo, porque si llegara al golfo de las Higüeras, más fueran de trescientas leguas las que descubriera. En este viaje del Almirante no se dicen más particularidades, ni cómo se le perdieron los navíos, porque en el III libro de esta General Historia está dicho este camino que el Almirante hizo. Como podéis haber notado, lector, fue de Poniente a Oriente, y al revés de la orden que he tenido para llegar al golfo de Urabá, por ser la forma de cómo el Almirante lo anduvo y los descubrió.

[4.7] Libro XXI, cap. viii: En consecuencia de la geografía y asiento de la Tierra Firme desde el golfo de las Higüeras, bajando la tierra de Yucatán a la costa de la Nueva España, hasta el rico de Pánuco, con quien confina la Nueva España a la parte del Norte; y de ahí adelante se dirá lo que hay hasta el Ancón Bajo, etc.[58]

4.7.1. Proseguiré desde donde acabé en el capítulo precedente, que fue en el golfo de Higüeras, que algunos atribuyen al Almirante primero don Cristóbal Colón, diciendo que él lo descubrió. Y no es así, porque el golfo de Higüeras lo descubrieron los pilotos Vicente Yáñez Pinzón y Juan Díaz de Solís y Pedro de Ledesma con tres carabelas, antes que el Vicente Yáñez descubriese el río Marañón, ni que el Solís descubriese el río de la Plata.

[4.8] Libro XXIII, cap. xi: Cómo Alvar Núñez Cabeza de Vaca fue por mandado de la Cesárea Majestad por su gobernador y capitán general al río de Paranaguazú, alias de la Plata, con una buena armada y con título de Adelantado.[59]

4.8.1. Solamente me desplace el título de Adelantado, porque, a la verdad, es mal augurio en Indias tal honor y nombre, y muchos de tal título han habido lastimado fin, como lo podemos ver por don Bartolomé Colón, primero Adelantado en Indias, hermano del primero Almirante, que ni dejó heredero ni cosa que de su persona permanezca.

[4.9] Libro XXVII, cap. i: En que se trata del viaje y descubrimiento que el capitán y piloto Juan de la Cosa hizo por la costa de la mar, Tierra Firme y en la provincia de

[58]Oviedo ca. 1565: Library of the Royal Palace of Madrid MS II-3041 / Oviedo 1959: 2.329.
[59]Oviedo ca. 1565: Library of the Royal Palace of Madrid MS II-3041 / Oviedo 1959: 2.370.

Cartagena y otras partes.[60]

4.9.1. Después del Almirante primero, descubridor de estas Indias (porque con verdad ninguno se puede llamar descubridor, sino continuadores) del descubrimiento a que don Cristóbal Colón dio principio y fundamento, antes con más razón se podrían algunos de los tales descubridores llamar alteradores y destruidores de la tierra, pues que su fin no era tanto de servir a Dios ni al Rey, como de robar; pero en las muertes que hubieron, se verá esto muy claro), un Juan de la Cosa, que vivía en el puerto de Santa María, hombre diestro en las cosas de la mar, y valiente hombre de su persona, y que como piloto había ganado hacienda en estas partes.

[4.10] Libro XXVIII, cap.i, Del suceso de Diego de Nicuesa, gobernador primero de Veragua e otras provincias, e de lo que paso, e de la maldad que el capitán Lope de Olano usó con él; e lo dejó perdido con pare de la gente e se volvió atrás desamparándole.[61]

4.10.1. E quedó por su teniente y capitán con hasta otros quinientos e cincuenta hombres, un hidalgo, pariente del mismo Nicuesa, que se llamaba Cueto, con el cual y los que allí quedaron, quedó concertado que le esperase allí, porque el iba con algunos de los pilotos que había primero llevado a aquella costa el Almirante viejo, don Cristóbal Colón cuando descubrió a Veragua (. . .) Y llegaron a Puerto Belo, que es uno de los mejores que hay en aquella costa, el cual nombre le puso Cristóbal Colón, que lo descubrió (. . .) E llevando su camino la vía del poniente, topó al capitán Lope de Olano, que volvía en el bergantín con que había acompañado al gobernador Diego de Nicuesa, e habíale dado cantonada, e lo dejaba perdido; porque al tiempo que pasaba por Veragua, un piloto que iba en el bergantín de Lope de Olano, dijo: Esta es Veragua, e yo vine aquí con el Almirante don Cristóbal Colón cuando descubrió esta tierra (. . .) Y este desleal capitán Lope de Olano, con mal pensamiento vino para atrás, la vía del Oriente, en busca de la gente que había quedado con el capitán Cueto, e reconoció a Veragua, e pasó adelante, e topó en la mar con el otro piloto que se dijo de suso, llamado Pedro de Umbría, que el Cueto enviaba a buscar al gobernador, porque era diestro en la costa, e fue uno de los pilotos del Almirante viejo (. . .); y en el río propio de Belén, al cual el Almirante primero así le había puesto el nombre, asentó este Lope de Olano e hizo un pueblo.

[4.11] Libro XXVIII, cap.iv: Cómo fue desde a mucho tiempo después de lo que se ha dicho de suso, por gobernador e capitán general a la provincia de Veragua, Felipe Gutiérrez, y del mal suceso de su gobernación e cargo.[62]

4.11.1 Para la continuación de esto de Veragua, digo que aquella provincia fue descubierta por el Almirante primero, don Cristóbal Colón, y porque estaba en reputación de tierra muy rica y en la verdad lo es, deseaba el Emperador nuestro

[60]Oviedo ca. 1565: Library of the Royal Palace od Madird MS II-3041 / Oviedo 1959: 3.130–131.

[61]Oviedo ca. 1565: Library of the Royal Academy of History of Madrid, *Papeles Varios de Jesuitas*, vol. 108 / Oviedo 1959: 3.175–176.

[62]Oviedo ca. 1565: Library of the Royal Academy of History of Madrid, *Papeles Varios de Jesuitas*, vol. 108 / Oviedo 1959: 3.187.

señor, que pues ya la provincia de Castilla del Oro, que está más al Oriente de Veragua en la costa de Tierra Firme, está poblada de cristianos, e asimismo otras provincias que están más al Occidente en la misma costa, que era razón que lo que está en medio, y como es dicho, tenido por rico, se poblase e continuase la conversión de los indios e la población de los cristianos. E para esto mandó a la visorreina de las Indias, doña María de Toledo, madre del almirante don Luis Colón, la cual estaba en la corte, que diese orden, pues Veragua cabía en la gobernación del Almirante su hijo, por la haber descubierto su abuelo el Almirante primero don Cristóbal Colón, que se poblase y enviase allí quien lo hiciese.

[4.12] Libro XXIX, cap.xxx: De las minas del oro y perlas y riquezas de la provincia de Cueva y Castilla del Oro, y del viaje de la Especiería desde Panamá a las islas de Maluco, y de la Puente Admirable, y otras cosas que pertenecen a la consecuencia historial.[63]

4.12.1. Pero pues venimos a hablar en las minas del Darién, como en parte que conviene, quiero desengañar a los que hubieren dado crédito al cronista Lucio Marineo en lo que dijo en aquella su obra de las *Cosas memorables de España*, en el libro XIX, en el capítulo que quiso hablar en estas Indias, sin verlas, no se contentando de haber dicho tantas cosas en lo de España (mal informado), en especial cuando quiso tratar de algunas particulares genealogías, en las cuales se apartó de lo cierto. Vino a las Indias entre sueños; y digo entre sueños, porque aunque durmiendo hablara, no pudiera decir tan al revés de la verdad lo que dijo; y por eso es menester que el que escribe lo que no ve, mire bien de quién se informa.

4.12.2. El dice que los Reyes Católicos enviaron a Pedro Colón con treinta y cinco naos y con gran número de gentes a descubrir otras islas, mayores mucho que las de Canaria, que tienen minas de oro, y se saca mucho en ellas y muy bueno. Y que como navegó sesenta días, llegó finalmente a tierras muy apartadas de España, en las cuales todos los que de acá van, afirman que hay antípodas debajo de nuestro hemisferio. Y cuanto a estos errores, digo que no fue Pedro, sino Cristóbal el Almirante Colón; y cuanto a las carabelas, fueron tres; y cuanto al viaje, yo le escribí en la primera parte de esta *General Historia de Indias*.

4.12.3. Fue opinión del Almirante primero, don Cristóbal Colón, y de otros cosmógrafos modernos, que hay estrecho de agua desde esta mar, que acá llamamos del Norte (en la costa de Tierra Firme), a la del Sur o austral, y aquel que hay ya le halló el capitán Hernando de Magallanes, como se dijo en el libro I, capítulo II de esta segunda parte, que es libro XX de la *General Historia de las Indias*. Pero acá, en estas otras costas de la Tierra Firme, no se sabe que le haya, sino estrecho de tierra y no de agua; y éste es el paso o traviesa que hay del Nombre de Dios a Panamá, o desde Careta a Acla, al golfo de San Miguel, por donde el Adelantado Vasco Núñez de Balboa descubrió la mar del Sur.

[63]Oviedo 1535–1549: Library of the Royal Academy of History MS 9/553, fols. 113–114 / Oviedo 1959: 3.329–331. Written in 1540 and updated in 1548.

[5] FROM *LA HISTORIA GENERAL Y NATURAL DE LAS YNDIAS*
TERCERA PARTE

[5.1] Libro XLIX, cap. xvi: En que el cronista da fin a este libro, y pone siete servicios que se han hecho en las Indias al Emperador Rey, nuestro señor, y al cetro real de Castilla; y son los siguientes.[64]

5.1.1. Entre las cosas que en esta *General Historia* yo hallo más bastantes y principales, son siete muy calificadas y dignas de perpetua memoria, y tales que no consienten ni puede haber olvido en ellas entre los que viven y han de venir al mundo después de nosotros, y son éstas:

5.1.2. La primera y principal de todas, y la que ha dado causa e ilustra las demás, es atribuida al primero Almirante don Cristóbal Colón, que descubrió estas Indias; con el cual ningún descubrimiento se puede comparar, ni mayor servicio se pudo hacer al cetro real y Reyes de Castilla Católicos, don Fernando y doña Isabel, en cuyo tiempo acaeció, y los reyes sus sucesores presentes y futuros en su señorío.

[5.2] Libro L, cap. xxx: En que se sigue una conclusión y descargo que el autor de estas historias da para su definición hasta el presente tiempo a los que vieren estas materias, para que sepan que en España, entre algunos latinos y personas graves y no de poca autoridad se platicó que el historiador de tan nuevas y peregrinas vigilias las debiera escribir en lengua latina. Y después que entre los tales fue altercado, culpándole unos y excusándole otros, no faltó entre ellos quien le escribiese a las Indias lo que acullá en España se había conferido a pro y a contra: a lo cual respondió con una letra suya lo que aquí en sentencia podéis ver, lector, y arrimaros a la opinión que os pareciese, con tanto que sin pasión y humanamente recibáis su disculpa con la ante reposada, tomando en vuestra mano el peso o balanzas de la justicia y la justificación del autor, dando a la razón y verdad el lugar que se le debe admitir, para lo cual mejor considerar y ponderar y mejor decidir en el propósito la verdadera sentencia, notad lo que dice.[65]

5.2.1. Yo no pasé a estas partes con los primeros españoles que la vieron; pero halléme en la corte de los Reyes Católicos, don Fernando y doña Isabel, de inmortal memoria, en el real y campo y cristiano ejército que tenían sobre la gran ciudad de Granada, cuando fue despachado, el año que he dicho, para esta empresa, el que tan loable efecto puso en ella. Y conocíle y vile muchas veces a él y a los demás principales que en ello se hallaron, como por el discurso de estos tratados lo digo; y soy llegado a tal edad, que comienzo a pasar de setenta años, y continuaré las historias de este jaez lo que Dios fuere servido que acompañen la vista, aliento, mano y disposición para escribir lo que más viniere a mi noticia.

[64]Oviedo ca. 1565: Library of the Royal Palace of Madrid MS II-3042, fols. 491 verso–492 recto / Oviedo 1959: 5.303–304. Written in early 1549, according to an explicit reference in the manuscript.

[65]Oviedo ca. 1565: Library of the Royal Palace of Madrid MS II/3042, fol. 547 / Oviedo 1959: 5.417. According to the title this passage was written while Oviedo was still in Hispaniola (before 1546); however, the chapter ends with a passage dated 1549 in Seville, which was probably added shortly before his return to Santo Domingo.

[6]

[6.1] FROM DIÁLOGO ON ALONSO DE CÓRDOBA, ALMIRANTE DE VALENCIA[66]

6.1.1. Su mujer se llamó doña (. . .) en la que hubo a su hijo e sucesor en estado don Santiago Almirante del reino de Valencia y marqués de Lista, el cual es digno de tal padre y a él muy semejante el cual caso con la Ilustre señora doña María Colón, marquesa de Guadalete hija del ilustre señor don Diego Colón, almirante segundo de Indias, e de su mujer la Ilustre señora doña María de Toledo, visorreina de las Indias, la cual señora marquesa es nieta de aquel famoso e ilustre don Cristóbal Colón Almirante primero y descubridor del nuevo orbe o segundo e nuevo imperio e mares e reinos incontables (. . .), por cuya industria vinieron a nuestro reino a hacer tan grande e tan poderoso el cetro real de Castilla.

[6.2] FROM DIÁLOGO ON PEDRO GONZÁLEZ DE MENDOZA, ARCHEBISHOP OF TOLEDO[67]

6.1.2. Podéis tener por cierto que no se concluyera este descubrimiento de la Indias sin el Cardenal. Porque Don Cristóbal Colón, primer Almirante de ellas, desconfiando de todos los medios que buscó para cumplir tal viaje y su deseo en sólo el Cardenal halló acogimiento y resultó del favor que este reverendísimo Prelado le hizo a España y a los reyes de ella tanto tesoro como todos sabemos y hemos visto con nuestros ojos, y por medio del Cardenal, el Rey y la Reina Católicos acogieron y recibieron a Colón y despacharon y armaron para su navegación.

[66] Oviedo ca. 1535–1552: unnumbered dialogue, Library of the Royal Academy of History of Madrid MS 9/4023, fol. 291 recto.

[67] Oviedo ca. 1535–1552: Library of the Royal Academy of History of Madrid MS 9/5387, fol. 416 recto.

[7] FROM *QUINQUÁGENAS DE LOS GENEROSOS E ILUSTRES E NO MENOS FAMOSOS REYES, PRINCIPES, DUQUES*. . .

Que escribió el capitán Gonzalo Fernández de Oviedo, alcaide de Sus Majestades de la fortaleza de la ciudad e puerto de Santo Domingo.

[7.1] Quinquágena II, estancia XXV[68]

7.1.1. San Jerónimo dice que más se recuerda la memoria de lo que los ojos ven que de lo que la oreja oye. Todos los hombres somos testigos de esa verdad, y es así y mejor se entienden las cosas vistas que las que se oyen o se leen. A lo menos de aquellas que los ojos corporales pueden ver. Antes que yo viese estas nuestras Indias, ni con oír al mismo Colón, primero descubridor de ellas, ni al piloto Vicente Yáñez Pinzón, que fue uno de los que se hallaron con él en el primero viaje que hizo a estas partes, ni con oír a fray Buyl, que fue el primer perlado que acá vino, ni oír a mosén Pedro Margarite, caballero de la Orden de Santiago, e a otros caballeros e hidalgos criados de los Reyes Católicos, que por su mandado vinieron con el mismo Almirante don Cristóbal Colón en el segundo viaje que acá vino, nunca pude sentir ni entender las cosas de las Indias hasta que las vine a ver, e entendí muy diferenciadamente lo que vi e veo de lo que antes había oído.

[7.2] Quinquágena III, estancia IV[69]

A Colón no es de dejarlo,
que estas Indias descubrió.

7.2.1. Razón es que al Almirante primero de estas nuestras Indias no le dejemos de poner en el número de los muy ilustres e famosos varones, pues emprendió tan grande empresa e salió con ella, e descubrió esta nueva orbe, o mundo, que hasta él estaba incógnito, en el cual, según la común opinión, ninguno habló ni escribió de los cosmógrafos, ni se navegaban estos mares e reinos de este imperio occidental. E así dijo el mismo Almirante en unos versos suyos: "Por Castilla e por León Nuevo Mundo halló Colón". No porque fuese nuevo ni más viejo que es lo que Tolomeo llamó Asia, África, Europa. Porque en aquellas tres partes pusieron todo lo del mundo, y aquellas y esto de nuestra Indias todo está en el mundo e es todo un mundo. Pero aquello no es esto ni esto aquello, y distintas son cada una de las tres viejo (quiero decir lo que aquéllos dijeron que era el mundo), y distinto e apartado de ellas es todo lo de acá. Así que el mundo viejo (quiero decir lo que aquéllos dijeron que era el mundo), le tasaron debajo de estos límites. Desde el estrecho de Gibraltar entrando por aquella puerta o mar que ay entre los dos montes Calpe e Abila, e corriendo la costa arriba hasta el río Nilo, y desde la misma puerta corriendo sobre estotra mano siniestra dentro del estrecho hasta el río Thanays, todo lo que hay entre esos dos ríos mirando al Oriente llamaron Asia. Todo lo que hay desde el dicho río Nilo hasta volver por el Mediterráneo hasta el estrecho de Gibraltar e salir de él al mar Océano e costa a costa corriendo al Sur e al Este hasta estar norte sin la tierra austral

[68]National Library of Madrid MS 2217, fol. 56 verso / Avalle-Arce: 1.300–301.
[69]National Library of Madrid MS 2219, fol. 9 verso / Avalle-Arce: 2.416–418.

derechamente del dicho río Nilo, todo aquello que está en medio llamaron y es la que África se dice. Todo lo que hay desde el río Thanays viniendo costa a costa hasta el dicho estrecho de Gibraltar, e saliendo de allí al mar océano, e volviendo bojando la tierra a la parte de septentrión, e subiendo al oriente hasta estar Norte-Sur con el dicho río Thanays, todo aquello es lo que llaman Europa. Y todas estas partes son diversas e apartadas de este otro mundo nuevo, o mejor diciendo, no nuevo mas cognito (sic. for 'incógnito') por los cristianos y nuestros cosmógrafos antiguos, hasta que la persona e industria de este Almirante lo mostró e enseñó al mundo el año de 1492 años. E por mandado de los Reyes Católicos don Fernando e doña Isabel, que ganaron a Granada, desde el campo e real que sobre ella tenían vino el dicho Colón al río de Saltes, del cual salió con tres carabelas a buscar estas mares e tierras incógnitas, e aquellos serenísimos Reyes le hicieron Almirante perpetuo de estas partes a él y sus sucesores, con título de mayorazgo. Al cual sucedió el segundo Almirante don Diego Colón, su hijo, e al segundo sucedió el tercero Almirante (que ahora lo es), don Luis Colón, hijo del dicho don Diego, segundo Almirante.

7.2.2. Así que esto de acá otra cosa es. No quiero aquí disputar si estas tierras e mares estaban escritas, porque lo que a eso toca yo lo tengo largamente dicho e probado en la *General Historia* que yo escribo como cronista de sus Majestades de estas partes. Pero digo e afirmo que en todo lo que he visto e oído e leído nunca hombre ni vasallo hizo a su rey e señor, ni a príncipe del mundo, tan señalado ni tan grande servicio como don Cristóbal Colón hizo a la corona real y Rey de Castilla. Porque así como un rey puede e suele dar una ciudad o villa, o un ducado o principado, o un reino a uno que quiere hacer grande, así este famoso nauta e Almirante don Cristóbal dio a Castilla un mundo lleno de reinos, e de donde tantos millones de oro e plata, e perlas e esmeraldas, se han llevado e llevan a España, que sin número ni estimación su valor.

7.2.3. Esto no es novedad, ni escribir de oídas, sino hablar de vista, que a Colón, primero Almirante, yo le vi muchas veces, e conocí a sus hijos e nietos, y los conozco, y cuarenta y dos años ha que curso e ando en estas Indias, e los veinte e dos ha que tengo esta fortaleza de la ciudad e puerto de Santo Domingo de la isla Española por sus Majestades como su alcaide e criado antiguo de su real casa. E creerse debe que lo que toca a Indias lo habré entendido, e no lo escribo desde la plaza Zocodover de Toledo, ni desde algún pueblo fuera de estas partes, como hoy escriben algunos desde España, dándonos a entender las cosas de las Indias sin haberlas visto.

MAPS

The Voyages of Columbus

—— 1st Voyage
— — 2nd Voyage
- - - 3rd Voyage
- — - 4th Voyage

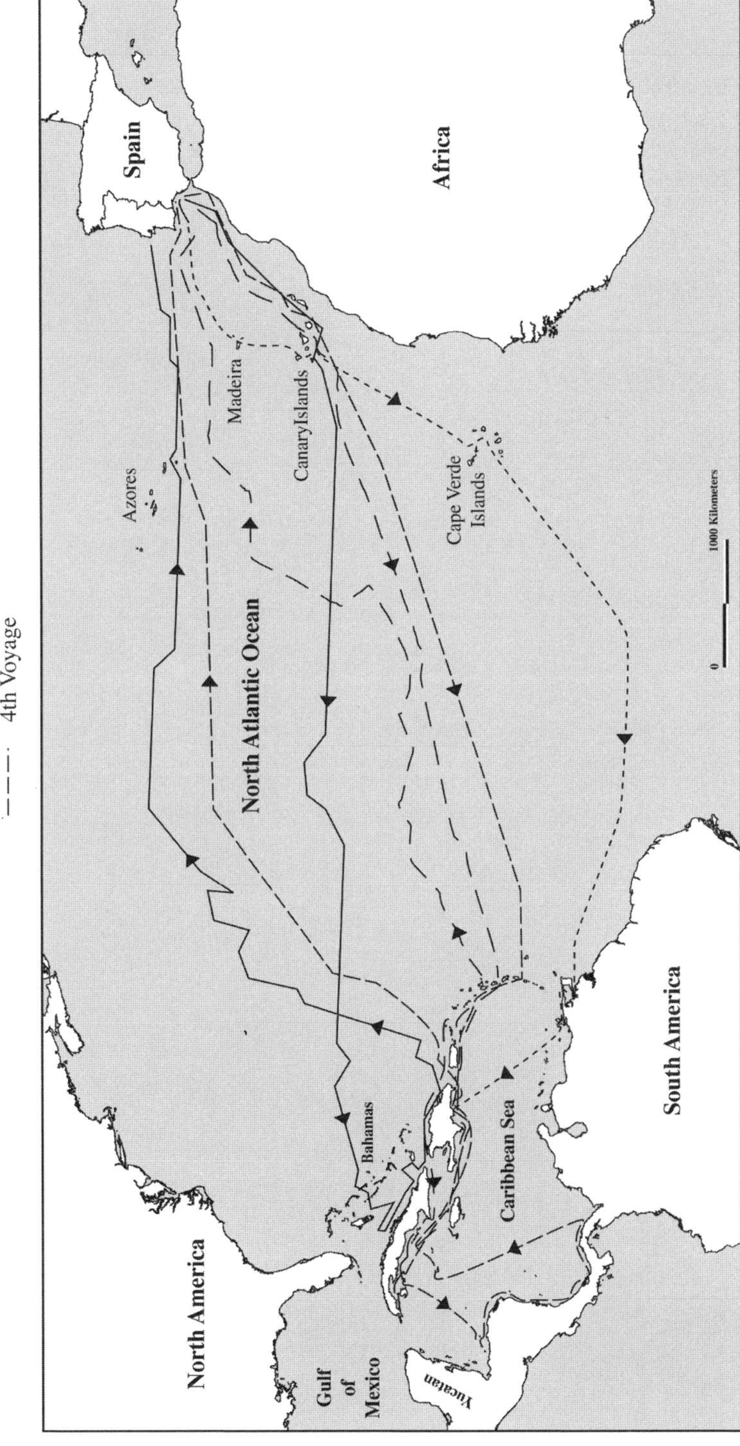

N
W
E
S
San Salvador
Bahamas
(Lucayos)
Samaná Cay
Havana
Cuba
Caicos Islands
Isla de los Pinos
Jardín de la Reina
Great Inagua (Babaque)
Yucatán
Cabo Cruz
Isabela
Española
Virgin Islands
Sevilla la Nueva
Azua
San Germán
San Juan
Santa
Cruz
Jamaica
San Juan
(Puerto Rico)
Antigua
Isla Beata
Santo Domingo
Monserrate
Guadalupe
Maríagalante
Dominica
Costa de las Orejas
Cabo Gracias a Dios
Caribbean Sea
Matininó
Barbados
Cabo de Vela
La Orchila (Is.)
Isla Margarita
Paria
Santa Marta
Trinidad
Cartagena
Santa María
de Belén
Veragua
0
500 Kilometers

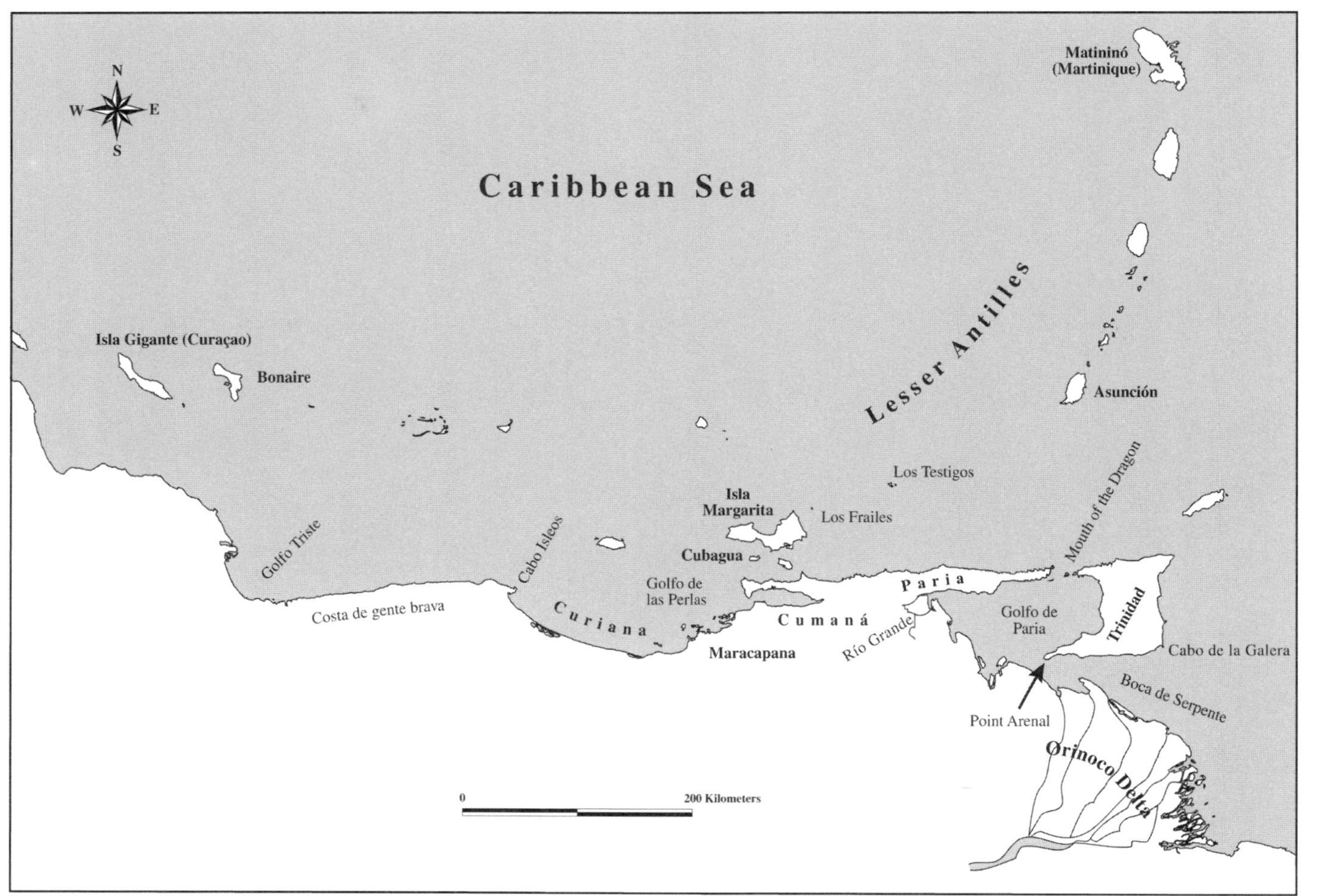
Matininó
(Martinique)
N
W
E
S
Caribbean Sea
Lesser Antilles
Asunción
Isla Gigante (Curaçao)
Bonaire
Los Testigos
Isla
Margarita
Los Frailes
Mouth of the Dragon
Cubagua
Golfo Triste
Cabo Isleos
Golfo de
las Perlas
Paria
Golfo de
Paria
Trinidad
Costa de gente brava
Curiana
Cumaná
Río Grande
Maracapana
Cabo de la Galera
Boca de Serpente
Point Arenal
Orinoco Delta
0
200 Kilometers

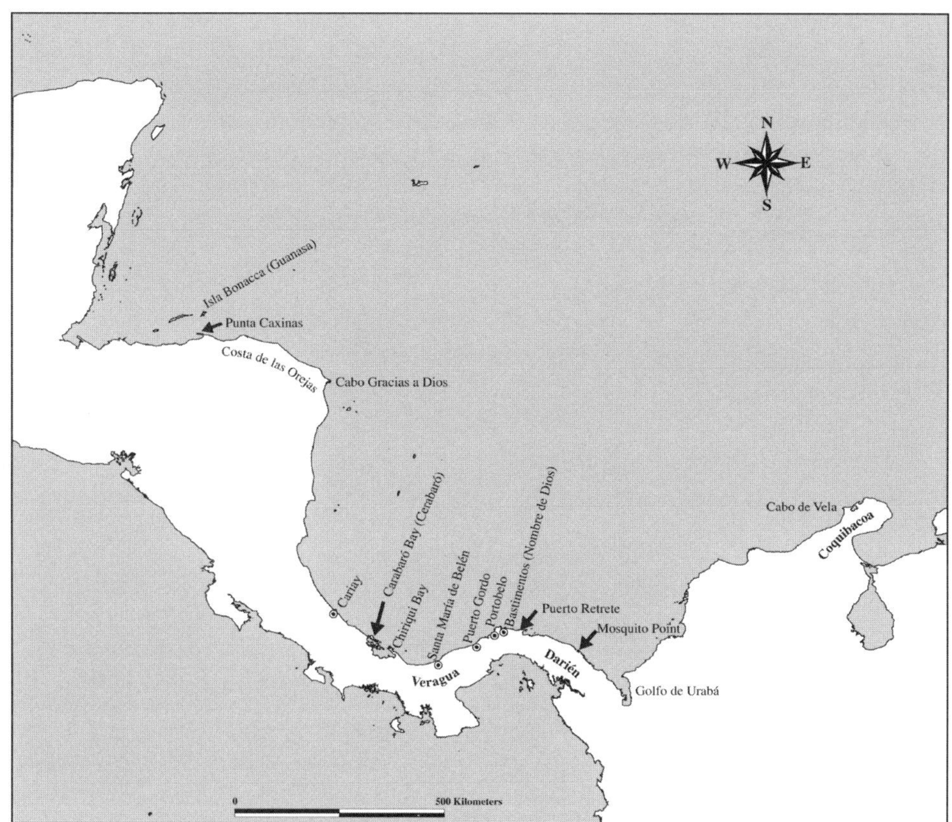
N
W
E
S
Isla Bonacca (Guanasa)
Punta Caxinas
Costa de las Orejas
Cabo Gracias a Dios
Cariay
Carabaró Bay (Cerabaró)
Chiriquí Bay
Santa María de Belén
Puerto Gordo
Portobelo
Bastimentos (Nombre de Dios)
Puerto Retrete
Mosquito Point
Veragua
Darién
Golfo de Urabá
Cabo de Vela
Coquibacoa
0
500 Kilometers

ILLUSTRATIONS

PL. 1. Oviedo's coat of arms as shown on the last page of the *Historia General y Natural de las Indias*, Seville 1535. A member of the royal bureaucracy both by birth and by office, Oviedo nonetheless felt an enduring attraction for the symbols and values of aristocracy. In 1525 he was granted the royal privilege to add the four stars of the Southern Cross, visible in the southern hemisphere where he was living, to his family arms. Another cross, the cross of Oviedo which crowns the helmet, marks his moral attachment to his fatherland, Asturias. The simultaneous emphasis on personal experience and tradition is typical of Oviedo's ideology. National Library, Madrid.

Epistola. Fo. .ccciij.

[illegible] suplico a. V. S. reuerendissima se acuerde como suele de con[illegible] las mercedes q̃ alas indias haze y en especial a aq̃lla nr̃a cibdad ⁊ ysla en la te[illegible] muy cla memoria ẽ todo lo q̃ le tocare pues q̃ es la madre ⁊ p̃ncipio ⁊ fundamẽto d̃ todas las republicas d̃ xp̃ianos q̃ ay ẽ idias. y especialmẽte ẽ dos cosas: la vna en q̃ los [illegible] q̃ para alla se proueyeren sean doctos y de buena casta ⁊ de aprouada y esperi[illegible] vida en virtudes: ⁊ q̃ residan en sus obispados: ⁊ lo mismo digo q̃ se guarde ẽ las elecciones delos juezes dela justicia ⁊ oficiales dela real haziẽda: porq̃ aũ que hasta agora por la bondad de dios ⁊ auiso de. V. S. assi se ha mirado si enesto ouiesse d̃scuy[illegible] visto esta q̃ tales andaran las ouejas si los pastores a quien fueren encomendadas no fueren quales los han menester/ ⁊ tanto es mayor el peligro q̃nto el camino es mas luengo y. V. S. reuerendissima tan apartado delo ver: ⁊ tanta dubda como ocurre en saberse aca la verdad. y por esto querria yo mõseñor reuerẽdissimo q̃. V. S. p̃mero q̃ estos pastores ⁊ oficiales aculla passassen fuesse de vista informado de sus personas ⁊ calidades: porque no ouiesse necessidad de llamar los despues para su castigo: y la con ciẽcia real de Cesar ⁊ la de. V. S. reuerẽdissima ⁊ dellos señores del cõsejo mas sin es crupulo estuuiessen: ⁊ los vezinos de aq̃llas partes mas seguros ⁊ pacificamẽte biuies semos a gloria ⁊ alabãça de jesu christo: el qual la reuerendissima ⁊ illustrissima perso na y estado de. V. S. largos tiempos prospere a su santo seruicio. De seuilla a treynta dias del mes de Setiembre: de. M. d. ⁊ treynta ⁊ cinco años.

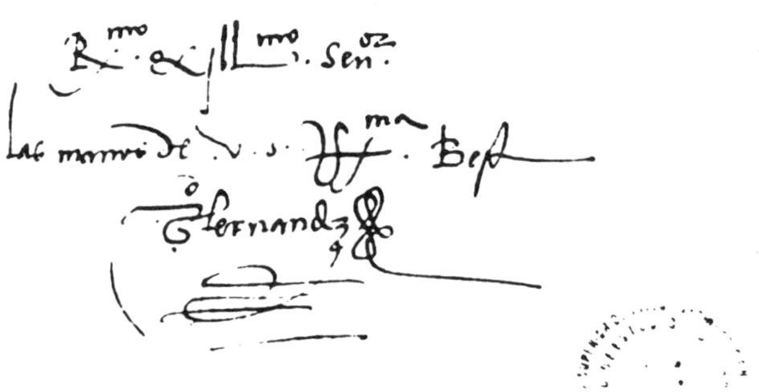

Pl. 2. Oviedo's autograph signature in the letter addressed to the president of the Council included at the end of the 1535 edition of the *Historia General y Natural de las Indias*. With this signature, Oviedo was simultaneously equating his writing to an official report submitted to the authority and making explicit his own authorial presence. National Library, Madrid; Biblioteca Nacional de Madrid.

Oviedo dela natural hy
storia delas Indias.
Con preuilegio dela
S.C.C.M.

PL. 3. Front page of *Oviedo de la Natural Historia de las Indias*, Toledo 1526. The classical motives and the imperial arms framing the title announce both the ideological framework of the work and the official value Oviedo claimed for his writing. The title, bearing Oviedo's name on the front, emulates works by ancient authorities—Pliny, in particular. Some copies are signed by hand on a space especially designed for that function, a sign of authorial self-awareness. John Carter Brown Library.

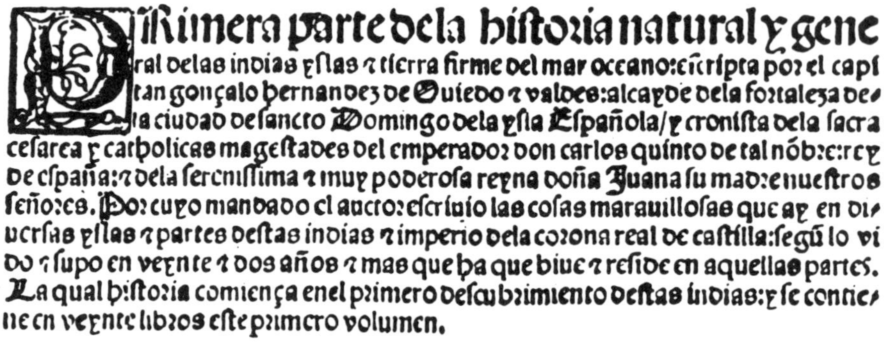

Primera parte dela historia natural y gene
ral delas indias yslas ꝛ tierra firme del mar oceano: escripta por el capi
tan gonçalo hernandez de Ouiedo ꝛ valdes: alcayde dela fortaleza dela ciudad de sancto Domingo dela ysla Española / y cronista dela sacra
cesarea y catholicas magestades del emperador don carlos quinto de tal nombre: rey
de españa: ꝛ dela serenissima ꝛ muy poderosa reyna doña Juana su madre nuestros
señores. Por cuyo mandado el auctor escriuio las cosas marauillosas que ay en di-
uersas yslas ꝛ partes destas indias ꝛ imperio dela corona real de castilla: segun lo vi
do ꝛ supo en veynte ꝛ dos años ꝛ mas que ha que biue ꝛ reside en aquellas partes.
La qual historia comiença enel primero descubrimiento destas indias: y se contiene en veynte libros este primero volumen.

PL. 4. Opening page of the first part of the *Historia General y Natural de las Indias*, Seville 1535, containing a brief statement about the author and the contents of the book. National Library, Madrid.

Libro

na delos hõbres. La hoja desta plãta es d'
ste talle a manera de vnos hierros d' lãças

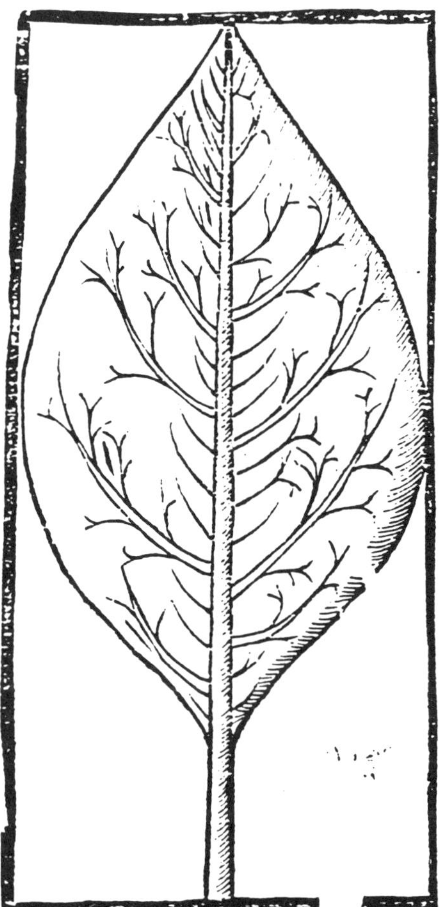

ginetas de azpe muy cortadores / y abiua-
dos delas pũtas q̃ se solian vsar ẽtre los ca
ualleros ẽla guerra y ẽtre los buenos mõte
ros: ⁊ a mi parecer no esta aq̃ mal contrahe
cha esta hoja, sino muy biẽ: ⁊ por la misma
mesura teniẽdo delante la misma ⁊ natural d'
esta excelente ⁊ salutifera planta. La q̃l al-
gũos llamã plãta o arbol d' balsamo nueuo.

¶ Capitulo. v. Dela yerua o planta llamada Perebecenuc.

En esta ysla Española ay vna
yerua o planta q̃ se dize perebe
cenuc: marauillosa y excelente
para llagas / ⁊ por muchos ⁊
por mi experimentada: dela q̃l
ay mucha cãtidad: ⁊ sin esta ⁊ las q̃ tengo di
cho creo yo q̃ deue auer otras yeruas ⁊ plã
tas ⁊ arboles innumerables apropiados
a nr̃as passiones ⁊ llagas humanas: po como los indios antiguos son ya muertos/
assi se ha acabado conellos el conoscimiẽto
d'stas propriedades ⁊ secretos d' natura / di
go delos q̃ estauã por los indios esperimẽ-
tados o sabidos: ⁊ todo lo q̃ agora se puede
dezir es poco ⁊ no biẽ entẽdido / por q̃ esta
generaciõ es tan auara dello poco q̃ saben
q̃ por ningun interesse ni biẽ q̃ se les haga q̃e
rẽ manifestar cosa d'stas: en special delas q̃
podriã aprouechar alos xp̃ianos si son me
dicinales. Y las q̃ se hã alcãçado a saber ha
sido no de volũtad d'los indios / sino por no
lo poder encobrir: y aũ q̃ algunas cosas he
oydo dezir q̃ son para diuersos remedios/
ni q̃rria ni acostũbro poner tpõ ẽ relatar co
sas confusas o no claras: y por tãto no dire
sino lo q̃ fuere muy notorio / o yo tuuiere ex
perimẽtado ⁊ visto assi como desta yerua o
plãta de q̃ agora hablo llamada Perebẽ-
cenuc / d' la q̃l ay muy grã cantidad en esta
ysla: ⁊ aũ ẽ partes dẽtro d'sta cibdad / y ẽlos
campos y eredamiẽtos tanta como d' todas
las otras yeruas / aun q̃ seã las verdolagas
q̃ no lo puedo mas ẽcarecer: por las muchas
q̃ aca ay delellas. Esta yerua tiene muchas
hojas anchas ⁊ agudas ẽlas puntas y en el
talle q̃rẽ parecer hierros d' lãças ginetas d'
los peq̃ños como si q̃siessen ẽseñar alos hõ
bres q̃ son para curar las heridas d'las tales
lãças o llagas. Sõ muy delgadas ẽ si estas
hojas y vocs ⁊ las pũtas d'llas algo mo-
das ⁊ los astiles o tallos en q̃ nacẽ estas ho
jas son assi mismo algo morados ⁊ d'la color
d'las pũtas d'las hojas / aũ q̃ algunas ay q̃
no son pũtiagudas ⁊ son algo mas romas:
po las vnas y las otras tienẽ los estremos
d' aq̃lla color ẽtre leonado ⁊ morado. Echa
vnas flores coloradas luẽgas ⁊ amari-

Pl. 5. Illustration of a *goaconax* leaf included in book 11, chapter 4, fol. 97 verso, *Historia General y Natural de las Indias*, Seville 1535. National Library, Madrid.

Segunda parte.

general ante del principio deste libro veynte donde dixe que continua
mi relacion hasta aquella tierra Septentrional que dizen del Labrador que esta en sesenta grados
desta parte de la linea equinocial.
Y con esto que es dicho se da fin a
este libro veynte, hasta que mas cosas se sepan de la Especieria, y sus
Magestades embien a aquella cõ-
quista y poblallo, pues que es de
la corona y cetro Real de Castilla.

Fin del Libro veynte.

general
y natural historia de las Indias, Islas y tierra firme del Mar
Oceano, del cetro y co-
rona Real de Castilla
y de Leon.

Comiença el prohemio
al Libro veynte y uno.

Geographia

PL. 6. Last page of the so-called Ayer copy of book 20, ca. 1557. Newberry Library, Chicago.

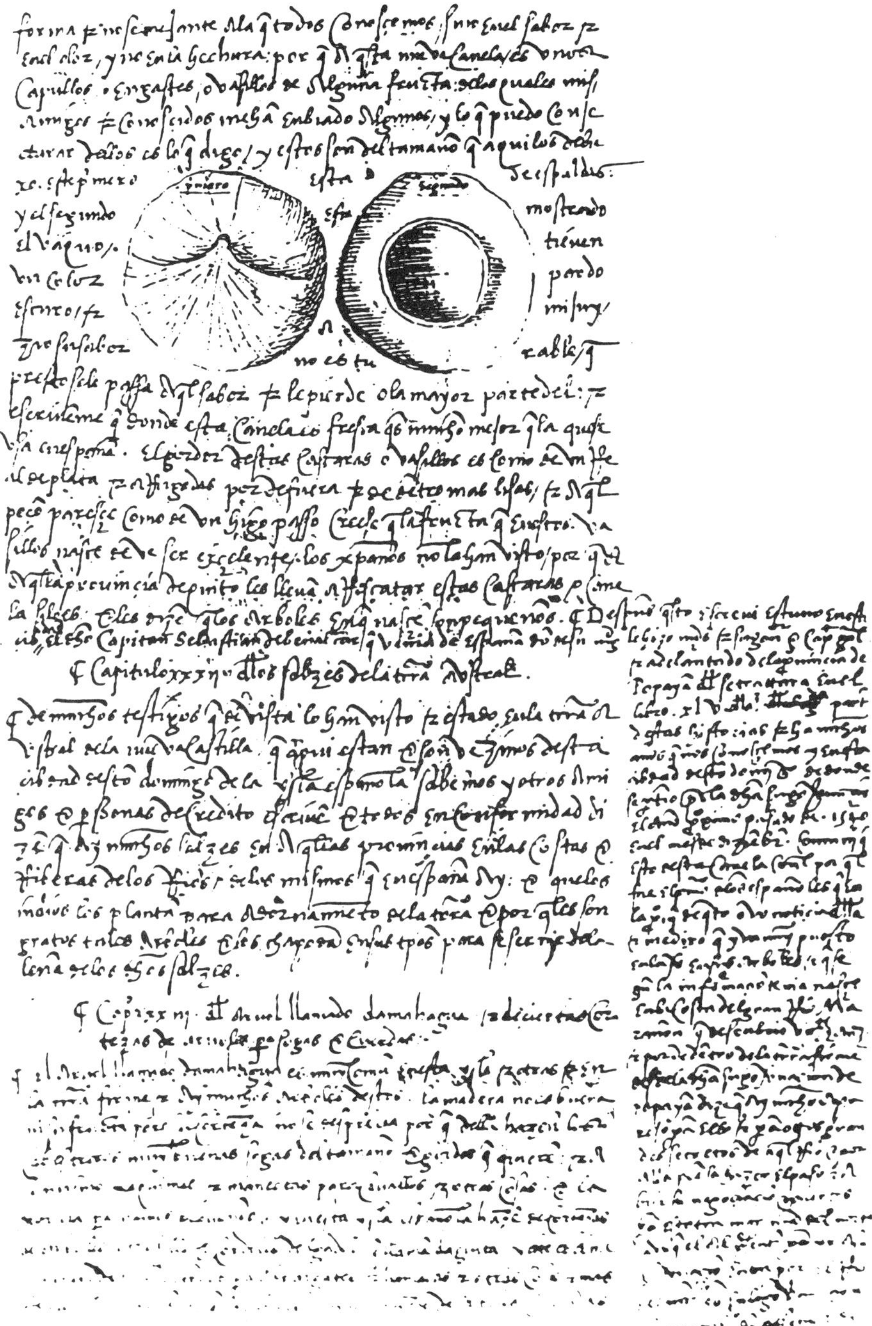

Pl. 7. Illustration of the so-called Quito cinnamon included in book 11, chapter 31. Huntington Library MS HM 177 vol. II, fol. 68 recto.

PL. 8. Illustration of the *perorica* included in book 11, chapter 8, Huntington Library MS HM 177 vol. II, fol. 79 recto.

PL. 9. Detail of the copy made by the end of the eighteenth century by Juan Bautista Muñoz of book 12 of the manuscript version of the *Historia General y Natural de las Indias*, today missing. Library of the Royal Academy of History, Madrid, Muñoz Collection A/34.

tieos hizieron señaladas mercedes: y en especial le confirmaron su preuilegio enla dicha Barcelona. a. xxviij. de Mayo de mil y cccc.xcij. y entre otras de mas de le hazer noble ⁊ dar titulo de almirante perpetuo destas Indias a el ⁊ a sus successores / por via de mayorazgo. y que todos los que del dependiessen: ⁊ avn sus hermanos se llamassen don: le dieron las mismas armas reales de Castilla y de Leon mezcladas ⁊ repartidas con otras que assi mesmo le concedieron de nueuo: aprouando ⁊ confirmando de su auctoridad real las otras armas antiguas de su linaje. E delas vnas ⁊ las otras formaron vn nueuo y hermoso Escudo de armas con su Timbre ⁊ deuisa / enla manera ⁊ forma que aqui se contiene: y se vee patente.

UN escudo cõ vn castillo de oro en cãpo de goles o sanguino cõ las puertas ⁊ vẽtanas azules: ⁊ vn leõ de purpura o morado ẽ cãpo de plata cõ vna corona de oro: la lengua sacada ⁊ rãpãte / assi como los reyes de castilla ⁊ de leõ los traen. Y aqste castillo ⁊ leõ hã destar enel chieph o cabeça del escudo: el castillo enla parte derecha / y el Leõ enla siniestra. Y de alli abaxo las dos partes restãtes del escudo todo / hã de estar partidas en mãtel: y enla parte derecha vna mar en memoria del grande mar oceano: las aguas al natural azules y blancas: ⁊ puesta la tierra firme delas indias / que tome quasi la circunferencia deste quarto / dexãdola parte superior ⁊ alta del abierta / de manera que las puntas desta tierra grande muestran ocupar las partes del medio dia ⁊ tramontana. E la parte inferior que significa

b ij

Pl. 10. Christopher Columbus's coat of arms, from *Historia General y Natural de las Indias*, Seville 1535, book 2, chapter 7, fol. 10 recto. National Library, Madrid.

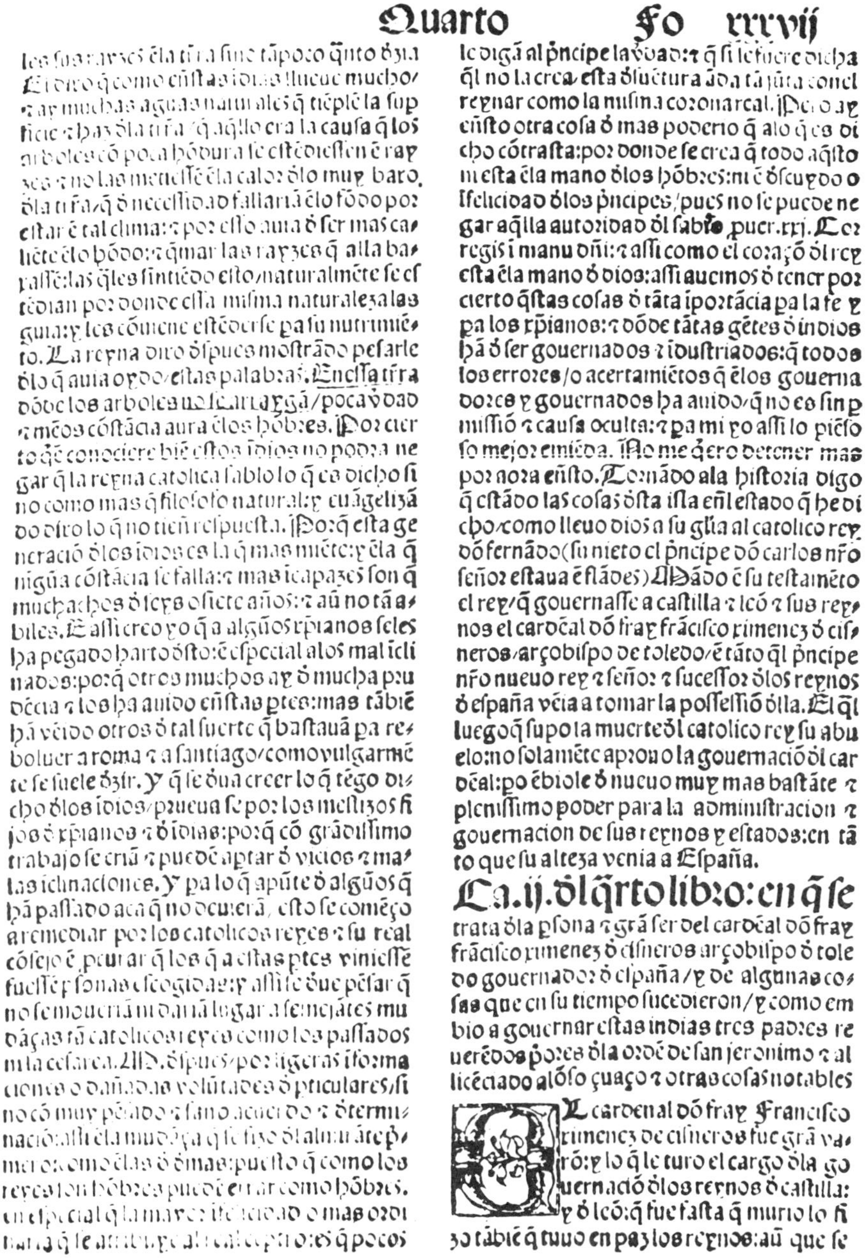

Quarto Fo. xxxvij

Ca. ij. dl qrto libro: en q se trata dla psona y grã ser del cardẽal dõ fray frãcisco ximenez d cisneros arçobispo d toledo gouernador d españa / y de algunas cosas que en su tiempo sucedieron / y como embio a gouernar estas indias tres padres reuerẽdos pores dla ordẽ de san jeronimo y al licẽciado alõso çuaço y otras cosas notables

PL. 11. Passage from book 4 of *Historia General y Natural de las Indias* (1535 edition, fol. 37 recto) containing Oviedo's negative perception of the native Americans. National Library, Madrid.

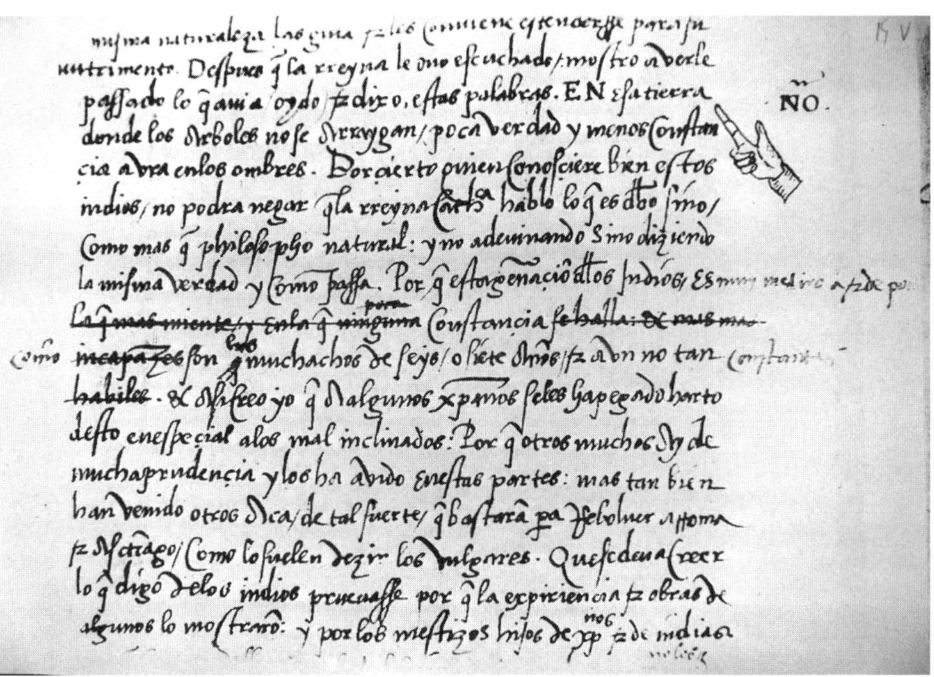

PL. 12. Passage from book 4 of the final manuscript version of *Historia General y Natural de las Indias* in which Oviedo moderates his former views on the native Americans. Huntington Library MS HM 177, vol. I, fol. 14 verso.

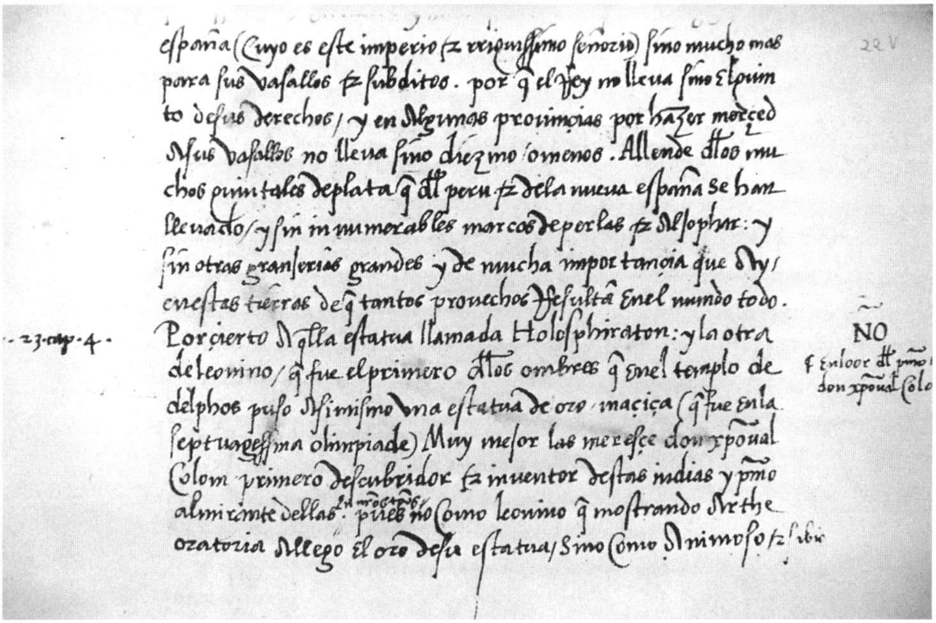

PL. 13. Passage from book 6 in the final manuscript version of *Historia General y Natural de las Indias* in which Oviedo praises Columbus. Huntington Library MS HM 177, vol .I, fol. 22 verso.

WORKS CITED

Amador de los Ríos, José
1851–1855 "Vida y Escritos de Gonzálo Fernández de Oviedo y Valdés" in *Historia General y Natural de las Indias*, vol. 1. Madrid.

Avalle-Arce, Juan Bautista
1974 "El Novelista Gonzalo Fernández de Oviedo, alias de Sobrepeña" in *Estudios de Literatura Hispanoamericana en Honor de J. A Arrón*, North Carolina Studies in the Romance Languages and Literature 158.23–55. Chapel Hill.

Ballesteros Baretta, Antonio
1942 "Don Juan Bautista Muñoz y la Historia del Nuevo Mundo," *Revista de Indias* 10.589–661.

Ballesteros Gaibrois, Manuel
1981 *Gonzalo Fernández de Oviedo*. Madrid.

Barnes, R. B.
1988 "Time, History and Reckoning" in *Prophecy and Gnosis*, 100–140. Stanford.

Beltrán de Heredia, Vicente
1970– *Cartulario de la Universidad de Salamanca*, 6 vols. Salamanca.

Bermejo, Jose Luís
1980 "Orígenes del oficio de Cronista Real," *Hispania* 145.395–409.

Brucioli, Antonio
1537–1538 *Dialoghi di Antonio Brucioli, della Philosophia Morale*. Venice.

Carrillo, Jesús
1997 "The Representation of the Natural World in the Early Chronicles of America: the 'Historia General y Natural de las Indias' by Gonzalo Fernández de Oviedo." Ph.D. diss., Cambridge University.

Casas, Bartolomé de las
1958 *Opúsculos, cartas y memoriales*, Biblioteca de Autores Españoles, vol. 110. Madrid.

1992 *Historia de las Indias* in *Obras Completas*, 14 vols, ed. Isacio Fernández Pérez, vols. 3–5. Madrid.

Contreras, Remedios
1988 "Intentos de publicación de la *Historia General de las Indias* anteriores a Amador de los Rios" in *América y la España del Siglo XVI*, ed. Fermín del Pino, 1.117–129. Madrid.

Donatini, Massimo
1980 "Giovanni Battista Ramusio e le sue *Navigazioni*. Appunti per una biografia," *Critica Storica* XVII, 1.55–101.

Fernández Armesto, Felipe
1991 *Columbus*. Oxford.

Fracastoro, Girolamo
1739 *Hieronymi Fracastorii veronensis Carminum editio*. Padua.

Gerbi, Antonello
1959 "El Claribalte de Oviedo," *Fenix* 6.378–390.

1978 *La Naturaleza de las Indias Nuevas. De Cristóbal Colón a Gonzalo Fernández de Oviedo*. Mexico.

Grafton, Anthony
1990 "Inventions of Traditions and Traditions of Invention in Renaissance Europe: The Strange case of Annius of Viterbo" in *The Transmission of Culture in Early Modern Europe*, ed. A. Grafton and Ann Blair, 8–38. Philadelphia.

Griffin, Clive
1988 *The Crombergers of Seville. The history of a printing and merchant dynasty*. Oxford.

Griffin, Nigel, ed. and trans.
1999 *Las Casas on Columbus: Background and the Second and Fourth Voyages*, with historical introduction by Anthony Pagden, Repertorium Columbianum 7. Turnhout.

Herrera y Tordesillas, Antonio de
1601 *Historia General de los Hechos de los Castellanos en las Islas y Tierra Firme del mar océano*. Madrid.

Humboldt, Alexander von
1914 *Cristóbal Colón y el descubrimiento de América*, trans. Luís Navarro y Calvo, 2 vols. Madrid

Jos, Emiliano
1940 "Fernando Colón y la Historia del Almirante," *Revista de Historia de América* 9.5–29.

Ligota, C. R.
1987 "Annius of Viterbo and Historical Method," *Journal of the Warburg and Courtauld Institutes* 50.44–56.

López de Gómara, Francisco
1555 *La Historia General de las Indias y Nuevo Mundo, con más la conquista del Perú y México*. Zaragoza.

1912 *Anales de Carlos V, Annals of the Emperor Charles V*, ed. and trans. Roger Bigelow Merriman. Oxford.

López Meneses, Amada
1958 "Andrea Navagero Traductor de Fernández de Oviedo," *Revista de Indias* 71.63–72.

López-Ocón, Leoncio
1989 "El patriotismo liberal de Marcos Jiménez de la espada en la conmemoración del IV Centenario de la empresa colombina" in *Ciencia Colonial en America*, ed. Antonio Lafuente and José Sala Catala, 379–395. Madrid.

1992 "Ciencia e historia de la ciencia en el Sexenio democrático: la formación de una tercera vía en la polémica de la ciencia española" in *Dynamis, Acta Hispanica ad Medicinane Scientiarumque Historiam Illustrandam*, vol. 12.87–103. Granada.

Marticorena, Manuel
1960 "Una traducción desconocida de Fernández de Oviedo" in *Estudios Americanos*, vol. 13, nos. 67–68, 299–300.

Merrim, Stephanie
1982 "The Castle of Discourse: Fernández de Oviedo's Don Claribalte (1519) or 'Los correos andan más que los caballeros,'" *Modern Language Notes* 97.329–346.

Muñoz, Juan Bautista
1780 Oviedo/adiciones y enmiendas a los libros 1–19. Library of the Royal Academy of History, *Colección Muñoz,* A/34.

Nader, Helen and Luciano Formisano, eds.
1996 *The Book of Privileges Issued to Christopher Columbus by King Fernando and Queen Isabel 1492–1502*, trans. Helen Nader, Repertorium Columbianum 2. Berkeley and Los Angeles.

Nava, M. Teresa
1985 "En torno a la historiografía indiana (1764–1768): La bibliografía americanista y la primera comisión de Indias," *Revista de Indias* 185.111–133.

1989 "La Real Academia de la Historia como modelo de unión formal entre el Estado y la cultura,"

Cuadernos de Historia Moderna y Contemporanea 8.127–155.

Navagero, Andrea
1718 *Opera Omnia*. Padua.

O'Gorman, Edmundo
1976 *La idea del descubrimiento de America. Historia de esa interpretación y crítica de sus fundamentos*. Mexico.

Otte, Enrique
1958 "Aspiraciones y actividades heterogéneas de Gonzalo Fernández de Oviedo," *Revista de Indias* 71.9–61.

Oviedo, Gonzalo Fernández de
1519 *Libro del muy esforzado cavallero de la Fortuna propiamente llamado Claribalte*. Valencia.

1526 *Oviedo de la Natural Historia de las Indias*. Toledo.

1532 *Cathálogo Real e Imperial de Castilla*. Library of the Royal Monastery of El Escorial, MS h-j-7.

1534 *Summario de le naturale et general Historia del'Indie occidentali composta da Gonzalo Ferdinado del Oviedo, altrimenti di Valdes*. Venice.

1535 *Primera Parte de Historia General y Natural de las Indias*. Seville.

ca. 1535–1549 *La historia natural y general de Yndias Yslas y Tierra Firme del mar océano en tres partes en quatro volúmenes repartida*. The so-called Monserrate Manuscript. Autograph manuscripts containing fragments of the work in the Library of the Royal Academy of History of Madrid MSS. 9/551, 9/553, 9/555, 9/554, 9/556 & 9/557; and in the Huntington Library in Los Angeles MS HM 177; 2 vols.

ca. 1535–1552 *Batallas y Quinquágenas escriptas por el capitán Gonzalo Fernández de Oviedo, criado del príncipe don Johan hijo de los Reyes Catholicos y coronista mayor de Indias, del Emperador Carlos V.* 2 vols. of original manuscripts: University Library of Salamanca MS 359 and Library of the Royal Academy of History MS 9/5387. Four later partial copies: Library of the Royal Academy of History of Madrid MS 9/4023; Library of the Royal Palace of Madrid MS II-2604; and National Library of Madrid MSS 3314-15.

ca. 1535 — *Relación de lo sucedido durante la prisión del rey Francisco de Francia*. National Library of Madrid, MS 8756.

1550 — Letter to Bishop Pedro La Gasca, Santo Domingo, 3 January 1550. Facsimile in the Huntington Library, PL.292.

1555 — *The Hystorie of the Western Indies*, trans. Richard Eden in *The Decades of the Newe Worlde and West Indies. Contayning the navigations and conquestes of the Spaniards*. London.

1556 — *Quinquágenas de los generosos e illustres e no menos famosos reyes, príncipes, duques (. . .) que escribió el capitán Gonzalo Fernández de Oviedo, alcaide de Sus Majestades de la fortaleza de la ciudad e puerto de Santo Domingo*, 3 vols. Autograph manuscript in the National Library of Madrid MSS 2217–2219.

ca. 1556–1557 — Ayer copy of book 20 of the *Historia General y Natural de las Indias* preserved in the Newberry Library.

1557 — *Libro XX de la segunda parte de la general historia de las Indias. Escripta por el Capitan Gonzalo Fernández de Oviedo y Valdes . . .* Valladolid.

ca. 1565 — *Historia General y Natural de las Indias*, 3 vols. The so-called Truxillos manuscript. Manuscript copy of extensive parts of Oviedo's original (Monserrate) by Andrés Gascó and his nephew Antonio Gascó. Vols. 1 and 3 in the Library of the Royal Palace of Madrid II/3041-42. Vol. 2 in the *Colombina* of Seville MS 83-6-15. Book 28 in vol. 108 of the Jesuit Collection of the Library of the Royal Academy of History.

ca. 1780 — Oviedo/Adiciones y enmiendas a los libros 1–19. Partial copies of the Monserrate manuscript by Juan Bautista Muñoz. Muñoz Collection A/34 in the Library of the Royal Academy of History.

ca. 1850	*Historia General y Natural de las Indias, islas y tierra-firme del Mar Océano. Copia manuscrita muy exacta del manuscrito original del autor, existente en Monserrate de Madrid. Hecha por D. José Amador de los Ríos (?), mediados del siglo XIX.* 3 vols. Library of the Hispanic Society of America in New York.
1851–1855	*Historia General y Natural de las Indias, islas y tierra firme del mar Oceano, por el capitán Gonzalo Fernández de Oviedo y Valdes, primer cronista del Nuevo Mundo*, 4 vols., ed. J. Amador de los Rios. Madrid.
1880	*Quinquágenas de la Nobleza de España*, ed. Vicente de la Fuente. Madrid.
1942	*De la Natural Historia de las Indias*, ed. Enrique Alvarez López. Madrid.
1959	*Historia General y Natural de las Indias*, ed. Juan Pérez de Tudela, Biblioteca de Autores Españoles, vols. 117–121. Madrid.
1959b	*Natural History of the West Indies by Gonzalo Fernández de Oviedo*, ed. Sterling A. Stoudemire. Chapel Hill.
1969	*De la Natural Historia de las Indias*, facsimile in honor of Sterling A. Stoudemire. Chapel Hill.
1974	*Las Memorias de Gonzalo Fernández de Oviedo*, 2 vols. Selection from the *Quinquágenas*, ed. Juan Bautista Avalle-Arce. Chapel Hill.
1983	*Batallas y Quinquágenas*, ed. Juan Pérez de Tudela. Madrid.
1986	*Sumario de la Natural Historia de las Indias*, ed. Antonio Ballesteros Gaibrois. Madrid.
1989	*Batallas y Quinquágenas*, ed. Juan Bautista Avalle-Arce.
1994	"Transcripción y edición del 'Cathálogo Real de Castilla' autógrafo inédito de Gonzalo Fernández de Oviedo y Valdés," ed. Evelia Romano de Thue-

sen. Ph.D. diss., University of California, Santa Barbara.

Pagden, Anthony
1993 *European Encounters with the New World from the Renaissance to Romanticism*. New Haven.

Peña y Cámara, José de la
1957 "Contribuciones documentales y críticas para una biografía de Gonzalo Fernández de Oviedo," *Revista de Indias* 69–70.603–705.

Pérez de Tudela, Juan
1952 Review of Edmundo O'Gorman's *La idea del descubrimiento*, *Revista de Indias* 12.147–150.

1957 "Rasgos del semblante espiritual de Gonzalo Fernández de Oviedo: la hidalguía caballeresca ante el nuevo mundo," *Revista de Indias* 69–70. 391–445.

1959 Vida y Escritos de Gonzalo Fernández de Oviedo" in *Historia General y Natural de las Indias*, vol. 1.I–CLXXV. Madrid.

Pérez Vilatela, L.
1993 "La onomástica de los apócrifos reyes de España en Annio de Viterbo y su influencia" in *Humanismo y Pervivencia del Mundo Clásico*, ed. J. M. Maestre, vol.1.807–819. Cadiz.

Phillips, William D., Jr., ed.
2000 *Testimonies from the Columbian Lawsuits*, trans. William D. Phillips, Jr. and Anne Marie Wolf, philological commentary by Mark D. Johnston, Repertorium Columbianum 8. Turnhout.

Pino, Fermín del
1988 "América y el desarrollo de la ciencia española en el siglo XVIII: tradición, inovación y representaciones a propósito de Francisco Hernández" in *América española en la Epoca de las Luces. Tradición—Innovación—Representaciones*. Madrid.

1990 "Utilidad y Honor Nacional en la Política Científica Ilustrada" in *Ciencia, Técnica y Estado en la España Ilustrada*, ed. J. Fernández Pérez and I. González, 31–43. Madrid.

Sanuto, Marin
1878 *Diarii*, vol. 52. Venice.

Sconza, M. Jean
1987–1988 "A Reevaluation of the *Siete edades del mundo*," *La Corónica* 16.94–112.

Schoenrich, O.
1949–1950 *The Legacy of Christopher Columbus. The historic litigations involving his discoveries, his will, his family and his descendents*, 2 vols. Glendale.

Tate, Robert B.
1970 *Ensayos sobre la historiografía peninsular del siglo XV*. Madrid.

1983 "Alfonso de Palencia y los preceptos de la historiografía" in *Nebrija y la Introducción del Renacimiento en España*, 37–53. Salamanca.

1994 "La Historiografía de los Reyes Católicos" in *Antonio de Nebrija: Edad Media y Renacimiento*, ed. Carmen Godoñer and Juan Antonio González Iglesias, 17–28. Salamanca.

1996 "The Rewriting of the Historical Past, *Hispania et Europa*" in *Historical Literature in Medieval Iberia*, ed. Alan Deyermond, 85–104. London.

Turner, Daymond
1966 *Gonzalo Fernández de Oviedo. An Annotated Bibliography*. Chapel Hill.

1983 "The aborted first printing of the second part of Oviedo's General and Natural History of the Indies," *Huntington Library Quarterly* 46.105–25.

1985 "Forgotten Treasure from the Indies: The Illustrations and Drawings of Fernandez de Oviedo," *Huntington Library Quarterly* 48.1–46.

Vega González, Jesusa
1983 *La Imprenta en Toledo*. Madrid.

Vega, María José
1994 "*Computatio Omnium Temporum*. La Edad del Mundo en la Historiografía Reformista" in *Antonio de Nebrija*: *Edad Media y Renacimiento*, ed. C. Ordóñez and J. A. González, 97–106. Salamanca.

Wagner, Klaus
1979 "Legajos y otras aficiones del inquisidor Andrés Gascó," *Boletín de la Real Academia de la Historia* 176.149–185.

INDEX TO INTRODUCTION AND TRANSLATION